Kinshasa in Transition

POPULATION AND DEVELOPMENT
A series edited by Richard A. Easterlin

PREVIOUSLY PUBLISHED:

Fertility Change in Contemporary Japan
Robert W. Hodge and Naohiro Ogawa

Social Change and the Family in Taiwan
Arland Thornton and Hui-Sheng Lin

*Swing Low, Sweet Chariot: The Mortality Cost of
Colonizing Liberia in the Nineteenth Century*
Antonio McDaniel

*From Parent to Child: Intrahousehold Allocations
and Intergenerational Relations in the United States*
Jere R. Behrman, Robert A. Pollak, and Paul Taubman

Anthropological Demography: Toward a New Synthesis
Edited by David I. Kertzer and Tom Fricke

*The Institutional Context of Population Change: Patterns of Fertility
and Mortality across High-Income Nations*
Fred C. Pampel

Birth Quake: The Baby Boom and Its Aftershocks
Diane J. Macunovich

Kinshasa in Transition

WOMEN'S EDUCATION, EMPLOYMENT, AND FERTILITY

David Shapiro

with

B. Oleko Tambashe

THE UNIVERSITY OF CHICAGO PRESS • CHICAGO AND LONDON

DAVID SHAPIRO is professor of economics, demography, and women's studies at Pennsylvania State University. He is coauthor of *The Agricultural Development of Zaire*. B. OLEKO TAMBASHE is research associate professor in the Department of International Health and Development and affiliate faculty at the Payson Center for International Development and Technology Transfer at Tulane University. For the past several years he has worked for the USAID-funded project Family Health and AIDS in West and Central Africa.

The University of Chicago Press, Chicago 60637
The University of Chicago Press, Ltd., London
© 2003 by David Shapiro and B. Oleko Tambashe
All rights reserved. Published 2003
Printed in the United States of America

12 11 10 09 08 07 06 05 04 03   1 2 3 4 5

ISBN: 0-226-75057-4 (cloth)

Library of Congress Cataloging-in-Publication Data
Shapiro, David, 1946–
    Kinshasa in transition : women's education, employment, and fertility / David Shapiro with B. Oleko Tambashe.
        p. cm. — (Population and development)
    Includes bibliographical references and index.
    ISBN 0-226-75057-4 (cloth : alk. paper)
    1. Fertility, Human—Congo (Democratic Republic)—Kinshasa.
    2. Women—Education—Congo (Democratic Republic)—Kinshasa.
    3. Women—Employment—Congo (Democratic Republic)—Kinshasa.
    4. Women—Congo (Democratic Republic)—Kinshasa—Social conditions.
    5. Women—Congo (Democratic Republic)—Kinshasa—Economic conditions.
    I. Tambashe, Oleko. II. Title. III. Population and development (Chicago, Ill.)

    HB1074.5.K5 S525 2003
    305.4'096751'12—dc21

                                            2002020412

For Sharon Shapiro and for Hélène Dembo

Contents

Illustrations

Tables

Preface

In 1988, we began what has become a long-term collaboration and partnership. At that time, sub-Saharan Africa was characterized as the only major region of the world in which fertility transition had not yet begun. We were interested in studying fertility in Kinshasa, a city that had been found in previous demographic surveys to have a quite high level of fertility. We felt that, if there were to be any signs of fertility decline among women in Kinshasa, those indications would most likely be present among better-educated women and women employed in the modern sector of the economy. Consequently, we submitted a grant proposal to the Rockefeller Foundation to study women's education, employment, and fertility behavior.

In 1990, with funding from Rockefeller to the University of Kinshasa's Demography Department (where Basile Tambashe was a faculty member) and a grant from the Fulbright Scholar African Regional Research Program to David Shapiro, we conducted a survey of women of reproductive age in Kinshasa as the first step in our study. We have used the resulting data set to write a number of research papers on these and other aspects of the economic and demographic behavior of families and households in the city. We have presented those papers at numerous conferences and seminars, and we have published a number of them in various journals. Early on, however, we decided that we would like to prepare a more comprehensive work, pulling together and extending our different papers, and also providing some historical background and context. This book is the result.

The major initial work on this book was done during the 1997-1998 academic year, when David Shapiro had a sabbatical leave from Penn State. The first four months of the sabbatical were spent at the Catholic University of Louvain in Belgium, and much of part 1 was drafted at that time. Early drafts of most of parts 2 and 3 were written during the latter portion of the sabbatical, during stays at the African Population and Health Research Center in Nairobi, Kenya, at the Institut de Formation et de Recherche Démographiques (IFORD) in Yaoundé, Cameroon, and with Basile Tambashe, who by then was working for Tulane University in Abidjan, Côte d'Ivoire.

A number of chapters draw in part from some of our earlier and ongoing joint work, including chapters 4, 5, 6, 7, 9, 10, and 11. In each of these cases, however, the chapters are significantly different from earlier published work. Most typically, these differences reflect a more in-depth and detailed treatment in the book.

We are very pleased with the final product. As indicated in the introduction, we believe that the book constitutes a thorough case study of the important and in many ways dramatic social, economic, and demographic transitions that have taken place in Kinshasa since the middle of the 20th century. We hope that it will be useful to scholars interested in these kinds of changes, which are taking place throughout sub-Saharan Africa.

Acknowledgments

Numerous organizations have contributed financial resources to make production of this book possible. The Rockefeller Foundation, the Fulbright Scholar African Regional Research Program, the Hewlett Foundation, the Fulbright-Hays Faculty Research Abroad Program, Penn State's Population Research Institute, the Spencer Foundation, the Population Council, the Research and Graduate Studies Office of Penn State's College of the Liberal Arts, Penn State's Global Fund, and Penn State's Department of Economics all provided financial assistance. The Demography Department of the University of Kinshasa was most hospitable during the 1989-1990 academic year, when our data collection in Kinshasa was carried out. Initial work on the manuscript took place at the Institut de Démographie at the Catholic University of Louvain (UCL) in Louvain-la-Neuve, Belgium; the African Population and Health Research Center in Nairobi, Kenya; and the Institut de Formation et de Recherche Démographiques (IFORD) in Yaoundé, Cameroon. Each of these organizations provided a very congenial and supportive environment that contributed greatly to the final product.

Likewise, we are indebted to numerous individuals whose assistance was instrumental. Gordon DeJong provided the initial support and encouragement that made our research possible, and Jan Hendrickson-Smith, Henk Meij, and Ron Crandall of the Population Research Institute's Computer Core put our own data set together so that we could carry out analyses of the 1990 data. Jeanne Spicer of the Computer Core also provided assistance with some of our analyses. Emile Berckmans of the Belgian Archives for the Social Sciences at UCL was incredibly helpful in providing access to and assistance with the data from the 1975 survey of Kinshasa, and Bernard Masuy at UCL was also a very helpful resource person with that data set.

Dick Easterlin provided insightful suggestions and encouragement both early on and when we had completed the first draft of the manuscript. Eliwo Akoto, Director of IFORD, provided support in multiple dimensions during a stay by David Shapiro in Yaoundé. A substantial number of students at Penn State worked on the data set and various elements of what eventually became chapters in this book, most notably Tim Devlin, Karli Sager, Tor Winston, Kokou Agbodoh, Tesfayi Gebreselassie, and Lisa Strunk. Very helpful comments on early versions of one or more of the various chapters were provided by David Ribar, Dominique Tabutin, Susan Watkins, Hilary Page, Eliwo Akoto, Dominique Meekers, Séraphin a Pitshandenge Ngondo, George Kephart, Deborah DeGraff, Sandy Remancus, and Claudia Vondrasek, and their assistance is gratefully acknowledged. We also received useful comments from two anonymous reviewers. The illustrations for the book were created by Tesfayi Gebreselassie, and the index was prepared by Anjabebu Asrat and Michael Maitland. Preparation of the book would not have been possible without the sterling assistance of Nancy Cole, whose dedication to getting the job done is unparalleled.

Last, but most definitely not least, are two personal acknowledgments. David Shapiro wishes to thank Sharon Shapiro. Without her continued support, patience, and marvelous sense of humor throughout the process, this book would not have been possible. Likewise, Basile Tambashe would like to thank Hélène Dembo, his wife, for her warm support and understanding.

Introduction and Overview

During the second half of the 20th century, there were tremendous changes in Kinshasa, the capital of the Democratic Republic of the Congo and the second-largest urban agglomeration in sub-Saharan Africa. As the city has grown from a population of around 300,000 in the mid-1950s to a population at present in excess of 5 million, women's education, employment, and fertility behavior have all been transformed substantially. This book documents and analyzes these changes, and, in so doing, it constitutes a detailed examination and case study of important social, economic, and demographic transitions. While our focus is on the dramatic changes that have taken place in Kinshasa, these transformations are presumably occurring in other cities in the region as well.

Fertility transition has only recently begun in sub-Saharan Africa. Up through the end of the 1980s, sub-Saharan Africa was the only major world region in which fertility transition at the level of national populations had not yet begun. During the 1990s, however, this situation changed considerably. A few countries showed strong evidence of fertility decline, and a number of other countries appeared to be at various early stages of fertility transition (Tabutin 1997; Cohen 1998; Shapiro and Tambashe 1999a). Even prior to the emergence of fertility decline at the national level, however, there were clear signs of fertility decline in urban areas (see Jolly and Gribble 1993), with fertility being especially low in capital cities as compared to other urban and rural areas (Cohen 1993). Indeed, urban places have been in the forefront of fertility transition in the region (Shapiro and Tambashe 1999a; Tabutin and Schoumaker 2001).

A key factor in this fertility transition is women's educational attainment, and a principal conclusion of the book is that women's access to secondary education in particular has played a significant role in initiating fertility transition in Kinshasa. In the 1950s and 1960s, ethnicity was an extremely important factor associated with fertility and fertility differentials in Kinshasa and elsewhere in the country. By the 1990s, however, educational attainment had replaced ethnicity as a key factor influencing fertility behavior.

Education, and again secondary education in particular, has been critical as well with respect to women's participation in employment and especially employment in the modern sector of the economy. However, context clearly plays an important role: in this case, poor macroeconomic performance and limited development of the country's economy since attaining independence in 1960 have constrained the extent of women's access to employment in the modern sector. At the same time, there has been a burgeoning of women's employment in the informal sector of the economy. The book documents how women's education is related to prospects for employment in the formal and informal sectors of the economy.

The themes just mentioned focus on key consequences of women's educational attainment—namely, fertility and employment behavior. The book also sheds light on determinants of women's education. We examine the preponderant role of household economic well-being as an influence on investments in children's schooling and consider gender differences in school enrollment and educational attainment and their relation to household economic well-being. Further, household composition, including both numbers and ages of siblings and presence of fostered-in children, also plays an important role in influencing educational investments in children. Through these household composition variables, in particular, one generation's fertility is seen to have effects on the following generation's educational attainment.

An additional mechanism by which fertility, education, and employment are linked is through solidarity networks. Within extended families, child fostering and exchanges of resources (particularly in support of children's schooling) are common. The existence of these practices means that individual households and their behavior cannot be viewed in isolation: the costs of fertility may be shared through child fostering and participation in solidarity networks. Further, these practices provide some children with improved access to educational opportunities. Better-educated women employed in the modern sector are disproportionately likely to be participating as donors in these networks.

In sum, then, the book seeks to trace important social, economic, and demographic changes that took place in women's lives in Kinshasa during the second half of the 20th century. Large-scale surveys undertaken in the city in 1955, 1967, 1975, and 1984 constitute the basis for tracking the evolution of education, employment, and fertility. A more detailed small-scale survey that we carried out in 1990 is used as the basis for more in-depth analyses of fertility, school enrollment and educational attainment, and employment and how these variables interact with one another to influence the economic and demographic behavior of families and households in Kinshasa. These different surveys are described in the appendix to this introduction.

A better understanding of the interplay among education, employment, and fertility in the past will give insights into likely changes in the future. The book concludes with an attempt to assess the consequences of both the longer-term changes that have been taking place and the acute economic crisis that the country has experienced since the early 1990s.

Overview of the Book

Part 1 gives a descriptive overview of education, employment, fertility, and mortality in the city over the 35-year span covered by the five different surveys. Chapter 1 provides pertinent background information on the context, describing the history of the city and its development, as the economy and the city's urban character evolved. The stagnation of the economy and the chronic economic crisis that began in the mid-1970s are discussed. The chapter also provides a demographic overview of the city going back to the mid-1920s, including information on the importance of migrants to Kinshasa and on the changes over time in the ethnic composition of the city's population.

Chapter 2 examines schooling and educational attainment as well as employment. The explosion in female schooling in Kinshasa that took place especially following independence is documented, and the increasing school enrollment of female and male youths as well as the rising educational attainment of adult women and men are examined over the period covered by the various surveys. Growth in overall employment and changes in the structure of employment by class of worker and by industry are reviewed. In brief, the chapter shows that employment has grown somewhat more slowly than has the city's adult population and that, especially since the mid-1970s, employment growth has been predominantly in the informal sector of the city's economy.

Levels and trends in mortality and fertility are examined in chapter 3, for the Congo as a whole as well as for Kinshasa. While mortality nationally appears for the most part to have declined over time, this has not been the case for Kinshasa, where mortality has apparently increased slightly. In contrast, fertility in the city was roughly stable from the mid-1950s to the mid-1970s and has fallen substantially since the mid-1970s from initially quite high levels (a total fertility rate of about 7.5), while there has probably been a modest decline in fertility nationally following a slight increase from the mid-1950s to the mid-1970s. As a consequence of these divergent trends, the mortality advantage that Kinshasa previously enjoyed (as compared to the rest of the country) has diminished, while the higher fertility that prevailed in Kinshasa has disappeared, and the city now most likely has lower fertility than the rest of the country.

Following the overview given in part 1, the chapters in part 2 provide detailed and in-depth analyses of selected key aspects of fertility behavior. Chapter 4 analyzes more extensively ethnicity, education, and fertility and their interactions over time in Kinshasa. The chapter highlights the fact that ethnic group differences in fertility (which were a prominent feature of the earliest demographic surveys) have diminished over time while substantial differences in fertility by educational attainment have emerged. Evidence presented on the links between education and fertility documents clearly the importance of secondary schooling when looking at fertility. The concluding substantive section of chapter 4 reports the results of multivariate analyses of fertility (number of children ever born) for both 1975 and 1990, controlling for ethnicity, education, and other socioeconomic factors, including employment status. The principal conclusions of the chapter are that education has supplanted ethnicity as a key factor influencing fertility in the city and that the growth in the fraction of women with at least mid-level secondary schooling has been an important factor contributing to the overall decline in fertility.

Chapter 5 examines the role of various family background factors in influencing the timing of three key fertility-relevant life course events: age at entry into sexual activity; age at first union; and age at first birth. Each of these events constitutes an important milestone in the transition to adulthood, and the timing of each is likely to have important socioeconomic and demographic consequences for women. Several dimensions of family background are considered in the analyses: father's schooling; mother's schooling; parental survival status; the respondent's number of siblings; the type of place where a woman grew up; her ethnic group; and her religious background. These factors are likely to influence a young woman's socioeconomic well-being while she is growing up, her socialization, and her tastes and attitudes. Event-history analyses are used to determine how characteristics of the family environment influence the behavior of young women with regard to initiating sexuality, nuptiality, and fertility. Parental educational attainment is generally shown to contribute to delayed transitions. Given the secular trend toward increased schooling of both women and men, these results suggest that, in the future, the onset of childbearing, in particular, will occur later than has been the case in the past.

Chapter 6 focuses on the proximate determinants of fertility. Following a brief review of the proximate determinants framework as suggested and developed by Bongaarts (1978) and modified by Jolly and Gribble (1993) to account for childbearing outside unions, we present formal analyses of the proximate determinants in Kinshasa. The chapter then provides additional multivariate analyses of several key proximate determinants: age at marriage; contraception; abortion; breast-feeding; and postpartum abstinence. These analyses help identify the pathways by which background characteristics and education, in particular, influence fertility. We also look at ethnicity and the compensating effects of the proximate determinants, documenting the fact that, despite the existence of numerous significant differences in behavior by ethnicity, these differences often tend to offset one another with respect to their impact on childbearing.

In chapter 7 we take a closer look at contraception and abortion. The observed decline in fertility has been concentrated among women with relatively high levels of education and women employed in the modern sector of the economy. These women, in turn, have comparatively low prevalence rates for modern contraception and a high reported incidence of abortion. The chapter includes detailed tabular data on contraception and abortion and their association with various characteristics of women. We look at knowledge and attitudes about and the practice of modern contraception and present data on the unmet need for contraception. Overall, the chapter suggests that modern contraceptives and induced abortion have been used as complementary fertility-control strategies by better-educated women and particularly those employed in the modern sector. These women are most likely to be in the forefront of the contraceptive revolution in Kinshasa, and the secular increase in women's education is thus expected to translate into both higher overall contraceptive prevalence and a more efficient mix of contraception methods.

Chapter 8 focuses on secondary education and fertility decline, with an emphasis on how and why education, and in particular secondary education, is so important to fertility decline. The chapter begins with an overview of the Easterlin framework for fertility analysis (Easterlin 1975; Easterlin and Crimmins 1985), and discusses—within the context of this conceptual framework—the pathways by which education and secondary education in particular are likely to influence fertility. Several of these factors, including delayed marriage and childbearing as well as contraception and abortion, were the focus of the earlier chapters in part 2. In addition, infant and child mortality and their inverse association with women's educational attainment, as well as ideal and desired fertility and women's aspirations for the education of their children, are discussed as factors contributing to the impact of secondary education on fertility. Evidence on these factors, both from Kinshasa and from Demographic and Health Surveys (DHS) conducted elsewhere in sub-Saharan Africa, is reviewed. The analysis shows that increased women's schooling—especially at the secondary level—is related to various proximate determinants of fertility and to the demand for children, the supply of children, and the motivation for and costs of fertility regulation so as to result in decreased fertility.

Part 3 provides more in-depth analyses of behaviors and issues related to education and employment. Gender differences in school enrollment and educational attainment in Kinshasa are examined in chapter 9, with particular emphasis on the impact of poverty, household demographic composition, and economic well-being more generally on investments in children's education and differences by gender in such investments. All else equal, investments in the educational attainment of girls in Kinshasa are not as substantial as the corresponding investments in the education of boys, and poverty has a substantial impact on the demand for schooling and on school enrollment and educational attainment. Young children from poor households are also more likely to delay initial entry into school. Later entry, lower subsequent enrollment rates, an increased likelihood of repeating grades and eventually dropping out, and, hence, slower progress in reaching given educational levels all appear to be consequences of coming from poor households. Overall, then, the impact of low economic well-being on the educational attainment of women and men appears to be an important mechanism contributing to the intergenerational transmission of poverty in Kinshasa.

Chapter 10 looks at resource transfers among households. Such transfers, which serve to redistribute income, may include migrant remittances, demand for (child) labor, and efforts to finance investments in human capital. The emphasis of the chapter is on financial transfers in support of children's schooling and child fostering. The solidarity networks within which these transfers occur are typically operative in a high proportion of extended families in Kinshasa: nearly three-quarters of households participate as donors of such transfers, recipients, or both. Such transfers draw attention to the limitations of considering individual households only as the decision-making units and the units of observation for analyzing economic and demographic behaviors. The extent of participation of households (as donors, recipients, or both) in these resource flows and the nature of these solidarity networks are described, and we also report results of multivariate analyses of factors associated with giving and receiving assistance for children's schooling and child fostering. Economic well-being, education, and household demographic composition are all found to influence participation in solidarity networks. The existence of solidarity networks has implications for the diffusion of the costs of childbearing and, hence, for fertility behavior.

In chapter 11 we take a closer look at education and employment in the formal and informal sectors. Detailed descriptive information on education and employment highlight the limited access of women to employment in the modern sector, even for women with higher levels of education. Multivariate analyses (multinomial logit regressions) document the effects of education, time since completing school, and other variables of interest on women's employment status in Kinshasa. Overall, there is a clear positive association between education and employment, and, the longer the duration since leaving school, the greater the likelihood of employment. There is also evidence that household demographic composition influences women's employment status.

Chapter 12 focuses on migrants to Kinshasa and examines the associations between migration and education, employment status, and economic well-being. For the most part, migrants came to Kinshasa when they were young, but almost 30 percent of them were 20 years of age or older when they moved to the city. While there are some migrants with relatively high levels of education, migrant women are substantially more likely than Kinshasa natives to have had little or no schooling, although, as a group, they appear to be distinctly better educated than women in their areas of origin. The migrant women are more likely to participate in the labor market than are women born in the city, and they appear to enjoy slightly greater economic well-being.

The concluding chapter first considers the changes that are likely to have taken place with respect to women's education, employment, and fertility over the course of the period since 1990. The descriptive data from part 1, in conjunction with the analyses of fertility in part 2 and investments in children's education in part 3, provide the basis for speculation concerning changes in fertility likely to come about simply as a consequence of continued increases in the educational attainment of adult women. At the same time, however, Kinshasa (like the rest of the country) experienced an acute and extended economic crisis beginning in the early 1990s and continuing up through the present, including the change of government in May 1997 following a relatively brief civil war and then renewed civil war beginning in August 1998. This crisis, characterized early on by annual rates of inflation of 2,000-3,000 percent and more, civil disorder in late 1991 and again in early 1993 and consequent shrinkage in the modern sector of employment, and declining real incomes, is likely to have had significant impacts on current and prospective fertility as well as on the education and employment of women. The impacts on fertility will be both direct (e.g., delayed entry into marriage or delayed initiation of childbearing associated with economic reversal) and indirect (e.g., reduced school enrollments as a consequence of economic crisis having future fertility implications). Overall, we anticipate that the fertility decline observed after the mid-1970s has most likely continued and perhaps even accelerated somewhat in the 1990s. We then assess the near-term prospects for the economy of the Congo and its capital and the likely future changes in the key variables that our study has focused on, within the context of an economy characterized by on-going economic crisis.

Appendix: The Various Surveys

The five surveys that have been used in this work were carried out in 1955, 1967, 1975, 1984, and 1990. The first four of these were massive demographic surveys, while the last was a small-scale survey that we ourselves conducted. In this appendix we give a brief description of each of these data-collection efforts.

In the 1950s, the Belgian government carried out a huge population survey in the Belgian Congo, under the direction of Anatole Romaniuk. The survey, which took place between May 1955 and February 1958, covered more than 1.36 million people, just under 11 percent of the total estimated population as of 1956 of nearly 12.8 million. In Kinshasa (then known as Leopoldville), the survey took place from May through August 1955 and covered nearly 44,000 individuals (Romaniuk 1968, table 6.1, p. 245).

For present-day Kinshasa, results of the survey were given in two separate reports: one for the Cité Léopoldville, with a reported total population of 285,881 (Congo Belge 1957a), and the other for the Territoire suburbain de Léopoldville, with a total population of 46,738 (Congo Belge 1957b). These two areas made up the district of Leopoldville. Since the latter area subsequently became part of the city and province of Kinshasa, our data analyses for 1955 typically combine data from these two reports.[1] In addition, particularly

---

[1] Kinshasa is at present composed of 24 communes. The "territoire suburbain" of 1955 included an urban zone (consisting of the present highly urbanized communes of Matete and

for data on fertility, we also draw heavily on information provided in the published work of Romaniuk (1967, 1968).

The next large-scale household demographic and socioeconomic survey of Kinshasa took place from September 1967 to January 1968, under the auspices of the Congolese Institut National de la Statistique and with assistance provided by the French government (Institut National de la Statistique 1969). The survey covered 10 percent of Kinshasa's urban population and determined that population to be 901,520. A subsequent survey estimated that Kinshasa's total population in 1967, including the rural communes not covered in the 1967 survey, was 945,000 (Houyoux and Kinavwuidi 1986, 6).

From mid-December 1974 through the end of June 1975, a third major demographic and socioeconomic survey of Kinshasa was undertaken (Houyoux and Kinavwuidi 1986). The survey, which was part of a broader study of the western part of the country carried out between 1974 and 1977 (République du Zaïre et al. 1977, 1978a, 1978b), covered 10 percent of the city's population and estimated that population at 1,635,600. In addition to the basic survey report, we have also had access to the survey data, through the Belgian Archives for the Social Sciences at the Catholic University of Louvain. Hence, in some of the tables and figures presented below, we indicate that numbers for 1975 were calculated from the data.

In the middle of 1984, the Congo (then known as Zaire) held its first and only national census since independence (the census is typically described in publications as the *Scientific Census of the Population, July 1984*). The definitive results of the census were published in 1991 (Institut National de la Statistique 1991a, 1991b) and gave the city's population as 2,664,309.

These four massive data-collection efforts are used extensively in the first four chapters of this book. In addition, we use data from a comparatively small-scale survey that we carried out from March to July 1990 (Tambashe and Shapiro 1991). These data are the basis for most of the analyses presented in parts 2 and 3. Our survey was not a general household demographic and socioeconomic survey; rather, it was focused on women of reproductive age (13-49, reflecting—at least at the low end—the age range used to study fertility in earlier surveys). Our sample consists of 2,450 women, and the sample was drawn after stratifying the population by three broad socioeconomic levels and by sector of employment.[2] We heavily oversampled women employed in the modern sector and have consequently used sample weights to generate all population estimates reported in this work. For a more complete discussion of the data-collection process and the data set, see Tambashe and Shapiro (1991).

N'djili) with a population of 30,325 and a "rural and mixed zone" (the remainder of the territory of the district of Leopoldville, now part of Kinshasa) with a population of 16,413.

[2] The three socioeconomic levels were high, medium, and low, containing (on the basis of preliminary 1984 census data) roughly 4, 36, and 60 percent of the city's population, respectively. Reflecting our interest in modern-sector employment, our stratification by sector of employment simply differentiated women employed in the modern sector from all other women.

Because our 1990 survey covers a much smaller sample than the earlier surveys did, standard errors are larger and the precision of estimates lower, particularly for certain subgroups (e.g., older women with higher levels of education). Despite this, however, we believe that, for the most part, the 1990 data provide a good indication of changes that took place after 1984. One obvious limitation of the 1990 data, however, is that there is no systematic information on men, so we are unable to go beyond the 1984 data in looking at the educational attainment and employment of adult males. However, we did collect information on the school enrollment status of youths aged 6-25 in the households in which our sampled women resided. Hence, in the descriptive data reported below, we have provided information for 1990 where such information was available.

Part I

Education, Employment, Fertility, and Mortality, 1955-1990: An Overview

Chapter 1. From Leopoldville to Kinshasa

A Very Brief History

In 1881, the American explorer Henry Morton Stanley, acting on behalf of King Leopold of Belgium, founded what was to become the city of Leopoldville on the banks of the Congo River. Geography determined the location: Leopoldville was established at the downstream end of an extensive network of river transportation in the Congo Basin, dominated by the thousand-mile stretch of the Congo River navigable up to what is now Kisangani and just before an extensive series of rapids (the Cataractes) renders the river non-navigable as it heads to its mouth at the Atlantic Ocean. It was part of the Congo Free State (essentially a private preserve of King Leopold) from 1885 to 1908. Under intense international pressure brought to bear on him because of abuses associated in particular with the rubber trade, King Leopold ceded the Congo Free State to the government of Belgium in 1908, and it became the Belgian Congo.

Figure 1.1 shows a map of the country at present, indicating the position of the city (now named Kinshasa) in the west. Administratively, Kinshasa is at present both a city and one of 11 provinces in the Congo, and it is made up of 24 communes. It is in fact a sprawling area of 9,965 square kilometers, or almost 3,850 square miles (Institut National de la Statistique 1991b, table 1), but the vast bulk of this area is very sparsely populated rural land.[1]

A remote outpost for most of its first 20 years, Leopoldville was connected to the Atlantic and ultimately to the rest of the world in 1898, when the railway linking it to the inland seaport of Matadi was completed. Establishment of the railway allowed Leopoldville to develop as a commercial center,

---

[1] One of the 24 communes (Maluku) accounts for 80 percent of the total land area, and another (N'sele) accounts for an additional 10 percent (Institut National de la Statistique 1991b, table 3). These two communes are essentially rural, and in the 1984 census they included only 3 percent of the population, representing a population density of nine persons per square kilometer.

14   Chapter 1

Fig. 1.1 Democratic Republic of the Congo

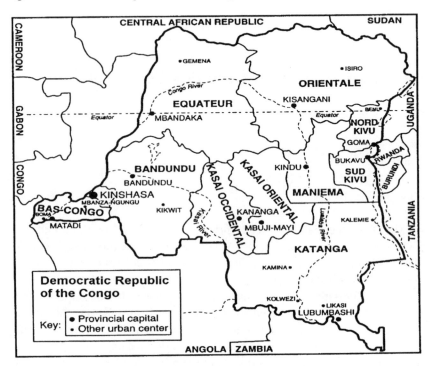

in particular as a transit point for rubber and other products from the interior of
the Congo bound for Europe and for goods imported from Europe and headed
for the interior. Thus, for example, between 1910 and 1930, the volume of
goods passing through the river port of Leopoldville each year grew from
19,000 tons to nearly 275,000 tons, representing almost a doubling every 5
years (Denis 1956, 588).

In 1923 Leopoldville became the capital of the Belgian Congo, and by the
end of the 1920s the city had become an important administrative center. The
growth of the city was rapid. Like many other emerging cities in sub-Saharan
Africa, Leopoldville was not located where human resources were plentiful,
and, hence, it was necessary to import workers to meet the growing demand for
labor. Recruitment of workers in rural areas served to attract Congolese men
to employment in the emerging modern economic sector (Dhanis 1953; Lamal
1954; Lux 1962). The Great Depression of the 1930s slowed the city's growth
briefly: 6,000 men were sent back to their rural areas of origin in 1930 and
7,000 more in 1932 in response to the corresponding sharp decline in demand
for labor (Denis 1956, 575). This forced return migration reflected the con-

siderable control over labor and unemployment exercised by the colonial authorities (see Capelle 1947), and it also emphasized the sensitivity to external events of this new urban center in sub-Saharan Africa.

The importance of external events was further highlighted with the onset of World War II. Supplies to Leopoldville were cut off, and, as a consequence, the city was obliged to develop its industrial base rapidly so as to become more self-sufficient. Labor recruitment was, as before, focused on finding men to work in the city's growing modern economy, and the colonial government strictly controlled migration to Leopoldville. However, the addition of considerable industrial activity to the city's existing commercial, transportation, administrative, and industrial activities resulted, not only in substantial diversification of the city's economy (Baeck 1956), but also in a doubling of the population between 1940 and 1945 and a doubling again between 1945 and 1950.

By 1960 the population of Leopoldville had reached roughly 400,000 (Houyoux and Kinavwuidi 1986, 19). When the Belgian Congo became independent in mid-1960, the controls on migration were effectively eliminated, and—fueled by the internal political strife of the early 1960s—the city began another period of rapid growth. This growth continued Leopoldville's sprawling geographic expansion, and it was accompanied by a variety of economic and social changes, including a rapid expansion of the informal or unstructured sector of the economy and the continuation of the substantial extension of schooling to women that had just begun near the end of the colonial period.[2]

From 1965, when General Joseph Désiré Mobutu seized power in a coup d'état, until the mid-1970s, the city (renamed Kinshasa in 1966 after one of the villages that existed near the site where Stanley first established Leopoldville) and the country experienced a period of political stability and economic growth. In the early 1970s, on the heels of this political and economic success, President Mobutu announced a policy to promote "authenticity." To further "authenticity," the president required citizens to abandon their European names in favor of African ones, he changed the names of many other cities throughout the country from their colonial designations to African names, and he changed the name of the country from Congo to Zaire. However, following the implementation in 1973 and 1974 of ill-conceived policies of Zairianization and radicalization (which essentially expropriated most businesses owned by foreigners and typically turned them over to unqualified Zairians, with very harmful and long-lasting adverse consequences) and the sharp decline in world copper prices that took place at roughly the same time,[3] the economy entered a period of protracted crisis from which it has not yet emerged.

[2] For more detail on the history of Leopoldville, see Capelle (1947), Baeck (1956), Denis (1956), Whyms (1956), and Mbumba (1982).

[3] Copper was the major source of export earnings and government revenues.

The chronic crisis that began in the mid-1970s was accompanied by stagnation in the modern sector of the economy and continued growth in the informal sector. Despite these problems, the population of the city continued to grow rapidly throughout the 1970s and 1980s. Economic growth and development were further hindered by a notoriously corrupt and poorly functioning public sector (some political scientists described the governance system as one of *kleptocracy*). During the 1980s, the country's government attempted, with assistance from the International Monetary Fund and the World Bank, to implement a series of structural adjustment programs aimed at improving the efficiency of operation of the public sector and encouraging the growth and development of the private sector. A number of economic reforms were adopted, but political support for structural adjustment was unsteady and had an "on-again, off-again" character.

Beginning in the latter half of 1990, the chronic economic crisis became acute. After a number of years during which inflation averaged 40-50 percent per year and real incomes declined substantially, suddenly very rapid inflation of 2,000-3,000 percent per year emerged as the monetary authorities effectively abandoned any efforts to adhere to the structural adjustment program. The ensuing economic crisis, occurring in the midst of a political crisis characterized by increasingly vocal calls for democracy and the ouster of President Mobutu, came to a head in late September 1991. Initiated by soldiers who had seen the real value of their salaries shrink to almost nothing, rioting, looting, and generalized civil disorder broke out, first in Kinshasa, then in urban centers throughout the country. This resulted in the withdrawal of foreign donors and in a considerable shrinkage of Zaire's and Kinshasa's fragile modern sector. A second round of looting and pillaging, this time solely by the military, took place at the end of January 1993.

Inflation continued at an accelerated pace after late 1991, reaching as high a rate as 500 percent in one month in Kinshasa at the end of 1993 and averaging 10,000 percent and more on an annual basis for much of 1993 and 1994. In 1995, and during the first half of 1996, inflation slowed to less than 20 percent per month, corresponding to well under 1,000 percent per year (Maton and Van Bauwel 1996).

By 1997 the national economy was a shambles. Industrial production had been reduced tremendously, as had mining production. Manufacturing activity was cut in half from 1990 to 1993-1994, while mining output fell by 60 percent over the same period. Both sectors showed slight improvement in 1995 and early 1996 but by mid-1996 were still operating at only 50-60 percent of their 1990 levels (Maton and Van Bauwel 1996). Kinshasa's economy likewise suffered greatly during the 1990s. Transportation from the countryside to the cities became increasingly difficult, food prices skyrocketed, and malnutrition became increasingly prevalent.

In brief, the chronic crisis that had characterized the Congo's economy since Zairianization in the mid-1970s became an acute crisis in the early 1990s. The political situation remained deadlocked until May 1997, when a rebellion begun in late 1996 with assistance from neighboring countries and led by Laurent Désiré Kabila succeeded in taking power from President Mobutu.

Not long after declaring himself president Kabila changed the name of the country back to Democratic Republic of the Congo. While his government showed early success in slowing inflation ("Un An après" 1998, 141), changing the economy so as to replicate the relative prosperity of the early 1970s has proved to be a far more difficult task. President Kabila found himself presiding over a country rich in mineral wealth and with substantial agricultural potential, but also one with a badly deteriorated transportation and production infrastructure, ruined by years of neglect, government corruption, and, more recently, extreme economic instability and civil war.

Exacerbating the difficulties confronting the Congo's government is a rebellion that broke out in the eastern part of the country in early August 1998. Rebels, assisted by some of President Kabila's former allies, have succeeded in capturing a significant share of eastern Congo. Hence, for the past few years, the government, with considerable assistance from several other sub-Saharan nations, has been devoting significant resources simply to its efforts to defeat the rebellion and remain in power.

In January 2001, President Kabila was assassinated by one of his own guards. His son, Joseph Kabila, a young and inexperienced army general, was quickly installed as the new president. The younger Kabila has seemed to be much more interested than his father was in finding a peaceful means of ending the ongoing civil war, although as of this writing the conflict continues. Even assuming that the civil war can be brought to a conclusion, it is apparent that massive investment and rebuilding will then be required if the new Kabila government is going to have any hope of reinvigorating the moribund Congolese economy.

A Demographic Overview

The evolution of Kinshasa's population over time up through 1984 is shown in figure 1.2. The graph documents the adverse effects of the Great Depression, the very rapid growth following the onset of World War II, and the considerable growth following independence in 1960. From 1930 to 1935 there was a decline in the city's population of nearly 30 percent. This decline was more than made up by 1940, and during the 1940s the average annual growth rate of the population of Kinshasa was approximately 15 percent, an extremely high figure. Estimated growth during much of the 1960s was in excess of 12

Fig. 1.2 Population of Kinshasa, 1925-1984

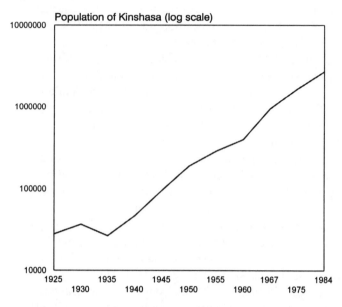

Sources: Congo Belge (1957a, table 1); Houyoux and Kinavwuidi (1986, 6); Institut National de la Statistique (1991b, table 01).

percent per year, and subsequent growth has slowed gradually: from over 7 percent per year for the period from 1967 to 1975 to roughly 5.5 percent per year for the period from 1975 to 1984.[4]

Projections for the period since 1984 typically have assumed continued growth in the neighborhood of 5-6 percent per year (Institut National de la Statistique 1993; Shapiro 1992), although the acute economic crisis of the 1990s may well have rendered these projections too high for much of the decade. Official projections published several years ago (Institut National de la Statistique 1993, table P.1.01, pp. 17-18) estimated that, by the year 2000, the city's population would be 6.06 million. These projections assumed that population growth would decline from 5.6 percent per year in 1985-1989 to 5.2 percent in 1990-1994 and to 4.7 percent in 1995-1999 (Institut National de la Statistique 1993, table I10, p. 52).

The most recent estimate of Kinshasa's population by the United Nations (1996) was for a 1996 population of 4.4 million. With 5 percent annual growth

---

[4] Boute and Saint Moulin (1978, 15) estimated that, for the period from 1956 to 1975, Kinshasa's average annual growth rate was 8 percent. This growth was divided equally between natural increase (the excess of births over deaths) and net migration.

subsequently, that estimate would imply a population in 2000 of 5.35 million. We estimate that, in the year 2000, the city's population was somewhere between about 4.9 and 5.7 million. The high end of this range is the outcome if one assumes 6 percent annual growth between 1984 and 1991 and then a reduction to 4 percent annual growth after 1991; assuming growth of 5 and 3 percent during each of the respective subperiods yields the lower estimate.[5]

As noted above, the early growth of Leopoldville was stimulated largely by labor recruitment. Since only men were being recruited, this led to a very sharp imbalance in the gender composition of the city's population during the colonial period. This imbalance, as well as related distortions to the gender composition of rural populations subject to heavy recruitment, was the source of some concern on the part of a number of observers (Charles 1948; Dhanis 1953; Lamal 1954). The colonial government began to address the issue following World War II by promoting a considerable amount of housing construction so as to accommodate more families in the city.

Figure 1.3 shows the gender composition of the city's population and the relative presence of children and how they have changed over time. During the 1920s there were only about 30 women per 100 men. This figure rose to 60 by the mid-1930s, reflecting the much more substantial decline in the male population than in the female population as a consequence of the Great Depression, and stayed in the range of 50-60 up through the mid-1950s. Although the improvement was noted by some observers (Capelle 1947), the continuing large gap led others during the colonial period to refer to the *mal démographique* of Leopoldville (Charles 1948). Between 1955 and 1967 the gap was substantially reduced, and further narrowing by 1975 meant that there were nearly 90 women age 15 and over for every 100 men in the same age range.

The shrinkage of the gender imbalance among adults was accompanied by growth in the proportion of the city's population represented by children (those under age 15): from only about 10 percent of the population in the late 1920s (when men made up 70 percent of the total population), their share grew to more than 35 percent by the mid-1950s and jumped to more than 50 percent by 1967, then fell slightly to 50 percent in 1975 and 46 percent in 1984. Reflecting the sharp changes pursuant to independence, the number of children per 100 women rose very rapidly between 1955 and 1967, from 156 to 243, and has declined subsequently.

The preceding considerations are summarized in figure 1.4, which shows

---

[5] Reliable data on the city's current population are not available. There were reports of out-migration from Kinshasa to rural areas during the early 1990s, and the possibility of both reductions in fertility and increases in mortality resulting from the acute economic crisis further reinforces our conviction that growth most likely slowed after 1990. Offsetting this, more recently, is the possibility of increased migration to the city in response to the ongoing rebellion.

Fig. 1.3 Population composition, 1925-1984

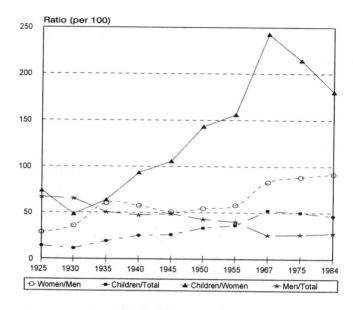

Sources: 1925-1950: Congo Belge (1957a, table 2); 1955: Congo Belge (1957a, table 9); 1967: Institut National de la Statistique (1969 table 6); 1975: Houyoux and Kinavwuidi (1986, table 1.1); 1984: Institut National de la Statistique (1991a, table 1).

Note: Children are ages 0-14.

population pyramids for the city in 1955, 1967, 1975, and 1984.[6] Although considerably lessened compared to the situation that prevailed prior to the mid-1930s (see figure 1.3), the gender imbalance was still quite evident in 1955. Males outnumbered females in each age group from age 15 on, and for those age 25 and older there were roughly twice as many men as women in each age group.

By 1967, however, the gender imbalance among adults had narrowed considerably. With the exception of ages 25-29, males outnumbered females beginning with the 10-14 age group, but only from age 35 upward was there a substantial excess of males over females. By 1975, much of this remaining imbalance had disappeared. Men outnumbered women in all age groups beyond 20-24, but only for those aged 40 and up were there about 50 percent more men than women in each age group. A similar picture is evident for 1984, except that the relatively large imbalances began at age 50 rather than age 40.

[6] The 1955 pyramid is, like the 1955 data in figure 1.3, for the Cité Léopoldville only, not the entire district. That is, data for the "territoire suburbain," where the gender imbalance was substantially smaller, are not included.

   In addition to the changes over time in gender composition, and visually even more striking, the pyramids displayed in figure 1.4 also document the changes in age composition. More specifically, the "artificial" character of the city's age structure in 1955, brought about by the heavy impact of labor migration, is evident from the relatively small cohorts aged 5-19, which stand in sharp contrast to the swollen cohorts (especially for males) of those aged 20-44. By 1967, and also for 1975 and 1984, the pyramids have a conventional shape for a high-fertility population, with a large base reflecting the considerable extent of childbearing and relatively smooth declines in moving from younger to older cohorts. Continued sex-selective migration to the city is still reflected in bulges in the pyramids for males of labor force age, but nowhere near the extent to which this had been the case during the colonial period.

Nativity and Ethnicity

The remainder of this chapter examines two additional characteristics of the city's population and how they have changed over time: the percentage of the population native to Kinshasa, by age group, and the ethnic origins of the population.[7] As may be seen in table 1.1, in 1955 only slightly more than one in four residents of Leopoldville had been born there. Further, the native-born population was extremely young, with 90 percent under the age of 15 and 95 percent under age 20. The population age 20 and over consisted almost entirely of migrants to the city. By 1967, the proportion of residents who had been born in Kinshasa had increased substantially, rising to nearly half. Compared to 1955, there were clear increases in every age group in the proportion born in the city, with the increases being greatest for those aged 10-19. This latter aspect reflects the elimination between 1955 and 1967 of the indentations at these ages in the city's age pyramid. However, the native-born group was still quite young.
   By 1975, the trend toward increasing proportions born in Kinshasa continued, and, by 1984, with further increases in every age group in the percentage born in Kinshasa, almost 60 percent of the city's population had been born there. Just over two-thirds of this group were under age 15, and 81 percent were under age 20. Over time, then, there has been a clear increase in the proportion of the city's population that is made up of individuals born in Kinshasa, and these individuals have been getting progressively more important in increasingly older age groups. Leopoldville in 1955 was a city populated by

---

[7] In looking at ethnicity, the focus is on African residents. In the mid-1950s the European population numbered about 15,000 (just over 5 percent of the total population) and had an age and gender composition very similar to that of the African population (Baeck 1956). As of 1984, the non-African population of Kinshasa was enumerated at just over 110,000, or a little more than 4 percent of the city's population (Institut National de la Statistique 1991a, table 2, p. 58).

Fig. 1.4 Population pyramids, 1955-1984

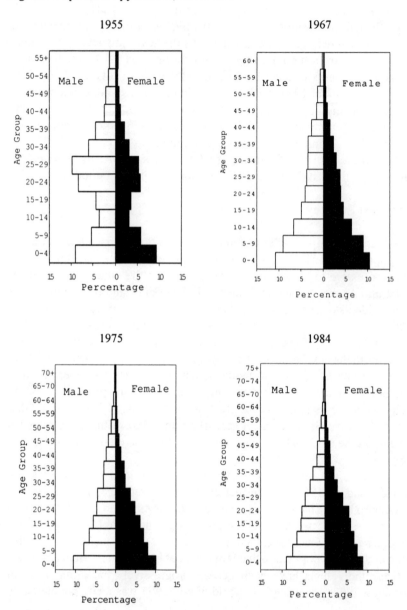

Sources: 1955: Congo Belge (1957a); 1967: Institut National de la Statistique (1969); 1975: Houyoux and Kinavwuidi (1986, table I.l, p. 33); 1984: Institut National de la Statistique (1991a, table 1, p. 56).

Table 1.1 Percentage of the Population Born in Kinshasa, by Age, 1955-1984

Age Group	Percentage Born in Kinshasa			
	1955	1967	1975	1984
0-4	80	89	92	95
5-9	56	73	78	88
10-14	41	71	65	79
15-19	18	39	49	64
20-24	5	20	31	47
25-29	2	10	15	33
30-34	1	5	10	23
35-44	1	2	6	13
45-54	1	2	4	7
55+	1	2	5	7
Total	26.5	47.1	49.7	59.4
	Percentage of Kinshasa-Born Population			
Under age 15	90	88	77	69
Under age 20	95	94	89	81

Sources: 1955: Congo Belge (1957a, tables 9 and 10); 1967: Institut National de la Statistique (1969, table 10, p. 35); 1975: Houyoux and Kinavwuidi (1986, annexe I.2, p. 69); 1984: Institut National de la Statistique (1991a, table 5, p. 61).

Note: The denominator for 1955 is restricted to those residing in Cité Léopoldville (comparable data for the "Territoire suburbain" were not published). The numerator includes those born either in Cité Léopoldville or in the "Territoire suburbain."

adults almost all of whom had been born and brought up in rural areas; Kinshasa in 1990 was a city with a substantial native-born adult population.[8] However, even in 1990 the majority of the population aged 20 and over undoubtedly consisted of migrants.

Accompanying the changing composition of the city's population in terms of place of birth has been a gradual shift with respect to the ethnic composition of the population. As shown in table 1.2,[9] ethnic groups from what is now the

[8] Among women in our 1990 survey, almost 40 percent of those aged 30-34, nearly half of those aged 25-29, and close to 60 percent of those aged 20-24 had been born in Kinshasa.

[9] Table 1.2 identifies broad ethnic groups that are important in Kinshasa and whose behavior with respect to fertility is analyzed in more detail in chapter 4 and subsequently. These groups are described in the appendix. Table 1.2 also shows the provinces of the country from which these groups come. In the Congo, those born in Kinshasa are classified according to their ancestral region of origin. Hence, the province of Kinshasa is not included in the table. Data on ethnic group from the 1967 survey report were not sufficiently detailed to be included in the table; however, the partial information provided in the report suggests that the ethnic composition in 1967 was intermediate between that of 1955 and that of 1975. Census reports from 1984 do not provide information on the ethnic origins of the population.

Table 1.2 Ethnic Composition, by Broad Ethnic Group, 1955-1990 (percentage distributions)

Group	Province(s) of Origin	1955	1975	1990
Bakongo North	Bas-Congo	8	10	8
Bakongo South	Bas-Congo	32	26	22
Kwilu-Kwango	Bandundu	15	26	37
Mongo	Equateur, Kasai Occidental, Bandundu	6	8	7
Ubangi	Equateur, Orientale	8	8	8
Luba and related	Kasai Occidental, Kasai Oriental	5	9	11
Other Congolese	Orientale, Kivu, Maniema, Shaba	2	2	2
Foreigners	Non-Congo	25	12	5
Total		100	100	100

Sources: 1955: Congo Belge (1957a, table 6); 1975: calculated from data; 1990: calculated from data.

Note: Data for 1955 and 1975 refer to the entire population; data for 1990 are for the population of women aged 15-49. The bulk of foreigners is made up of people from Angola, who represented 21, 11, and 4 percent of the total population in 1955, 1975, and 1990, respectively.

Province of Bas-Congo (to the west and south of the city) accounted for about 40 percent of Leopoldville's population in 1955.[10] The vast majority of this group, in turn, came from the portion of Bas-Congo Province that is south of the Congo River and close to the city. A smaller number originated in the portion of the province that is north of the river, which for the most part is located farther from the city. Another quarter of the population in 1955 consisted of non-Congolese Africans, more than 85 percent of whom were from neighboring Angola. The only other group with as much as 10 percent of the city's population was the Kwilu-Kwango group[11] from Bandundu Province immediately to the east of the city, from which considerable labor had been recruited for Leopoldville (Dhanis 1953; Lamal 1954).

[10] The data in the table for 1955 are limited to Cité Léopoldville because only partial data were provided on the ethnic origins of residents of the "territoire suburbain" (for principal tribes). However, since the principal tribes from the Bakongo South and Bakongo North groups alone accounted for 39 and 9 percent of the total "territoire suburbain" population, respectively, these two groups combined accounted for a little over 40 percent of the total (Cité Léopoldville and "territoire suburbain") population. Angolans represented an additional 9 percent of the "territoire suburbain" population, and another 5 percent can be identified as coming from the Kwilu-Kwango group. The remaining 39 percent of the "territoire suburbain" population, for which ethnic group cannot be identified given available data, most likely (on the basis of geographic proximity) were from the Bakongo South, Kwilu-Kwango, and/or Mongo groups.

[11] This designation represents a fairly heterogeneous amalgamation of smaller ethnic groups that are grouped together largely on the basis of their geographic origin (the Kwilu and Kwango Districts constitute the southernmost two-thirds of Bandundu Province). For further discussion of the different ethnic groups, see the appendix.

By 1975, the growth of migration to Kinshasa from elsewhere in the Congo had resulted in a sharp drop in the share of the city's African population that consisted of people from outside the country and a more modest decline in representation of those from the nearby Bakongo South group. The largest increase was for individuals from Kwilu-Kwango, and the share of the population represented by the Luba and related group had nearly doubled. These changes continued up through 1990, by which time foreigners from elsewhere in Africa had become only a small proportion of the population, the Kwilu-Kwango group had surpassed the two Bakongo groups combined, and the Luba and related group had further increased its share of the city's population.

Overall, then, Congolese have made up an increasingly larger portion of the city's total population over time. In addition, there has been a clear trend toward increased diversity of the Congolese population of Kinshasa, with notable reductions in the proportion of residents from Bas-Congo, very substantial increases in the representation of ethnic groups from Kwilu-Kwango in Bandundu, and increased representation of the Luba group from the more distant provinces of Kasai Occidental and Kasai Oriental. Two other groups, the Mongo and the Ubangi peoples, primarily from the north of the country, have each maintained a fairly stable share of the city's population over this period. These six groups, which represented almost three-quarters of Leopoldville's population in 1955, accounted for 93 percent of Kinshasa's population in 1990.

Chapter 2. Education and Employment

Because of the fact that the black woman is not sufficiently educated, she can not participate in an effective manner in the evolution of our country. —A.-R. Bolamba

From Colonial Limits on Schooling to Postindependence Explosion to Economic Crisis

During most of the colonial period, access to schooling for Congolese women was extremely limited. At the outset, this policy reflected in large part an effort to meet the rapidly growing needs of the colony for (male) office workers in government and in the private sector as well as the growing demand for skilled and semiskilled labor (Bolamba 1949; Hulstaert 1951; Mukadi 1979). In the early 1920s, a commission on education established by the minister of colonies recognized the importance of providing schooling to women (Mukadi 1979). Despite this, however, the schooling of females continued to lag far behind that of males. The absence of women teachers was also cited as a factor contributing to the delay in the schooling of girls (Bolamba 1949; Hulstaert 1951).

The provision of schooling to boys and young men had, by the end of World War II, resulted in the emergence of a growing class of educated Congolese men (so-called *évolués*). However, the continued imbalance between the schooling of males and that of females began to attract considerable attention. In addition to the factors cited above, several observers have argued that, among many Congolese parents, there was a lack of interest in having their daughters attend school (Bolamba 1949; Hulstaert 1951; Comhaire-Sylvain 1968). Many parents simply did not see the point. For example, Comhaire-Sylvain (1968, 17), discussing the situation in Leopoldville in 1945, notes, "A mother who was told to send her daughters to school responded: 'After school will they go and work in an office? No. Hence, it's not worth it.'"

By the early 1950s there were numerous voices, Belgian as well as Congolese, calling for a vastly increased effort on the part of the colonial government to provide schooling for girls as well as for boys (Bolamba 1949; Bukasa 1951; Wassa 1951; Van Bulck 1956). The desirability of such an effort, particularly in urban areas, was emphasized by Baeck (1956, 626-627): "The gap between the level of evolution of women and men is still very large. Women, more than men, remain attached to the traditional milieu. . . . There is no doubt that the promotion and the emancipation of the indigenous woman are the necessary conditions for harmonious evolution in the urban milieu."[1]

Following independence, there was a considerable push to promote increased schooling of the population, with emphasis on provision to girls as well as to boys. During the 1960s, the country's school enrollments grew at roughly twice the pace of the population at large, and this rapid growth, accompanied by increasing proportions of female students, persisted during the 1970s (Kikassa 1979).[2] After independence as well as before, Kinshasa benefited from its privileged position as the country's capital, and, hence, has consistently had distinctly higher school enrollments and educational attainments than have been seen elsewhere in the country.

Chronic economic problems created severe difficulties for the education sector during the 1980s. There were sharp reductions in national budgets for education associated with structural adjustment efforts, and, in response to deterioration in the public education system, private schools mushroomed throughout Kinshasa, particularly at the primary level.[3] Despite the economic problems, enrollment rates in the city continued to increase, and the educational profile of the population changed dramatically.[4]

School Enrollment and Educational Attainment

Figure 2.1 shows school enrollment rates for 5-year cohorts of school age, separately by gender, and gender differences in enrollment rates, for the five surveys from 1955 through 1990.[5] In considering the structure of enrollment

---

[1] Many of the calls for educating women were oriented, not toward providing training that would equip them to enter the labor market, but rather toward giving them the opportunity and knowledge to become better mothers and housewives. See, e.g., Bolamba (1949) and Bukasa (1951).

[2] This very rapid growth in school enrollments after independence characterized, not only Kinshasa and the Congo, but also numerous other countries in Africa, Asia, and Latin America (Colclough with Lewin 1993, table 1.1, 14).

[3] Data from our 1990 survey indicate that 28 percent of enrolled youths aged 6-9 were in private schools, as were 14 percent of students aged 10-14.

[4] The continued growth in enrollments in Kinshasa is notable. Numerous countries in Africa and Latin America experienced economic difficulties in the 1980s, and increased private costs of education resulting from structural adjustment programs frequently resulted in declining enrollment rates during the decade in many of these countries (Colclough with Lewin 1993).

[5] Data on school enrollment for 1990 are based on information collected on the enrollment status of more than 8,500 youths aged 6-25 residing in the households of survey respondents. Because data were not collected on the enrollment status of 5-year-olds, for purposes of figure 2.1 we have assumed that they have not yet begun school. Since the normal age for beginning school is 6, this assumption seems most plausible.

rates at any point in time, it is clear that peak enrollment takes place among those aged 10-14. In part this reflects the inclusion of 5-year-olds in the youngest group, but it also reflects delayed entry to school. That is, many students begin their studies, not at the "normal" age of 6, but instead a year or two later. When overall enrollments are low (e.g., as was the case in 1955), those aged 5-9 have the second-highest enrollment rates, while, at higher overall enrollment levels (as in 1975 and later), the enrollment rates are greater for the 15-19 age group than for those aged 5-9.

Reflecting the effort made by colonial authorities following World War II to bring increasing numbers of girls in urban areas into the education system (Bukasa 1951, 175-176), by the mid-1950s over a third of girls in Kinshasa aged 5-9 and almost 60 percent of those aged 10-14 were enrolled in school. Enrollment was much lower among those aged 15-19, however: not quite 10 percent were in school in 1955 (figure 2.1a). There was a very rapid expansion in enrollment rates between 1955 and 1967, with more than a doubling taking place in the overall enrollment rates of those aged 5-24.[6] Of particular note during this period were substantial increases in female enrollment rates for those aged 5-19, such that almost 90 percent of girls aged 10-14 and more than 35 percent of females aged 15-19 were enrolled in school in 1967.

Continued expansion of enrollment of females aged 15-19 is evident between 1967 and 1975, and, in the latter year, over 10 percent of young women aged 20-24 were in school. Moving forward to 1984, there are further increases in enrollment rates for the youngest and oldest age groups, in particular, and enrollment of young women in their early 20s continued to increase up through 1990.[7]

Overall, then, the period from 1955 to 1990 witnessed quite substantial increases in female school enrollment. Very high enrollment rates for those

---

[6] The high enrollment rates for those aged 5-9 in 1967 are largely a consequence of the timing of the survey. The 1967 survey was carried out principally during the last quarter of the calendar year and, hence, at the outset of the school year. By contrast, the 1975 and 1990 surveys were carried out later in the school year and early in the calendar year, and the 1984 census refers to essentially the end of the school year. Since age is calculated by subtracting the year of birth from the survey year, this means that a survey carried out late in the calendar year, like the 1967 survey, will count as 6-year-olds children who were eligible to begin school at the outset of the school year. However, a survey conducted early in or midway through the calendar year will count as 6-year-olds children who were only age 5 when the school year began. Hence, absent any other changes, the latter survey will find lower enrollment rates by age for the 5-9 age group. Indeed, examination of enrollment rates by individual years of age in 1967 and in 1975 reveals that, among those age 6, enrollment rates in 1967 were 39-45 percent, compared to only 11-12 percent in 1975. Further, below age 15, the rates for children age x in 1967 are very close to the rates for children age $x + 1$ in 1975.

[7] Because of frequent grade repetitions as well as delayed entry to school, it is typically the case that students in their early 20s are still in high school. In 1984, for example, 87 percent of young women aged 20-24 who were students had not completed high school. The corresponding figure for their male counterparts was 83 percent (Institut National de la Statistique 1991a, table 9, p. 67).

Fig. 2.1 School enrollment rates by age group, 1955-1990

a. Females

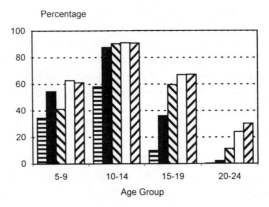

b. Males

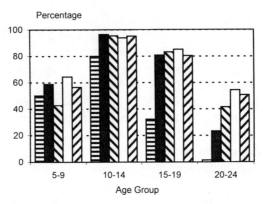

c. Gender differences

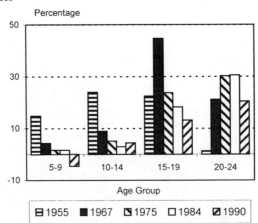

☐ 1955 ■ 1967 ◼ 1975 ☐ 1984 ◩ 1990

Sources: 1955: Congo Belge (1957a, table 21); 1967: Institut National de la Statistique (1969, annex 15); 1975: calculated from data; 1984: Institut National de la Statistique (1991a, tables 1, 9); 1990: calculated from data.

Note: Male enrollment rate minus female enrollment rate.

aged 10-14 were reached early on (by 1967), while enrollment rates for the 5-9 and 15-19 age groups increased over time up through 1984, and enrollment rates for those aged 20-24 continued to increase through 1990.

For males there is a similar general pattern to changes in enrollment rates over time, as shown in figure 2.1b. The most obvious difference is that the rates for males are consistently higher than are those for females. In addition, the pace of change is more rapid for males in the 15-19 age group (e.g., the 80 percent level is reached early, in 1967), and the increased enrollment rates of young women aged 20-24 after 1984 are not matched by increases in enrollment rates of young men in this age group.[8]

Gender differences in enrollment rates in 1955 were relatively large for those aged 10-14 and 15-19 and distinctly smaller among children aged 5-9 (figure 2.1c). The much narrower gender gap in enrollment for the youngest cohort that is apparent in the 1955 cross section reflects in large part the fact that, as of 1955, increased access of females to schooling was a quite recent phenomenon.

As is evident from figure 2.1c, the modest gender gap in enrollment of children aged 5-9 in 1955 narrowed substantially by 1967, in 1975 and 1984 it was very small, and in 1990 it was actually negative. There has been a similar decline in gender differences in enrollment among those aged 10-14. As of 1990, enrollment rates of boys under age 15 were higher than those of girls under age 15, but only slightly so. Reflecting larger gains for males than for females, the gender gap in enrollment of 15-19-year-olds widened sharply between 1955 and 1967, dropped almost as sharply by 1975, and has continued to decline since. Among those aged 20-24, a gender gap of note emerged in 1967, widened as of 1975 and 1984, and then narrowed by 1990.

In effect, then, as enrollment rates rose over time for both males and females, there was a clear tendency for gender gaps in enrollment eventually to diminish. These reductions began with the youngest age groups and spread progressively to older age groups. For the two oldest age groups there was in fact a widening of gender differences during the period examined, but in each case there is evidence of subsequent narrowing of the differences.

A somewhat closer look at enrollment rates is provided by the enrollment profiles by single year of age shown in figure 2.2.[9] As explained in note 6 above, the timing of the 1967 survey resulted in inordinately high enrollment rates for those under age 10 in particular. Taking this into account, the figure may be summarized by noting that, over time, for both females and males, the

[8] Indeed, the numbers show a decline in enrollment of males aged 20-24 between 1984 and 1990, from 54.5 percent to 51.3 percent. It is possible that this accurately reflects what took place, and, in particular, it may show the effects of prolonged economic crisis in reducing the incentives for young men to invest in education. However, it is useful to recall that the 1990 survey was a comparatively small one. Consequently, we prefer to be conservative in assessing the change since 1984 and, thus, simply note the absence of any increase.

[9] Data for 1955 were not available for single years of age, and data for 1984 were not available for single years of age above age 19.

middle portion of the enrollment profile remained fairly stable and that the left and right sides of the profile drifted upward.

That is, enrollment rates of 10-14-year-olds were high throughout the period from 1967 to 1990 (and well above the rates prevailing in 1955). Among children aged 6-9, a distinct increase in the rates took place between 1975 and 1984, suggesting that delayed entry to school was becoming increasingly less common during this period. For those aged 15 and over, there were slight differences by gender in the evolution of enrollment rates. Among females, enrollment rates rose from 1967 to 1975 for those aged 15-17 and then did not change much subsequently, while for ages 18 and above there appears to have been a more steady increase in enrollment rates throughout the period being examined. Among males, by contrast, there were already high enrollment rates in 1967 up to age 18 or so, and these rates did not increase much subsequently. Beyond age 18 there were increases in enrollment rates up through 1984 but no further increases afterward—if anything, there appears perhaps to have been a slight decline between 1984 and 1990.

The trends of rising enrollment rates and narrowing gender differences in enrollment over time influenced the educational attainment of the adult population as well. However, the impact was gradual. This may be seen in table 2.1, which shows the educational attainment of the population aged 20 and over, by age and gender, in 1955, 1967, 1975, and 1984.[10] There are several clear implications of the data. Consider first a cross-sectional perspective. In any given year younger cohorts have higher levels of schooling than do their older counterparts. This phenomenon may be seen most easily by considering variations in the percentages with no schooling or in the percentages with secondary schooling or higher as one moves across cohorts (age groups). Thus, for example, in 1967, among women age 30 and over, 73 percent had never been to school, and only 7 percent had been to secondary school or higher, while, among those aged 20-24, the corresponding figures were 38 and 23 percent, respectively.

The rising levels of educational attainment of successive cohorts at each observation point reflect the increased provision of schooling over time. Hence, for any given age group, educational attainment rises as one moves from earlier to later years. This increased exposure to schooling is evident as well from considering the time-series changes through the years in the educational profile of the adult population. That is, in each successive period covered by the table, the adult population has distinctly higher levels of educational attainment than in the preceding period. In 1955, for example, more than 85 percent of women aged 20 and over had never been to school, and this percentage dropped to 61 in 1967, to 42 in 1975, and to 26 in 1984. Conversely, fewer than 2 percent of adult women had gone beyond primary school in 1955, whereas the corresponding percentages in 1967, 1975, and 1984 were 12, 24, and 44,

---

[10] Age groups and schooling categories differ slightly from year to year, reflecting differences in the nature of the available data.

Fig. 2.2 Enrollment rates by age, 1967-1990

a. Females

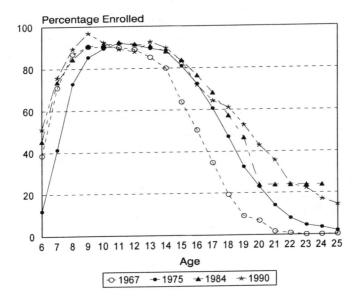

b. Males

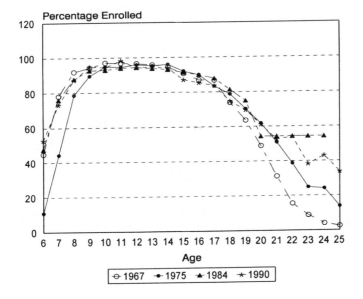

Table 2.1 Educational Attainment of the Population Aged 20 and over, by Age and Gender, 1955-1984 (percentage distributions)

Age Group	Females			Males		
	None	Primary	Postprimary	None	Primary	Postprimary
			1955			
20-24	78.9	17.5	3.6	35.1	53.0	11.9
25-29	84.9	13.2	2.0	39.5	50.4	10.1
30-34	87.4	11.4	1.2	44.2	46.1	9.7
35-44	90.3	8.6	1.0	50.7	41.6	7.7
45-54	94.8	5.2	0.0	65.6	29.3	5.1
55+	96.0	4.0	0.0	73.5	23.2	3.4
Total	85.7	12.4	1.9	45.6	45.2	9.2

Age Group	Females				Males			
	None	Primary	Secondary	Higher	None	Primary	Secondary	Higher
				1967				
20-24	37.7	39.3	22.6	0.4	7.5	25.9	64.1	2.5
25-29	57.4	30.5	11.3	0.8	13.7	40.8	41.2	4.3
30+	73.0	20.1	5.8	1.1	30.8	44.2	21.7	3.4
Total	61.2	27.0	11.0	0.9	23.2	40.0	33.3	3.4
				1975				
20-24	16.0	38.7	44.4	0.9	2.3	18.5	74.8	4.4
25-29	29.7	41.9	27.4	0.9	3.6	26.4	61.0	9.2
30-34	43.8	39.8	16.0	0.4	5.9	34.5	48.7	10.9
35-39	58.8	33.1	7.9	0.2	9.6	44.5	38.1	7.8
40-44	64.3	31.0	4.6	0.1	12.7	51.3	31.7	4.3
45-49	74.3	22.7	3.0	0.0	19.6	52.1	25.7	2.7
50-54	76.7	19.4	3.7	0.2	23.3	51.3	21.6	3.8
55+	88.7	9.3	1.9	0.2	48.2	39.5	11.1	1.3
Total	42.1	34.4	22.7	1.0	11.0	34.9	47.8	6.3
				1984				
20-24	7.5	25.4	63.3	3.8	2.7	13.3	73.7	10.3
25-29	13.0	30.3	52.7	3.9	3.6	14.4	64.3	17.7
30-34	20.8	36.8	39.5	2.9	5.4	17.4	60.7	16.5
35-39	33.9	38.6	26.3	1.2	8.2	24.0	52.7	15.1
40-44	48.5	34.5	16.1	0.9	11.9	33.7	42.7	11.7
45-49	60.3	28.7	10.5	0.7	15.8	44.9	31.7	7.5
50-54	69.7	22.6	7.2	0.5	22.0	45.4	28.8	3.8
55-59	72.8	23.2	4.0	0.0	27.9	43.7	25.9	2.5
60+	85.6	10.8	3.6	0.0	46.0	36.6	15.7	1.7
Total	26.3	29.9	41.1	2.7	9.3	23.1	55.3	12.3

Sources: 1955: Congo Belge (1957a, table 21), Congo Belge (1957b, table 15); 1967: Institut National de la Statistique (1969, annexe XV, p. 171; annexe VIII, pp. 158-160); 1975: calculated from data; 1984: Institut National de la Statistique (1991a, table 8, p. 65).

respectively.[11] These are very substantial changes, occurring over a comparatively short time span.

An additional observation of note concerns the gender gap in educational attainment. In each period covered, males have higher schooling levels than do females. However, there is a clear tendency toward diminution of this gender gap over time. For example, in 1955 men aged 20 and over were nearly 5 times more likely than women to have gone beyond primary school (9.2 percent compared to 1.9 percent). By 1967, this ratio had fallen to almost 3, and it fell further to about 2.3 in 1975 and to just over 1.5 in 1984. This narrowing of the gender gap in educational attainment, in turn, reflects in large part the more rapid growth in school enrollments of females than in enrollments of males.

While the gender gap overall has been narrowing, one area that has not seen much narrowing is the relative proportions of women and men with higher education. Across surveys, and across cohorts within surveys, proportions of both men and women with postsecondary education rose over time. However, for the most part they rose at least as rapidly for men as for women.[12] Hence, the magnitude of the relative differences has not diminished, and the absolute differences have grown as the overall proportions with postsecondary education have increased.

It is worth reiterating that, within the Congo, Kinshasa has traditionally drawn a disproportionate share of resources devoted to schooling. This can readily be seen by considering the educational attainments of young adults aged 20-24 as of the 1984 census (Institut National de la Statistique 1991a, 31, 65). In Kinshasa, five-sixths of males and two-thirds of females in this age group had completed at least some secondary schooling, and under 3 percent of males and 8 percent of females had no schooling. By contrast, among those aged 20-24 in the remainder of the country, just under half of males and less than one-fifth of females had been to secondary school, while over 13 percent of males and nearly 42 percent of females had no schooling.

In effect, the 1984 schooling distribution for 20-24-year-old females outside Kinshasa was quite similar to the 1967 schooling distribution in Kinshasa for females that age, while for males the 1984 figures for those outside

[11] Consideration of the cross-sectional and time-series data jointly reveals what at first glance may appear to be an anomaly: variability in the schooling of a given birth cohort over time. That is, e.g., 16 percent of 20-24-year-old women in 1975 had no schooling, while, 9 years later, 21 percent of women aged 30-34 (almost the same birth cohorts) had no schooling. Conversely, while 79 percent of 20-24-year-old women had no schooling in 1955, 20 years later the corresponding percentage for 40-44-year-old women had fallen to 63 percent. These variations reflect the effects of migration: in the first case, female migrants to Kinshasa between 1975 and 1984 who were aged 20-24 in 1975 had lower schooling levels than women that age who resided in Kinshasa in 1975, while, in the second case, female migrants between 1955 and 1975 who were aged 20-24 in 1955 had higher schooling levels than those residing in Kinshasa in 1955.

[12] The one exception to this statement is across cohorts among the younger age groups in 1984. Higher education was not yet completed for those aged 20-24, in particular. However, whether one considers the age range 20-39 or 25-39, there does appear to be some improvement, moving from older to younger age groups, in the percentage of women with higher education relative to that of men.

Kinshasa entailed slightly lower levels of educational attainment than those for males that age in Kinshasa in 1967. From this perspective, then, educational attainment in the rest of the country may be seen as lagging behind that in Kinshasa by perhaps 17-20 years.

Finally, note the magnitude of the changes over time in the educational attainment of the "typical" adult. In 1955, a woman in Kinshasa would most likely never have been to school, while, by 1984, the modal group in the education distribution of women is the secondary level. For men, in 1955, there were almost equal percentages of those with no schooling and those with primary schooling; by 1984, the majority of men had secondary schooling.[13] Hence, over a period of less than 30 years there were huge changes in the education levels of both women and men.

Changes over Time in the City's Economy

As noted in chapter 1, the location of the city of Leopoldville was based on geographic considerations linked to river transportation. As the city grew and developed, the mismatch between its physical location, where the demand for labor was growing rapidly, and the location of supplies of potential workers necessitated recruitment of workers from rural areas (Lux 1962). While in early times especially these workers were often from the relatively nearby Cataractes District of what is now the province of Bas-Congo, recruitment of workers also took place in more distant locales (see Dhanis 1953; Lamal 1954). Colonial authorities took considerable care to regulate labor migration to the city so that the inflows of migrants corresponded to the availability of job opportunities (Capelle 1947), and, when labor demand diminished, as in the Great Depression of the 1930s, workers no longer in demand were sent from the city back to their rural areas of origin.

In brief, then, the situation during the colonial period was one in which migration to Leopoldville was tightly controlled so as to ensure that adult male residents of the city had employment.[14] A direct consequence of this policy was that employment rates among males in the city were extremely high, and the vast bulk of employment consisted of salaried employment in the rapidly growing modern sector of the economy. While there were concerns about illegal migrants in the city, the number of such individuals was generally thought to be fairly limited (Capelle 1947), at least until near the very end of the colonial period (Houyoux and Kinavwuidi 1986, 4).

However, with independence also came an end to effective controls on

---

[13] Note, however, that, among those with secondary schooling in 1984, there was still a distinct gender gap: women were almost equally divided between those with 1-4 years of secondary schooling and those with 5-6 years, while two-thirds of men had attained 5-6 years (Institut National de la Statistique 1991a, table 8, p. 65).

[14] Residents of Leopoldville during the colonial period were required to have documents in their possession, issued by the colonial Office of the Black Population, verifying that, indeed, they had legitimate employment in the city.

internal migration. The city began to grow rapidly again during the 1960s, but, in contrast with previous growth spurts, this growth was no longer linked directly to the expansion of salaried employment in the modern sector. The political turmoil of the early 1960s in the Congo also contributed to the especially rapid growth of Kinshasa at that time. There were relatively large migrant flows from Katanga Province in the south from 1960 to 1962 and from the Kasais and from Bandundu and Equateur Provinces to the east and north of Kinshasa from 1963 to 1965 (Houyoux and Kinavwuidi 1986, 6). In any case, the "divorce" between population growth and modern-sector employment growth resulted in a period of relatively rapid growth of employment in the informal sector during the early years of independence.

By the late 1960s, a measure of political stability had been restored to the country, and, for several years, the economy showed signs of sustained growth. As noted earlier, however, the Zairianization and radicalization measures adopted in 1973 and 1974, in conjunction with the sharp fall of the price of copper, began a long downward slide for the economy that continued throughout the 1970s and 1980s and became acute in the 1990s. Modern-sector employment from the mid-1970s until the early 1990s tended to grow only very slowly (Lokota 1992), so—as was the case in the early 1960s—the informal sector served to pick up the slack and absorb a considerable proportion of Kinshasa's potential labor force. While reliable data are not available to measure employment at present, it seems clear that, since 1991, Kinshasa's modern sector has shrunk substantially while the informal sector has continued to grow very rapidly.[15]

Employment Growth and Structure

Data on the levels of employment and employment growth, separately by class of worker (salaried and independent)[16] and by gender, are shown in table 2.2. Consider first the data on total employment in the lower third of the table. Over the period from 1955 to 1984 total employment increased almost fivefold. During this same period, the city's population increased eightfold, and the population aged 15 and over increased almost sevenfold. Over the long haul, then, the level of total employment has failed to keep pace with the growth of the population and of the potential labor force, implying increased rates of unemployment and nonemployment.[17]

The growth of total employment and its component parts during various periods since 1955 highlights the effects of changing economic circumstances. From 1955 to 1967, when the population aged 15 and over was growing by 6 percent per year, total employment grew by less than half that rate. In addition,

[15] A prominent foreign industrialist in Kinshasa, interviewed in late 1994, indicated that employment in the more than 20 firms that he controlled had fallen by 25 percent since 1991.

[16] *Independent* as shown in the table includes unpaid family workers and apprentices.

[17] Some of the increased nonemployment is, of course, a direct consequence of the increased school enrollment of teenagers and young adults.

reflecting the relaxing of controls on migration and the "divorce" between modern-sector employment and migration, the rate of growth in the number of independents was two and a half times more rapid than the growth rate of salaried employment. This, in turn, signals much more rapid growth in informal-sector employment as compared to modern-sector employment.[18]

Between 1967 and 1975, by contrast, total employment grew slightly more rapidly than did the population aged 15 and over (10.0 percent per year vs. 9.4 percent per year). The growth of salaried employment took place at a slightly slower pace than did the growth of the potential labor force, while employment of independents grew at a rate almost twice as great as that for salaried employment. After 1975, however, the effects of the country's emerging economic crisis are readily apparent: while total employment grew at a rate comparable to the growth rate of the potential labor force, the growth rate of salaried employment was very low, being only about one-fifth the growth rate of the number of independents.

Hence, the economic crisis was characterized by an accelerated shift in the composition of employment toward increasing proportions of informal-sector workers. In 1955, independents represented only 10 percent of total employment. This figure increased to 14 percent in 1967 and 22 percent by 1975, and, between 1975 and 1984, it almost doubled, rising to 41 percent.

Consideration of the gender differences shown in table 2.2 reveals that the most rapid increases in employment have been those of women. The rate of growth of female employment was three to five times that of male employment in each period covered by the table. Overall, women's share of total employment increased from less than 2 percent in 1955 to nearly 30 percent by 1984. And, while female salaried employment actually grew more rapidly than employment of female independents between 1955 and 1967, after 1967, as well as for the full period, female employment growth was more heavily concentrated in the informal sector.

Associated with the growth and changing structure of employment in terms of class of worker has been a substantial shift in the industrial structure of employment (table 2.3). In 1955, fully half the employment in Leopoldville was in manufacturing and construction (secondary sector), while most of the other half was in the tertiary sector. Over the next 12 years, the balance between these two sectors shifted dramatically: employment in the secondary sector fell to less than 30 percent of the total, predominantly reflecting a sharp

---

[18] Although a very small number of independents may be found in the modern sector, the vast majority work in the informal sector. Salaried workers may be either in the formal or in the informal sector, constituting virtually all workers in the former and a minority of those in the latter. Elsewhere, it has been estimated that, in 1987, just over a quarter of the total employment in the informal sector consisted of salaried workers and that a similar fraction of all salaried workers in Kinshasa were employed in the informal sector (Shapiro 1992). Thus, while the distinction between salaried and independent workers is by no means identical to the distinction between the modern and the informal sectors, it is the case that more rapid growth in the number of independents than in the number of salaried workers is a clear sign of expansion in the relative importance of employment in the informal sector.

Table 2.2 Total Employment and Employment Growth, by Class of Worker and Gender, 1955-1984

Year	Employment (000)			Annual Growth Rates (%)		
	Total	Salaried	Independent	Total	Salaried	Independent
Males						
1955	114.7	104.2	10.5	—	—	—
1967	150.6	130.2	20.4	2.3	1.9	5.7
1975	283.2	245.7	37.5	8.2	8.3	7.9
1984	408.0	301.2	106.8	4.1	2.3	12.3
Females						
1955	1.8	0.6	1.2	—	—	—
1967	7.2	5.4	1.9	12.2	20.1	3.9
1975	55.1	17.5	37.6	29.0	15.8	45.2
1984	167.4	39.0	128.4	13.1	9.3	14.6
Total						
1955	116.5	104.8	11.7	—	—	—
1967	157.8	135.5	22.3	2.6	2.2	5.5
1975	338.3	263.2	75.1	10.0	8.7	16.4
1984	575.4	340.9	234.5	6.1	2.9	13.5

Sources: 1955: Congo Belge (1957a, table 30) and Congo Belge (1957b, table 20); 1967: Institut National de la Statistique (1969, table 73, p. 118; and annexe XX, p. 179); 1975: Houyoux and Kinavwuidi (1986, table III.11, p. 175); 1984: Institut National de la Statistique (1991a, table 14, p. 74; and table 10, p. 68).

Note: Totals do not always equal sum of components owing to rounding. Growth rates shown for a particular year refer to the period since the preceding year.

decline in the absolute number of workers in construction, while tertiary-sector employment increased to two-thirds of total employment. Growth in employment in general services (including public-sector employment) was especially large. These trends continued through 1984, by which time barely one-sixth of total employment was in manufacturing or construction, while nearly three-fourths of total employment was in the tertiary sector.[19]

Of particular significance is the substantial increase after 1975 in the proportion of the workforce engaged in commerce. Wholesale and retail trade are included in commerce, and, hence, those in commerce may be in either the formal or the informal sector. Informal-sector commerce, consisting most frequently of petty trading, is the area that grew tremendously during this period. Total employment grew by 70 percent from 1975 to 1984, while

[19] Differences across the various surveys in the coverage of Kinshasa make it difficult to assess changes in the importance of primary-sector employment (predominantly agriculture). The 1955 and 1984 data included agricultural workers residing on the outskirts of the city, often in essentially rural areas of the province of Kinshasa. The 1967 and 1975 surveys, by contrast, did not include these more remote residents and, hence, tend to understate the extent of primary-sector employment in the city as a whole.

Table 2.3 Employment by Industry, 1955-1984

Industry	1955	1967	1975	1984
	Employment			
Agriculture	4,372	2,610	18,270	50,350
Mining	816	370	1,090	2,020
Manufacturing	32,834	33,700	64,350	75,530
Construction	25,228	13,350	22,340	21,870
Water/electricity	0	2,110	4,310	4,960
Commerce	16,804	25,770	70,360	215,940
Banks	0	4,490	7,890	9,190
Transport & comm.	16,828	22,790	43,300	53,020
Services-general	9,240	39,120	80,150	132,590
Services-personal	9,733	10,930	25,920	a
Don't know	0	2,520	350	9,920
Total	115,855	157,760	338,330	575,400
	Percentages			
Agriculture	3.8	1.7	5.4	8.8
Mining	0.7	0.2	0.3	0.4
Manufacturing	28.3	21.4	19.0	13.1
Construction	21.8	8.5	6.6	3.8
Water/electricity	0.0	1.3	1.3	0.9
Commerce	14.5	16.3	20.8	37.5
Banks	0.0	2.8	2.3	1.6
Transport & comm.	14.5	14.4	12.8	9.2
Services-general	8.0	24.8	23.7	23.0
Services-personal	8.4	6.9	7.7	a
Don't know	0.0	1.6	0.1	1.7
Total	100.0	100.0	100.0	100.0
	Percentage Distributions by Sector			
Primary	4.5	1.9	5.7	9.1
Secondary	50.1	29.8	25.6	16.9
Tertiary	45.4	66.7	68.6	72.2
Don't know	0.0	1.6	0.1	1.7
Total	100.0	100.0	100.0	100.0

Sources: 1955: Congo Belge (1957a, table 33) and Congo Belge (1957b, table 21); 1967: Institut National de la Statistique (1969, table 61, p. 108; and table 62, p. 109); 1975: Houyoux and Kinavwuidi (1986, table III.14, p. 178; and annexe III.10, pp. 205-212); 1984: Institut National de la Statistique (1991a, table 11, p. 69; and table 10, p. 68).

Note: Total employment for 1955 is lower than that listed in table 2.2 owing to omission from this table of 624 salaried females for whom data were not available. Reported data for 1984 include unemployed workers. The reported totals have been revised downward proportionately for this table so as to correspond to employment and hence eliminate unemployed individuals.

a Data for 1984 group all service workers together.

employment in commerce tripled and accounted for more than 60 percent of the growth in total employment. This rapid growth of employment in commerce reflects household survival strategies in which increased participation in the informal sector of the economy seeks to counter the effects of both limited job opportunities in the modern sector and declining real incomes of wage and salary workers.

There were increases in informal-sector participation in commerce for men as well as for women. In 1975, 56 percent of those in commerce were male, and 44 percent of these males were independents. Among women in commerce in 1975, 91 percent were independents. By 1984, women outnumbered men in commerce, reflecting much more rapid relative growth for women, and 56 percent of males as well as 93 percent of females in commerce were independents (Institut National de la Statistique 1991a, table 15).

Employment by Age and Gender

A complementary perspective on employment is provided by the data reported in tables 2.4 and 2.5. More specifically, employment rates by age and gender are shown in table 2.4. For males, variations in these rates over time in large measure reflect fluctuations in the strength of the city's economy. Nearly 90 percent of males aged 15 and over were employed in 1955; among those aged 25 and above, the figure was 94 percent. Twelve years later, employment rates of males aged 15 and over had fallen to 67 percent. This overall drop reflected very substantial declines for those aged 15-24, many more of whom were in school in 1967 than had been the case in 1955, and modest declines for older men. Among those aged 25 and over, the decline in the employment rate was much smaller, to 88 percent.

By 1975, the overall employment rate of males aged 15 and above had fallen modestly, primarily as a consequence of reduced employment among those in their early 20s (a group whose school enrollment rate rose from 41 to 54 percent between 1967 and 1975). Reflecting the economic expansion of the late 1960s and early 1970s and also the fact that the adverse consequences of Zairianization had not yet had much impact on the Kinshasa labor market, the employment rate of males aged 25 and over had actually risen slightly, to almost 90 percent. By 1984, however, after a decade of poor economic performance, employment rates had fallen in every age group but the youngest, and only 80 percent of men aged 25 and over were employed.

Over the full period, then, the percentage employed by age for males shows sharp reductions right away for those under age 25 and modest declines initially for those aged 25-29, primarily reflecting increased school enrollment. After 1975, however, there are further large reductions in the employment of younger men (ages 20-29) as well as moderate declines in the employment of those aged 30 and over, due largely to the deterioration of the economy.

The employment experience of women has been quite different from that of men. There has been a steady increase over time in women's economic

Chapter 2

Table 2.4 Percentage Employed, by Age and Gender, 1955-1990

Age Group	Males				Females				
	1955	1967	1975	1984	1955	1967	1975	1984	1990
15-19	53.2	5.5	5.5	5.9	2.0	a	2.4	5.2	9.5
20-24	91.2	49.5	39.0	29.1	1.7	a	11.5	18.5	27.2
25-29	94.1	85.3	84.5	66.7	1.9	a	15.9	32.1	43.4
30-34	93.9	91.1	94.1	84.7	2.0	a	17.8	37.7	55.4
35-44	95.6	92.5	96.2	90.3	4.5	a	21.7	40.5	56.3
45-54	93.9	82.0^b	94.5	87.8	4.1	a	28.5	43.3	52.2^c
55+	83.1	—	65.0	61.5	8.5	a	19.6	32.5	—
Total 15+	89.0	66.7	63.0	55.7	2.6	3.8	13.7	25.5	34.2^d
Total 25+	93.9	88.2	89.5	79.7	3.1	3.7	20.0	37.1	50.4^e

Sources: 1955: Congo Belge (1957a, tables 30 and 9), Congo Belge (1957b, tables 20 and 6); 1967: Institut National de la Statistique (1969, table 58, p. 106 [males]; and annexe XX, p. 179 [females]); 1975: Houyoux and Kinavwuidi (1986, annexe III.2, p. 196 [males]; and annexe III.3, p. 197 [females]); 1984: Institut National de la Statistique (1991a, table 10, p. 68); 1990: calculated from data.

[a] Data not available.
[b] Ages 45 and above.
[c] Ages 45-49.
[d] Ages 15-49.
[e] Ages 25-49.

activity.[20] While this increase has taken place among all age groups, it has been greatest among women aged 25-54 (see figure 2.3). In effect, then, women's employment was much less tied to fluctuations in the state of the city's economy than was men's employment. Overall, one-fourth of women aged 15 and over and 37 percent of those aged 25 and over were employed in 1984, and by 1990 these figures (with an upper age limit of 49) had risen to 34 and 50 percent, respectively.

The data shown in table 2.5 document the increase that has taken place over time in the share of total male employment represented by independents.[21] In 1955, fewer than 1 in 10 employed males in Leopoldville worked as an independent; by 1984, this figure had increased to 1 in 4, with the bulk of the increase occurring after 1975. Between 1975 and 1984, the percentage of employed males who were independents rose in every age group and most dramatically for workers under age 30.

---

[20] Because the 1990 survey probed for information on the economic activity of women, it is possible that the employment rates for 1990 reported in table 2.4 are biased upward somewhat compared to the rates for the earlier general surveys, which did not probe for this information. However, the rapid growth in female employment rates from 1975 to 1984 and the persistence of economic difficulties throughout the 1980s suggest to us that the continued growth after 1984 implied by our data is a good representation of the actual situation.

[21] Here and elsewhere in this work, we consider only the primary employment of individuals. In fact, the economic crisis since the mid-1970s resulted in an explosion of independent secondary activities in the informal sector, representing an effort to offset the effects of declining real salaries. These activities are not well measured, however, and they are not examined here.

Table 2.5 Percentage of Employed Workers Who Are Independent, by Age and Gender, 1955-1990

	Males			Females			
Age Group	1955	1975	1984	1955	1975	1984	1990
15-19	3.2	17.7	54.3	28.0	33.6	81.0	98.1
20-24	4.0	13.0	38.6	44.4	32.4	70.5	91.3
25-29	5.5	9.6	29.5	77.8	52.3	65.2	87.1
30-34	9.6	12.2	24.6	87.0	72.2	70.3	85.9
35-44	12.4	13.3	19.7	73.5	88.0	83.4	86.8
45-54	19.9	14.5	21.1	81.0	91.8	92.1	81.8[a]
55+	28.7	20.3	32.8	81.8	93.1	94.1	—
Total 15+	9.2	13.2	26.2	67.1	68.1	76.7	88.2[b]
Total 25+	11.2	13.1	24.2	78.7	77.9	77.7	86.4[c]

Sources: 1955: Congo Belge (1957a, tables 30 and 9), Congo Belge (1957b, tables 20 and 6); 1975: calculated from data; 1984: Institut National de la Statistique (1991a, table 14, p. 74); 1990: calculated from data.

[a] Ages 45-49.
[b] Ages 15-49.
[c] Ages 25-49.

Fig. 2.3 Percentage employed, by age group, women aged 15-54, 1955-1990

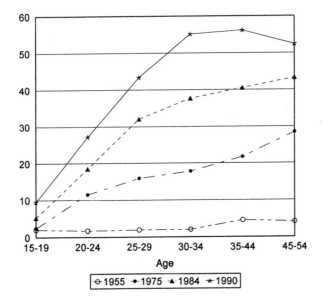

Among women, by contrast, independents have constituted the major share of total employment throughout the years. For females as for males, however, the slowdown in the growth of modern-sector economic activity after 1975—reflected in the slow growth of salaried employment shown in table 2.2 —translates into clear increases in the proportion of all employed workers who are independents. As was the case for males, these increases are most apparent among those under age 30.

For both males and females, the growth in the share of employment represented by independents reflects rapid growth of the informal sector in the face of grossly inadequate employment opportunities in the modern sector. Access to modern-sector jobs clearly became especially difficult for young workers as time went by. As of 1990, then, *prior* to the onset of the acute economic crisis, the Kinshasa labor market already showed signs of an economy in distress.

Chapter 3. Levels and Trends in Mortality and Fertility

This chapter provides an overview of mortality and fertility in Kinshasa during the period from 1955 to 1990. For comparative purposes, we also examine estimates of mortality and fertility for the entire Congo over this same period. Although our broader focus in this study is on fertility, knowledge of mortality experience is very important for understanding changes in fertility behavior (Easterlin 1996; Easterlin and Crimmins 1985). The first part of the chapter thus looks at levels and trends in mortality as reflected in estimates from different surveys and sources. This is followed by an overview of levels and trends in fertility. A concluding section goes into more detail on fertility and examines changes over time in numbers of children ever born by age and in age-specific fertility rates.

Mortality Levels and Trends

Estimates of mortality in Kinshasa and the Congo are shown in table 3.1. Owing to concerns about possible misreporting of mortality, these estimates are all generated via indirect methods.[1] The UN figures are, as we shall discuss below, part of broader population estimates and projections that attempt to take into consideration demographic estimates from national data sources.

Romaniuk's estimates for the mid-1950s make it clear that mortality was substantially lower in Kinshasa than in the rest of the country, with both the crude death rate and the infant mortality rate in the city being less than half their corresponding national values and life expectancy at birth being almost 50 percent higher in Kinshasa than in the country at large. In part, this reflected a more general phenomenon of lower death rates and higher life expectancy in urban as compared to rural areas of the Congo (Romaniuk 1968, tables 6.22

---

[1] We have not produced mortality estimates for Kinshasa for 1990 from our own survey data because our relatively small sample, restricted to women of reproductive age, is inadequate for this purpose.

Table 3.1 Mortality Estimates for Kinshasa and the Congo, 1955-1990

Year	Crude Death Rate	Infant Mortality Rate	Life Expectancy
Kinshasa			
1955	11.6	78	57.0
1967	9.9	91	55.7
1975	15	135	47-54.1
1984	12.6	104	53
1990	NA	NA	NA
Congo			
1955	26	165	39.5
1967	NA	NA	NA
1975ᵃ	17.0	NA	46.4
1984	16.8	137	47
1990	15.1	100	51.5

Sources: 1955: Romaniuk (1968, table 6.37, p. 312; and p. 335); 1967: Institut National de la Statistique (1969, 64); 1975: Houyoux and Kinavwuidi (1986, 102-103 [Kinshasa]), République du Zaïre (1978b, table 7.2.2, p. 149 [higher estimate of life expectancy for Kinshasa, Congo]); 1984: Institut National de la Statistique (1991c, 20-21); 1990: United Nations (1998, 560).

Note: NA = not available.

[a] Data in this row refer to results from the 1974-1977 surveys of the west of the country and pertain to the three provinces of Bas-Congo, Bandundu, and Kasai Occidental, a portion of Equateur Province, and Kinshasa.

and 6.36), presumably as a consequence of the more ready availability of modern health care services. In addition, however, Kinshasa experienced lower mortality than did other urban areas.

The mortality estimates for subsequent years suggest that there has been some convergence over time, with the differences between Kinshasa and the rest of the country narrowing. More specifically, as reflected in the estimates in the top half of the table, for the nearly 30-year period for which estimates of mortality in Kinshasa are available, some deterioration is suggested. There is an increased crude death rate and reduced life expectancy, both on the order of less than 10 percent, and a distinctly larger increase in the infant mortality rate, amounting to 33 percent. At the same time, however, there is no clear trend in mortality in Kinshasa across the various subperiods. The estimated crude death rate first declined, then increased, and then declined somewhat, ending up in 1984 at a level slightly higher than that estimated for 1955. Infant mortality rate estimates increased through 1975, then declined between 1975 and 1984, ending (in 1984) at a level one-third higher than that for 1955. Life expectancy at birth, in turn, appears to have diminished modestly over the entire period under consideration, with perhaps some increase from 1975 to 1984.

The changes across subperiods appear to be inconsistent for the period from 1955 to 1967 since the crude death rate fell while infant mortality rose and life expectancy fell. This apparent inconsistency may be due, at least in part, to the effects of changing age composition. That is, the crude death rate is a measure that is influenced by the age composition of the population, while the other two mortality measures are not. Since we saw in chapter 1 that the period from 1955 to 1967 was characterized by a sharp increase in the proportion of children in the city's population, and since children aged 5-14 tend to have especially low death rates in a population, this compositional effect could help account for a declining crude death rate accompanied by increasing infant mortality and declining life expectancy. For the additional subperiods for which estimates are available for Kinshasa, we see increased mortality initially (1967-1975) followed by decreasing mortality (1975-1984).

In contrast to the overall increased mortality estimated for Kinshasa, figures for the entire country all indicate continued improvement over time,[2] both for the entire period and for the different subperiods.[3] Between 1955 and 1990, the crude death rate and the infant mortality rate both fell by about 40 percent, while life expectancy at birth rose by 30 percent. Again, then, with decreasing mortality nationally and slightly increasing mortality for Kinshasa, the differences between the two have diminished over time. In 1984, the last year for which estimates are available for both the capital and the entire country, the crude death rate and the infant mortality rate were both about 25 percent lower in Kinshasa than in the Congo, while life expectancy at birth was nearly 13 percent higher. Although we do not have estimates for mortality in Kinshasa as of 1990, we believe that, between 1984 and 1990, the city continued to experience somewhat lower mortality than the rest of the country.

Fertility Levels and Trends

Estimates of fertility in Kinshasa from available data sources are shown in the top panel of table 3.2. Romaniuk's estimates for 1955, adjusted for under-reporting of births, present a picture of a high-fertility population, with a total fertility rate of about 7.5.[4] By comparison, as indicated in the lower panel of the

[2] UN estimates for the Congo for the period from 1950 to 1955 are quite close to those reported in table 3.1 for 1955, being 25.6 for the crude death rate, 166 for the infant mortality rate, and 39.1 for life expectancy at birth (United Nations 1998, 560). For the periods corresponding to the intervening years in the table, the UN estimates typically reflect lower mortality (e.g., for 1980-1985, the UN estimates for the three mortality measures are 16.2, 107, and 49.9, respectively). The general pattern of declining mortality over time is, thus, evident in the UN estimates, but, in contrast to the estimates shown in the table, the UN figures indicate a smoother decline.

[3] While no national surveys were undertaken between the mid-1950s and 1984, there was a large-scale study done in the mid-1970s covering the western part of the country (République du Zaïre et al. 1977, 1978a, 1978b) and including the six largest cities in the region as well as smaller urban centers and rural areas. The 1975 Kinshasa survey was part of the broader Enquête Démographique de l'Ouest du Zaïre study (known by its French acronym, EDOZA), which was carried out between 1974 and 1977.

[4] The unadjusted data, as reported by Romaniuk (1967, table II.1, p. 55), yielded a crude birth rate of 52.2, a general fertility rate of 244, and age-specific fertility rates that implied a total fertility rate of 6.68. Hence, Romaniuk's adjustments increased the first measure by 2.5 percent and the latter two measures by 12-13 percent.

table, for the entire country the level of fertility was distinctly lower: the total fertility rate was estimated to be 5.91, with a crude birth rate of 45.2 per 1,000 and a general fertility rate of 203 (Romaniuk 1967, 1968). In a departure from the more typical pattern, fertility was higher in Kinshasa and in other urban areas of the Belgian Congo in the 1950s than in rural areas, with estimated crude birth rates of 55 in urban areas and 43 in rural areas (Gouvernement Central de la République du Congo 1961; Romaniuk 1967, 1968).

The urban-rural differential in part reflected the presence of high levels of sterility and childlessness in certain rural areas in the northern parts of the country. Among women aged 35-44, for example, roughly 40 percent of those in the Tshuapa and Equateur Districts in Equateur Province and almost 45 percent of those in the Bas-Uele and Haut-Uele Districts in Orientale Province were childless. The corresponding figure for both Kinshasa and the Congo was 22 percent (Romaniuk 1968, table 6.47, p. 331). The northern part of the Congo, with its low level of fertility and high proportions childless, was part of a broader "infertility belt" stretching from Cameroon to southern Chad and including the Central African Republic (Retel-Laurentin 1974).

In addition, Romaniuk argued that the system of family allowances for salaried workers that prevailed in Kinshasa in the 1950s, a massive housing construction program, improved health care and especially prenatal care and hospital births, and efforts to combat venereal disease all contributed to the especially high level of fertility in the city as compared to elsewhere in the Congo (Romaniuk 1967, 162-167).[5] Further, Sala-Diakanda (1980, 205) has suggested that selective migration of high-fertility women may also have been a contributing factor.

Associated with this high fertility was early and near-universal marriage. In 1955, among young women in the city aged 15-19, 62 percent were married, while more than 90 percent of those aged 20-24 were in a sexual union. This reflected the low levels of women's schooling: fewer than 10 percent of young women aged 15-19 were enrolled in school, and enrollment was negligible at higher ages. Fully 64 percent of those aged 15-19 had not received any schooling, and (as shown in table 2.1 above) the same is true of between 79 and 95 percent of those in older cohorts of women of reproductive age.

As noted earlier, Kinshasa in 1955 was predominantly a city of migrants, particularly among those of reproductive age. Nearly three-quarters of the city's population had been born outside the city, including more than 80 percent of those aged 15-19 and more than 95 percent of those aged 20-49 (cf. table 1.1 above). In assessing the high fertility of the urban areas, Romaniuk (1967) emphasized the youthfulness of the urban-born population and noted that "the mentality [in urban areas] is essentially rural and traditional, at least in regard to procreation" (186). Similarly, in his summary he stated that "the rather

---

[5] The high levels of sterility among certain of the Congo's ethnic groups were convincingly linked to relatively high levels of venereal disease by Romaniuk (see Romaniuk 1961; Romaniuk 1967, chap. 10). See also Retel-Laurentin (1974).

Table 3.2 Fertility Estimates for Kinshasa and the Congo, 1955-1990

Year	Crude Birth Rate	General Fertility Rate	Total Fertility Rate
		Kinshasa	
1955	53.5	275	7.51
1967	51.6-60	243-282	NA
1975	48.9-54.9	250-261	7.5
1984	51.5	230	7.7
1990	NA	198	5.67
		Congo	
1955	45.2	203	5.91
1967	NA	NA	NA
1975[a]	44.6	218	6.3
1984	48.1	229	6.7
1990	45.3-48	NA	6.09-6.70

Sources: 1955: Romaniuk (1968, table 6.48, p. 333); 1967: Institut National de la Statistique (1969, 65-66); 1975: Houyoux and Kinavwuidi (1986, 114 [high estimates of crude birth rate and general fertility rate; no estimate given for total fertility rate]), Sala-Diakanda (1980, table 36 [low estimates of crude birth rate and general fertility rate and TFR estimate] [Kinshasa]), Tabutin (1982, table 1 [Congo]); 1984: Institut National de la Statistique (1991c, 21 [crude birth rate] and 18 [total fertility rate]), general fertility rate is estimated based on crude birth rate and the population of women aged 15-44 given in Institut National de la Statistique (1991a, table 1); 1990: calculated from survey data on births during the 5 years preceding the survey (Kinshasa), United Nations (1991, 602 [low estimate]), United Nations (1998, 560 [high estimate Congo]).

Note: NA = not available. (For 1967, no estimate of the TFR was provided for Kinshasa, and no estimates exist for the entire country other than the UN estimates; for 1990, the data are insufficient to permit calculation of the crude birth rate.)

[a] Data in this row refer to results from the 1974-1977 surveys of the west of the country.

profound social transformations that the African city has been subjected to do not, however, seem to have notably affected the attitudes of urban dwellers with regard to procreation" (324).

Estimates of fertility in Kinshasa from the 1967 and 1975 surveys shown in table 3.2 suggest that, over the 20-year period following the 1955 survey, there was little change in the overall level of fertility.[6] As noted earlier, there were no national surveys carried out during this period, but results from the large-scale Enquête Démographique de l'Ouest du Zaïre (EDOZA) study done in the mid-1970s and covering the western part of the country (République du Zaïre et al. 1977, 1978a, 1978b) provide a good indication of what was happening elsewhere in the country. These figures are reported for 1975 in the bottom panel of table 3.2.

[6] The existence of a range of estimates for both the crude birth rate and the general fertility rate in 1967 and 1975 complicates comparisons over time. However, the 1955 estimates of these measures fall within the ranges for 1967, and, for the birth rate, this is true for 1975 as well. With an estimated total fertility rate in 1975 essentially equal to the corresponding estimate for 1955, *little change in the overall level of fertility* seems like a reasonably accurate characterization.

In order to assess changes over time, Tabutin (1982, table 1) used Romaniuk's (1967) estimates and determined that, in the west of the country, as of the mid-1950s, the crude birth rate had been 46.4, the general fertility rate was 211, and the total fertility rate was 6.2. Hence, in the 1950s, fertility measures for the west of the country were slightly higher than the corresponding national figures, with the differences being on the order of 3-5 percent. Comparing these figures for the west from the 1950s with those from the 1970s makes it clear that, overall, there was a small increase in fertility (2-3 percent), as measured by the general fertility rate and the total fertility rate. This increase presumably reflected reductions in sterility in the northwestern part of the country (Sala-Diakanda 1980; Tabutin 1982).

The estimates for Kinshasa from the 1984 census reported in table 3.2 suggest continuation of the more or less horizontal trend. The implication is that fertility in Kinshasa did not change very much between 1975 and 1984: the reported crude birth rate is comparable to or slightly lower than that for earlier years, the estimated general fertility rate is somewhat lower, and the reported total fertility rate is slightly higher. For the Congo, the fertility estimates from the 1984 census are all higher than the 1975 estimates.

In marked contrast to the census estimates for Kinshasa, our survey data indicate that there was a notable decline in fertility by 1990.[7] Relative to the figures for 1975, the estimates for 1990 show fertility having declined by more than 20 percent. More specifically, the fall in the total fertility rate was 24 percent, while the drop in the general fertility rate was almost 21 percent if the low estimate from 1975 is used and 24 percent if the high estimate is used. Compared to the 1984 census estimates, the 1990 general fertility rate is almost 14 percent lower, and the 1990 total fertility rate shows a reduction of more than 26 percent. Such a sharp decline in fertility over a 6-year span is simply not plausible: either the 1984 census numbers are incorrect, or our 1990 fertility estimates are flawed.

We believe that the fertility estimates for 1984 are flawed. Multiple census reports (e.g., Institut National de la Statistique 1991c, 18) note that those estimates were generated using the FERTCB procedure of MortPak-Lite, a UN demographic software package (United Nations 1988). This procedure uses information from a single survey on the average number of children ever born to women by age group, employing a technique first suggested by Mortara (1949) for populations with constant fertility. This approach presupposes that fertility has remained stable in the recent past, however, and it is clear that applying the procedure when fertility has in fact been falling will yield incorrect estimates.

---

[7] The fertility estimates for 1990 are direct estimates based on reported birth histories for the 5-year period preceding the survey, whereas earlier estimates were generated using indirect methods. If the direct approach that we used for 1990 is applied to the 1975 data, the resulting estimated total fertility rate is 7.2, or 4 percent lower than the figure of 7.5 reported in table 3.2. Hence, using a direct approach for both years implies a drop in fertility in excess of 20 percent.

Consider, for example, what happens when the procedure is used with data from different surveys done in Kenya, where fertility has fallen sharply since at least the latter part of the 1980s. Applying the procedure to data on children ever born from the 1978 Kenya Fertility Survey (part of the World Fertility Surveys [WFS]) yields an estimated total fertility rate of 8.03—which is quite close to the survey estimate of 8.11 (African Population Policy Research Center 1998). However, when applied to the 1989 Kenya Demographic and Health Survey (DHS) data, the procedure generates an estimated total fertility rate of 8.06, well above the survey estimate of 6.7. Similarly, when applied to the 1993 Kenya DHS data, the single-survey procedure of FERTCB produces an estimate of the total fertility rate of 7.68, substantially higher than the DHS estimate of 5.4. *These results indicate that use of FERTCB with data from a single survey when fertility has been falling will yield inaccurate, misleading, and increasingly erroneous estimates of fertility.*

In the following chapter, we argue that changes in the educational attainment of the female population, particularly with respect to exposure to secondary schooling, and associated changes in the timing of entry of women into marriage have brought about a decline of fertility in Kinshasa (see also Shapiro 1996). Hence, we do not believe that the census estimates provide a good indication of fertility in Kinshasa as of 1984, given the other changes that were well under way at the time of the census.

As shown in the bottom panel of table 3.2, the census estimates reported a national total fertility rate of 6.7 (Institut National de la Statistique 1991c). This represents an increase of 13 percent as compared to the level that prevailed in the mid-1950s and an increase of 10-12 percent vis-à-vis the level that may be presumed to have existed in the mid-1970s.[8] Such an increase might reflect changes in proximate determinants of fertility, such as reduced durations of breast-feeding and postpartum abstinence, shortening birth intervals, and, consequently, increasing fertility (see Romaniuk 1980; Lesthaeghe 1989b).

Alternatively, given the problems that we have just seen with the procedure used to estimate fertility, it is possible that the national census estimates are incorrect and, instead, that fertility nationally has been either stable or perhaps declining slightly rather than increasing. As shown in the first part of this chapter, it appears that there has been a long-term downward trend in mortality in the Congo. As Easterlin (1996) and Easterlin and Crimmins (1985) have argued, declining mortality should lead ultimately to lower fertility, as couples determine that fewer numbers of births are required to achieve any given number of desired children surviving to adulthood.

---

[8] The slight increase in fertility in the western part of the country documented by Tabutin (1982) from the EDOZA study may be assumed to characterize the trend nationally, both because the west constituted a significant share of the total national population and because the lowered incidence of sterility should have had an impact in the northeast of the country as well as in the northwest. Overall, these considerations suggest that, as of the mid-1970s, the total fertility rate nationally was probably on the order of 6.0 or 6.1.

In addition, we have shown elsewhere (Shapiro 1996; Shapiro and Tambashe 1997a; see also chapter 4 below) that women in Kinshasa with secondary education tend to have significantly lower fertility than do those with only primary schooling or no schooling. The strong tendency for women with secondary education to have distinctly lower fertility has been documented for a number of countries in sub-Saharan Africa (Ainsworth et al. 1996), and analysis of data from other cities surveyed in conjunction with the EDOZA study in the 1970s reveals that this phenomenon is pertinent elsewhere in the Congo besides Kinshasa (Shapiro and Tambashe 2001a). This suggests that the growth over time in the proportion of women with secondary education should exert downward pressure on overall fertility. As of 1984, it is unlikely that this effect was very large since only 16 percent of women of reproductive age (15-49) nationally had secondary schooling. However, with nearly 25 percent of 15-24-year-olds and 17 percent of 25-29-year-olds having reached the secondary level, it seems likely that there was some effect.

Indeed, as indicated by the range of figures provided in the last row of table 3.2, as recently as 1991 the UN estimates for the country showed a total fertility rate of 6.09. This estimated rate had been stable for the period from 1970 through 1985, after having been just below 6.0 for most of the two decades prior to 1970 (United Nations 1991, 602). These estimates are, it may be noted, consistent with the data from the mid-1970s for the western part of the country. Following publication of the census estimates in 1991, however, the UN estimates were revised so as to be compatible with the census figures. Hence, more recent UN estimates show a total fertility rate of 6.0 for the period from 1950 to 1965, with a small increase to 6.1 in 1965-1970, moving to 6.3 in 1970-1975, to 6.5 in 1975-1980, and to 6.7 in 1980-1985, then holding steady at 6.7 for the period from 1985 to 1995 (United Nations 1998, 560).

In sum, then, while it is possible that the total fertility rate in the Congo is as high as 6.7, we believe that a strong case can be made for fertility being lower (see Shapiro and Tambashe 2001a). Further, we are convinced that the census estimate of a total fertility rate of 7.7 for Kinshasa is excessive. Indeed, it is useful in this regard to consider results from the 1988 Contraceptive Prevalence Survey (CPS) of Kinshasa (Bakutuvwidi et al. 1991, 47-48). On the basis of reported fertility in the 12 months preceding the survey, the CPS yielded an estimated total fertility rate of 5.52, slightly lower than our estimate of 5.67 for 1990. To allow for the possibility of underreporting of births, the authors also used a MortPak-Lite procedure and generated an estimate using an indirect approach.[9] That estimate was 6.23, or 13 percent higher than the direct estimate. Even this higher estimate, however, is considerably below the census figure of 7.7, by nearly 20 percent. Again, then, the census estimate of fertility for Kinshasa seems to be unduly elevated.

[9] The procedure generates an adjustment factor based on parity (P) and fertility (F) of women in different age groups. The adjustment factor used in this case (1.13) was based on the average of P/F for women aged 20-24 and aged 25-29 (Bakutuvwidi et al. 1991, 48).

Changes in Fertility by Age Group

A summary of cumulative childbearing and how it has changed over time is provided by figure 3.1, which shows differences by age group in the reported number of children ever born for 1955, 1967, 1975, 1984, and 1990.[10] In 1955, reported fertility rose steadily with age to 3.74 for women aged 35-44 and then fell to just under 3 for those aged 45-54. These relatively low levels reflect the high incidence of childlessness in these two age groups (22 and 36 percent, respectively) as well as underreporting of births, typically thought to entail failure to report births of children who have grown up or left home or who subsequently died and presumed to be especially prevalent among older women (Romaniuk 1967, 49; United Nations 1967, 31).

By 1967, the average number of children ever born had risen for women in each age group between the ages of 15 and 44. The increase was very modest among those aged 15-19, but there were substantial increases for all other age groups. In percentage terms, these increases were on the order of 45-50 percent, and, among those aged 35-44, reported fertility had risen to almost 5.7.

Corresponding data for 1975 show further increases in reported fertility for women aged 35 and over, while there were modest declines for women in the younger age groups. The largest average reported number of children ever born was just over six (more than 50 percent higher than in 1955), reflecting substantial declines in childlessness (to be documented and discussed in the following chapter).[11] For ages 25 and older, cumulative fertility in 1975 clearly exceeded that reported in 1955, while, among younger women, reported fertility was distinctly lower for the age group 15-19, in which the school enrollment rate had increased considerably during the 20-year period.

The 1984 census data indicate that the increases in reported fertility among the two oldest age groups that had emerged between 1955 and 1975 continued through the mid-1980s, particularly among women aged 45-49. For women aged 20-34, by contrast, there were declines in the reported number of children ever born between 1975 and 1984. The reduction was quite modest for those aged 30-34 but more substantial among the two younger age groups in this span, amounting to a decline of 11 percent for those aged 25-29 and 19 percent among those aged 20-24.

By 1990, the cumulative fertility of women in each of the age groups from age 20 to age 34 showed further reductions as compared to 1984, particularly so for those aged 25-34. By contrast, the average number of children ever born had risen among women aged 35-49, reaching almost 7.5 for those aged 45-49. As will be seen in chapter 4, this widening of differentials by age group in

[10] Data on this variable for 1967 were provided only up through the 40-44 age group.
[11] In fact, the maximum was 6.3 for women aged 40-44. These women have been grouped with those aged 35-39 in order to provide data comparable to the information available from 1955. The oldest age group reported on in the figure consists of women aged 45-54 in 1955 and 45-49 in the subsequent years.

Fig. 3.1 Average number of children ever born, by age group, 1955-1990

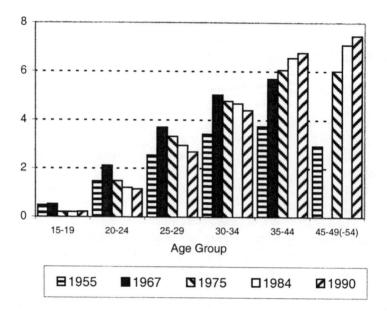

Sources: 1955: Romaniuk (1967, table II.4, p. 58); 1967: Institut National de la Statistique (1969, 63); 1975: calculated from data; 1984: Institut National de la Statistique (1991a, table 6, p. 62); 1990: calculated from data.

number of children ever born largely reflects differences by age group in the extent of exposure to secondary education.

A further perspective on changes in fertility by age group is provided by figure 3.2, which shows age-specific fertility rates for the three survey years 1955, 1975, and 1990.[12] The rates for 1955 shown in the figure are the reported age-specific fertility rates (Romaniuk 1967, table II.1) adjusted upward so as to produce the same total fertility rate of 7.51 estimated by Romaniuk.[13] The age-specific fertility rates from the 1975 survey, as well as those from our 1990 survey, are based on the reported fertility histories for the 5 years preceding each of the surveys. In the case of the 1975 survey, as mentioned earlier, this

---

[12] Data on age-specific fertility rates were not available for 1967. Given the problems discussed above concerning the 1984 fertility estimate for Kinshasa, we have not used the data for 1984.

[13] The adjustment was proportional across all age groups. If, as suggested above, underreporting of births was more common among older women, then the proportional adjustment overstates somewhat the age-specific fertility of younger women and understates that of older women. In addition, we have further adjusted the 1955 data, which were reported in 10-year intervals beginning with age 35. The adjustments in this case were based on the 5-year age-specific fertility rates for 1970-1974, designed to reproduce the ratios across 5-year age groups while retaining the same overall total fertility rate.

Fig. 3.2 Age-specific fertility rates, 1955, 1970-1974, and 1985-1989

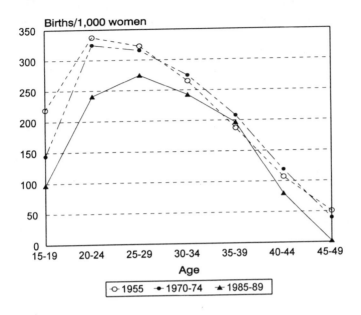

Sources: 1955: Romaniuk (1967, table II.1); 1970-1974 and 1985-1989: calculated from reported births for the 5 years preceding each survey.

procedure yields an estimate of the total fertility rate of 7.2, or 4 percent lower than the figure reported in table 3.2.

Figure 3.2 shows a clear decline in fertility of 15-19-year-olds between 1955 and the early 1970s. From age 20 on, however, the age-specific fertility rates in the two years were quite similar. Between the early 1970s and the late 1980s, by contrast, there were more substantial changes at both the low and the high ends of the age range. Rates for those under age 30 (and especially for those aged 20-24) declined substantially, and there was also a drop in fertility for women aged 30-34. Further, age-specific fertility rates of women aged 40 and over appear to have fallen sharply as well.

Overall, then, the period from the early 1970s to the late 1980s was one during which the total fertility rate appears to have declined by more than 20 percent (on the basis of the same methodology being applied to both surveys, with no adjustment for underreporting of births or age misreporting).[14] Further, the declines appear at both the lower and the upper ends of the age distribution. Caldwell et al. (1992) have suggested that fertility decline in sub-Saharan

[14] To the extent that underreporting of births or misreporting of age is more prevalent among women with low levels of education, these problems will have been more significant in 1975 than in 1990. If underreporting is more common among women with little or no schooling, then the actual decline in the total fertility rate would be greater than that implied by the unadjusted data reported here.

Africa will be as large among younger women as among older women, as unmarried younger women seek to avoid pregnancies and enforced marriage and young married women seek to maintain or lengthen birth intervals. Our 1990 data indeed show generally greater declines in age-specific fertility rates among younger women than among older women.

Part II

Socioeconomic and Proximate Determinants of Fertility

Chapter 4. Ethnicity, Education, and Fertility: 1955-1990

In the overview of fertility from 1955 to 1990 that was presented in chapter 3, we saw evidence of fertility decline in Kinshasa during the latter portion of that span, after 1975. As we shall see in this chapter, at the outset of the period, there were quite substantial differences in fertility by ethnic group, while the educational attainment of women was extremely low. As time went by, differences in fertility by ethnic group diminished, while increased schooling of girls and young women eventually raised the education level of adult women, was associated with a distinct pattern of fertility differences by education group, and ultimately resulted in declining fertility.

This chapter provides analyses of ethnicity, education, and fertility and their interactions over time in Kinshasa. A major theme of the chapter is that education has supplanted ethnicity as a key factor influencing fertility in the city. This is not to say that ethnicity does not matter for fertility behavior: as will be apparent from the analyses presented in chapters 5 and 6, early life course transitions and proximate determinants of fertility are frequently significantly related to ethnicity, all else equal. However, for reasons that will be discussed in chapter 6, it is fair to say that, for the most part, by 1990 ethnicity was distinctly less important than educational attainment in contributing to observed differences in childbearing behavior among women in Kinshasa.

We begin with a look at data on fertility differentials by ethnicity and education and how they have changed between 1955 and 1990. Then we briefly examine childlessness and marriage, two variables that have changed substantially over time, those changes being closely linked to changing fertility differentials by ethnicity and education. This is followed by a section providing detailed descriptive information on the educational attainment of women of reproductive age and evidence on the links between education and fertility. This evidence documents clearly the importance of secondary schooling when looking at fertility. We also present additional descriptive information on the spread of secondary schooling to the adult female population and on the relation between ethnicity and educational attainment. The last substantive section as well as the appendix to the chapter report the results of multivariate analyses of fertility (number of children ever born), controlling for ethnicity, education, and other factors. These analyses focus on how ethnic group fertility differentials are influenced once educational attainment is taken into consideration and on fertility differences by educational attainment, all else equal.

Fertility Differentials by Ethnicity and Education

As shown in chapter 3, the overall level of fertility in Kinshasa in the mid-1950s was quite high. At the same time, however, there were substantial differences in fertility among the different ethnic groups in the city. In brief, Kinshasa residents who were originally from those parts of the country where fertility was low and sterility was high tended themselves to have relatively low fertility, while residents from areas not affected by sterility did not have low fertility. That is, in the city, as well as elsewhere in the country, ethnic group differences in fertility were closely linked to variations across ethnic groups in the incidence of venereal disease and, hence, infertility (Romaniuk 1967, 1968).

The magnitudes of these differences by broad ethnic group are shown in the first column of data reported in table 4.1.[1] The Ubangi and Mongo women (originally from the north of the Congo) had especially low fertility, with general fertility rates that were only 59 percent and 75 percent of the city average, respectively. Bakongo women had above-average fertility, by 7 percent for those originally from Bas-Congo Province south of the Congo River and by 37 percent for those from Bas-Congo Province north of the river. The remaining two groups, those from the Kwilu-Kwango Districts and the Luba and related group, both had general fertility rates that were somewhat lower than the average for the entire city.

Between 1955 and 1975 the overall fertility level in Kinshasa remained fairly stable. However, considerable change took place in the fertility behavior of the different ethnic groups in the city, as may be seen by comparing the first two columns of data in table 4.1.[2] The general fertility rates of the two Bakongo

[1] For details on the composition of these broad ethnic groups, see the appendix. Data on fertility by ethnic group were not available for 1967 or 1984. The overall 1955 general fertility rate for the city shown in table 4.1 is 11 percent below the figure reported in table 3.2 above because the data in table 4.1 have not been adjusted for underreporting of births. Data adjusted by ethnic group within Kinshasa are not available. However, while the level may thus be too low, the table does give a good indication of the magnitudes of the differences by ethnic group.

[2] The citywide figure of 240 given in table 4.1 for 1975, based on reported fertility for the 5-year period preceding the survey, is a bit below the previously published estimates of 250 and 261 shown in table 3.2. If the general fertility rate is calculated on the basis of reported births for a 1-year period only (1974), the resulting figure is 247, closer to the earlier estimates. However, since inspection of the data suggests that (for 1990 as well as for 1975) there is a tendency to overstate the number of births in the calendar year preceding the survey and correspondingly to

Table 4.1 General Fertility Rates by Broad Ethnic Group, 1955, 1975, and 1990

Ethnic Group	1955[a]	1975[b]	1990[c]
Bakongo North	335	238	172
Bakongo South	261	229	178
Kwilu-Kwango	214	263	219
Mongo	182	226	182
Ubangi	145	220	172
Luba and related	232	267	235
All women[d]	244	240	198

[a] Births per 1,000 women aged 15-45. Calculated from data on fertility of principal tribes in Congo Belge (1957a, table 18) and Congo Belge (1957b, table 12). Since only principal tribes are covered (i.e., the data are not exhaustive), the ethnic group categorizations are not complete. However, the data on principal tribes included approximately 86 percent of the total population, and we are confident that the numbers reported here provide a good indication of fertility differences by broad ethnic group.
[b] Births per 1,000 women aged 15-44. Calculated from the 1975 survey data, based on reported fertility for the 5 years preceding the survey.
[c] Births per 1,000 women aged 15-44. Calculated from the 1990 survey data, based on reported fertility for the 5 years preceding the survey.
[d] Includes women not in the six major broad ethnic groups. For the six groups only, the GFR in 1955 was 244, the same as the overall level; in 1975 it was 243, slightly higher than the citywide figure; and in 1990 it was 200, just above the average for all women.

groups declined, with a 29 percent drop for the North group and a 12 percent reduction for the South group. However, these declines were offset by increases for the other four groups. Most notable in this regard was the increase of more than 50 percent in the general fertility rate of Ubangi women and the nearly 25 percent increase for Mongo women, bringing these two groups to fertility rates corresponding to more than 90 percent of the citywide average.

Overall, the range of differences in fertility had narrowed considerably. For the general fertility rate of a particular group relative to the rate for all women in the city, the range shrank from 59-137 percent in 1955 to only 92-111 percent in 1975. In addition, in contrast to the considerable diversity across the six ethnic groups that had prevailed in 1955, by 1975 there was substantially more similarity across groups. In effect, there were two groupings in the latter year: the Luba and Kwilu-Kwango women had become the high-fertility groups, with general fertility rates about 10 percent higher than the overall average, and the other four groups were clustered fairly closely together, with general fertility rates ranging from 92 to 99 percent of the overall rate. The large reduction in the dispersion of fertility by ethnic group is evident from the fact that the standard deviation of the six rates fell from 60 in 1955 to 18 in 1975. This change mirrored what was going on elsewhere in the country (Sala-Diakanda 1980, table 24, p. 146). Presumably, the narrowing of differentials reflected reductions in the incidence of sterility as a consequence of public

understate the number during the next-to-last calendar year prior to the survey, we use a longer period for our fertility estimates so as to minimize the effects of such misreporting.

health efforts to combat venereal disease during the 1950s and 1960s (Bruaux et al. 1957; Sala-Diakanda 1980).

By 1975, however, a new factor had emerged associated with distinct differences in fertility: women's educational attainment.[3] As shown in the first and third columns of data in table 4.2, clear differences in fertility by schooling level were evident. In a pattern that has been observed in a number of countries in sub-Saharan Africa (United Nations 1986; Jolly and Gribble 1993; Ainsworth et al. 1996), the highest fertility was actually that of women with primary schooling, and there were progressively lower levels of fertility for women with secondary education or higher as educational attainment increased beyond the primary level.[4] The higher fertility of women with primary schooling has been attributed to a reduction in the periods of postpartum abstinence and breast-feeding associated with acquisition of primary schooling (Lesthaeghe 1989b; Oni 1985; Janowitz and Smith 1984; Romaniuk 1980).

Since increased education beyond the primary school level was associated with sharply lower fertility, one might expect that the rapid expansion of women's schooling following independence would have affected fertility. However, women with at least some secondary education represented less than one-third of the total number of women of reproductive age and were disproportionately concentrated in the youngest age groups.[5] This limited their impact on the overall fertility level, and, as we shall see in the following section, the substantial reductions in sterility that took place between 1955 and 1975 undoubtedly put offsetting upward pressure on fertility. More broadly, the massive exposure of women to schooling between 1955 and 1975 had been most heavily concentrated at the primary level, and, since women with this level of schooling had the highest fertility, it is not surprising that the overall level had failed to decline (Shapiro 1996).[6]

---

[3] With respect to education and fertility, no information is available from the 1955 data, simply because the educational level of women was so low that this variable was not analyzed (as suggested by the data reported in table 2.1 above, about 85 percent of women aged 20-54 had never been to school). Information was provided on literacy rather than schooling in the 1955 survey, but this information was not related simultaneously to fertility. Likewise, data on education and fertility were not included in the 1967 survey report.

[4] The one exception to this statement is for the general fertility rate (GFR) of university-educated women, which is slightly greater than the GFR of women with 5 or 6 years of secondary education (although the total fertility rate—TFR—is distinctly lower). This apparent anomaly reflects the fact that university-educated women were heavily concentrated in the peak ages of childbearing. That is, for the sample as a whole as well as for women with 5-6 years of secondary schooling, a little more than half in the age range 15-49 were 20-34 years old, while, among university-educated women, the corresponding figure was nearly 70 percent. This bulge in the age distribution at ages at which fertility is highest would inflate the GFR while not having an impact on the TFR.

[5] Among young women aged 15-24, fully 46 percent had at least some secondary schooling in 1975. Among women aged 25-49, by contrast, the corresponding figure was only 17 percent.

[6] This point will be developed more fully below.

Table 4.2 Fertility by Educational Attainment, 1975 and 1990

	General Fertility Rate		Total Fertility Rate	
Educational Attainment	1975	1990	1975	1990
None	251	221	7.56	6.04
Primary	269	242	7.74	6.75
Secondary 1-2	204	213	6.99	6.59
Secondary 3-4	193	176	6.52	5.29
Secondary 5-6	138	174	3.85	4.48
University	144	103	3.31	3.52
All women	240	198	7.20	5.67

Note: Data for 1975 are based on reported fertility histories for the period from 1970 to 1974; data for 1990 are based on the reported fertility histories for the period from 1985 to 1989.

Indeed, while Sala-Diakanda's analyses of the fertility of married women in Kinshasa failed to find any impact of schooling among those aged 45-54, they did find that schooling was significantly negatively related to the fertility of wives aged 25-34. In a prescient statement, Sala-Diakanda suggested that, in the city, the importance of ethnic identity as a factor influencing fertility might well diminish progressively over time and yield its place to individual factors such as schooling (Sala-Diakanda 1980, 217).

Estimates of general or total fertility rates by educational attainment are not available from the 1984 census. However, as shown in table 2.1, between 1975 and 1984 there was a substantial rise in the proportions of women of reproductive age who had been to secondary school or beyond. In the peak ages of childbearing (20-34), over two-thirds of those in the youngest 5-year age group had at least some secondary schooling, as did more than 55 percent of those aged 25-29 and over 40 percent of those aged 30-34. Given the fertility differences by schooling level that prevailed in 1975, the sharp increase in women's educational attainment that took place between 1975 and 1984 would presumably be expected to result in some decline in fertility, all else equal.

As noted in the previous chapter, such a decline in fertility is evident in the 1990 data. It is clear from table 4.1 that, relative to the situation in 1975, the fertility of each of the different ethnic groups declined. The drop was greatest for the Bakongo North group and smallest for the Luba and related group. As in 1975, the Luba and Kwilu-Kwango women constituted the ethnic groups with relatively high fertility, while the other four groups had fertility below the average for the city as a whole. The range of differences widened slightly to 85-116 percent, and the standard deviation rose a bit to almost 25. The two Bakongo groups and the Mongo and Ubangi groups all had general fertility rates that were 85-90 percent of the city average, while the Kwilu-Kwango group's general fertility rate was 8 percent above the overall average, and that of the Luba group was 16 percent higher.

With respect to the different educational attainment groups (table 4.2), between 1975 and 1990 there were clear declines in the fertility of those with no or only primary schooling, and reductions were most common as well for those with 1-4 years of secondary schooling. Among women with the two highest levels of schooling, it appears that there were modest increases in fertility.[7] Overall, the pattern of differences by educational attainment remained essentially the same in 1990 as it had been in 1975, with the highest fertility being that of women with primary schooling and fertility falling progressively as schooling increased beyond the primary level. Because the educational attainment of the female population of reproductive age had increased dramatically, particularly at the secondary level, fertility overall declined.

Childlessness and Marriage

In the previous chapter, we noted that, in the 1950s, differences in fertility among ethnic groups in Kinshasa, were, like those between fertility in Kinshasa and fertility elsewhere in the country, linked to variations in the incidence of sterility. Further, it was stated that, over the succeeding 20 years, these differences diminished in magnitude. The changes for Kinshasa are evident in figure 4.1, which shows the proportion of women who were childless, by age group, for the period from 1955 to 1990.

It is apparent from the graph that there was a remarkable drop in childlessness among women aged 30 and older after 1955. For each of the three oldest groups shown, childlessness fell sharply from 1955 to 1967, there was a 65-70 percent decline in childlessness between 1955 and 1975, and there appear to have been further declines after 1975.[8] Among the younger age groups, by contrast, there was a substantial increase in the proportion of women who were childless up through 1975 for those aged 15-19 and up through 1984 for those aged 20-24. This growth in childlessness is closely linked to the growth over time in the percentage enrolled in school for women in these two age groups, as may be seen in figure 4.2.

This strong positive association between childlessness and school enrollment among younger women in fact reflects the link between increased access to schooling and a reduced propensity to be married. That is, while fertility out-

---

[7] Because two different measures of fertility are used in table 4.2, whether fertility for a given education group rose or fell between 1975 and 1990 is not always apparent. For two of the six groups, the changes in the two fertility measures were in opposite directions. Reflecting the observations in n. 4 above about age composition effects, the statement in the text puts weight on the TFR estimates rather than the GFR estimates for university-educated women.

[8] For 1967 and 1990, the maximum age for which data are available is 49. Hence, in the figure, the oldest group for those years is 45-49 rather than 45-54. Among the relatively small number of women aged 45-49 who were interviewed in 1990, none reported themselves as childless. For the years for which available data permit calculation for ages 45-49 and 50-54 separately as well as combined (1975 and 1984), the percentage childless among those aged 45-54 is only slightly higher (by 2.0 and 0.8 percentage points, respectively) than that for those aged 45-49.

Fig. 4.1 Percentage childless, by age group, 1955-1990

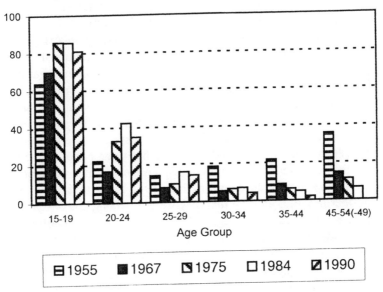

Sources: 1955: Congo Belge (1957a, table 20), Congo Belge (1957b, table 14); 1967: Institut National de la Statistique (1969, annexe XI, table 3); 1975: calculated from data; 1984: Institut National de la Statistique (1991a, table 6); 1990: calculated from data.

Fig. 4.2 Percentage childless by percentage enrolled, ages 15-19 and 20-24, 1955-1990

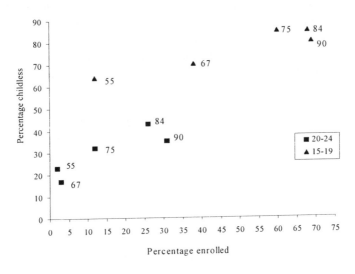

Sources: See figure 2.1 and figure 4.1.

side marriage is certainly not insignificant in Kinshasa, the vast majority of births occur to married women. Hence, as is the case more generally, marriage in Kinshasa is a key proximate determinant of fertility.

In Kinshasa, as elsewhere in sub-Saharan Africa, marriage may take a number of different forms. Van de Walle (1993) has argued that marriage in this setting is often "a process," with resulting ambiguity regarding exactly when a woman becomes married. The various surveys carried out in Kinshasa have typically enumerated married women in monogamous unions, in po-lygynous unions, and in consensual or de facto unions (*union de fait*), with women describing their own marital status in response to a single question. Our more detailed survey in 1990 determined that a number of women who indi-cated that they were not married in response to an initial question on marital status (comparable to the questions in the large-scale surveys) did, in response to further probing, indicate that they were in an ongoing sexual union (and, hence, at risk of becoming pregnant).[9] However, for purposes of comparability, here we identify as married women in 1990 only those who indicated that they were married in response to our initial question on marital status.

The percentage of women married, by age group and by survey year, is shown in figure 4.3 for women aged 15-29. For the youngest of these women, there was a sharp drop from 1955 to 1967 and another steep decline, to less than 20 percent, between 1967 and 1975. There were continued more moderate decreases after 1975 as well; overall, by 1990 only 12 percent of young women in this group were married compared to 62 percent in 1955. Among women aged 20-24, there were slower and more steady declines throughout, with the largest absolute decrease occurring between 1975 and 1984. The percentage married essentially was cut in half over the period, from 91 to 46. There were also declines in the percentage married among those aged 25-29, with the largest being between 1955 and 1967 and again between 1975 and 1984.[10] However, these reductions were more modest than those for the younger groups, with the result that, between 1955 and 1990, the percentage married fell from 93 to 75.

Among women aged 30 and over, changes in the percentage married during this 35-year span were both more modest and less characterized by trends. There was a slight decline from 88 percent to 82 percent married for women aged 30-34, while, among those aged 35-44, the percentage married fluctuated within the narrow range 81-85, with the maximum value in 1975. The percentage married among women aged 45-54 fluctuated between 67 and 71 up through 1984 and appears to have declined by 1990 (only 64 percent of

---

[9] The issues surrounding the definition of *marital status* and in particular the implications of alternative definitions will be explored more fully in chapter 6 below.

[10] It is worth noting that the decreases in proportions married between 1975 and 1984 would imply, all else equal, a reduction in fertility. Clearly, this implication is not consistent with the 1984 census estimates indicating that fertility during that period was more or less stable.

Fig. 4.3 Percentage of women married, by age group, ages 15-29, 1955-1990

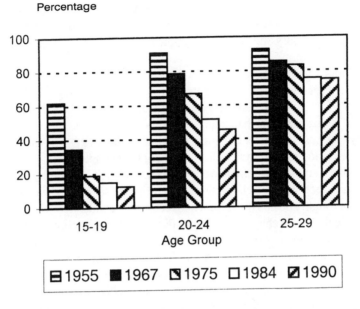

Sources: 1955: Congo Belge (1957a, table 12b), Congo Belge (1957b, table 7); 1967: Institut National de la Statistique (1969, table 14); 1975: Houyoux and Kinavwuidi (1986, table I.7, annexe I. 5); 1984: Institut National de la Statistique (1991, table 3); 1990: calculated from data.

those aged 45-49 were married in 1990, and typically these women have had a higher percentage married than those aged 50-54).

Overall, then, there were very substantial declines over time in the percentage of young women (under age 25) who were married. There were also noteworthy reductions in the percentage of women aged 25-29 who were married and small declines in the likelihood of 30-34-year-old women being married. Within the full period, it is also noteworthy that, for women aged 20-29, there were particularly large reductions in proportions married between 1975 and 1984. Given that ages 20-34 have constituted the peak ages of fertility in Kinshasa throughout this period and that married women have much higher fertility rates than do unmarried women, these changes in marital status are quite consistent with the argument made above that fertility in Kinshasa has declined since 1975.

Further Evidence: Education and Fertility, Ethnicity and Education

As a prelude to considering the relation between education and fertility in more detail, it is useful to examine closely what happened to the educational attainment of women of reproductive age between 1975 and 1990—the period during which fertility declined. Table 4.3 shows educational attainment by age group for each year. In each age group, there was a decline in the percentage of women with no schooling, and typically (especially from age 25 on) this decline was substantial. There were corresponding increases in the proportion of women with secondary and higher education and in the median years of education of each age group.

Among women aged 35-49, between about half and two-thirds in each age group had received no schooling or only primary schooling in 1990, and the median years of education ranged from 3 to 6. In 1975, well over half the women in this age range had not been to school at all. Among women aged 20-34, by contrast, the increased educational attainment between 1975 and 1990 consisted principally of a shift from primary to secondary schooling. In 1975, between 55 and 84 percent of women in each of the 5-year age groups in this range had received no schooling or only primary schooling, while, by 1990, between roughly 60 and 80 percent had received secondary education or higher.

Recall that, in chapter 3, we saw (figure 3.1) that, in considering the number of children ever born by age group, between 1975 and 1990 these numbers decreased for women aged 20-34 and increased for women aged 35-49. That is, declining fertility was evident among those groups in which substantial proportions of women had received some secondary education, and increasing fertility prevailed within the groups in which the bulk of the increase in schooling was concentrated at the primary level.

Now we may consider more detailed evidence on the association between education and fertility, provided in table 4.4. The table shows the average number of children ever born to women aged 15-49, by age and schooling, for both 1975 and 1990. A number of the means for 1990 as well as several of those for better-educated women in 1975 are based on relatively small sample sizes and, hence, should be considered with some caution. Despite this, however, there are some clear patterns in the table that are evident both in 1975 and in 1990. First, in comparing fertility differences by schooling and holding age constant, it is apparent that women with primary schooling tend to have the highest levels of fertility, followed by women with no schooling.[11]

Among those who have gone beyond the primary level, the average number of children ever born typically declines steadily as educational attainment increases, with women with the highest level of secondary schooling showing a sharp drop as compared to those with lower levels of secondary schooling and university-level women having the lowest fertility. In this regard,

---

[11] Among women aged 20 and over, there are 12 sets of within-age-group comparisons of schooling differentials in the number of children ever born that can be made, and, in a majority of these cases, women with primary schooling have the highest fertility. If the different schooling groups are rank ordered within each of these age groups according to the reported number of children ever born, the mean rank for women with primary schooling is 1.4, while that for women with no schooling is 2.3. By comparison, for those with 1-2 years of secondary school the mean rank is 2.7, while it reaches 3.4 for women with 3-4 years of secondary education.

Table 4.3 Educational Attainment by Age Group, Women Aged 15-49, 1975 and 1990 (percentage distributions)

Age Group	Year	None	Primary	Secondary 1-2	Secondary 3-4	Secondary 5+	Median Years
15-19	1975	7.0	47.2	33.9	10.6	1.3	6
	1990	2.6	24.2	36.9	30.5	5.8	8
20-24	1975	16.0	38.7	20.9	16.7	7.7	6
	1990	4.2	15.5	21.2	34.9	24.2	9
25-29	1975	29.7	41.9	12.2	11.4	4.8	4
	1990	6.9	23.3	19.5	26.0	24.2	9
30-34	1975	43.8	39.8	6.3	8.3	1.7	2
	1990	7.1	31.6	20.2	23.5	17.7	8
35-39	1975	58.8	33.1	3.8	3.6	0.6	0
	1990	10.2	44.5	18.3	14.2	12.7	6
40-44	1975	64.3	31.0	2.5	1.9	0.3	0
	1990	18.2	53.3	14.4	9.3	4.8	4
45-49	1975	74.3	22.7	1.5	1.4	0.2	0
	1990	28.7	39.0	1.2	29.3	1.8	3
15-49	1975	29.5	39.8	17.5	10.1	3.1	5
	1990	6.3	26.0	23.8	27.4	16.5	8

Note: The secondary 5+ group includes those with university education.

Table 4.4 Mean Number of Children Ever Born, by Age Group and Educational Attainment, Women Aged 15-49, 1975 and 1990

Age Group	Year	None	Primary	Secondary 1-2	Secondary 3-4	Secondary 5-6	Univ.	Total
15-19	1975	0.43	0.22	0.14	0.12	0.18	—	0.20
	1990	0.41+	0.37	0.18	0.16	0.09+	—	0.22
20-24	1975	1.78	1.85	1.44	0.92	0.56	0.35	1.50
	1990	1.56+	1.85	1.44	1.13	0.59	0.21*	1.15
25-29	1975	3.40	3.53	3.39	2.99	2.08	1.35	3.34
	1990	2.97*	3.52	3.50	2.36	1.79	1.25	2.69
30-34	1975	4.72	5.00	5.04	4.61	3.85*	2.69+	4.83
	1990	4.99+	4.96	4.21	4.12	3.56	2.62	4.31
35-39	1975	5.77	6.32	5.76	6.22	4.13+	—	5.96
	1990	7.11+	6.75	6.16*	6.43	4.58*	3.56+	6.26
40-44	1975	6.15	7.00	6.44	6.05*	—	—	6.42
	1990	7.76+	8.02*	8.58+	7.14+	4.52+	—	7.82
45-49	1975	5.95	6.49	5.36*	6.96*	—	—	6.07
	1990	7.72+	7.87+	—	6.74+	—	—	7.47
15-49	1975	4.48	2.81	1.30	1.78	1.16	1.01	2.89
	1990	4.30	3.68	2.12	1.88	1.65	1.20	2.50

— 　Fewer than 10 observations.
+ 　10-24 observations.
* 　25-49 observations.

it is interesting to note that, for a number of cells in the table for women under the age of 35, average fertility in 1975 is quite close to that in 1990.

Overall, the average number of children ever born to women aged 15-49 in 1975 was 2.89, while the corresponding figure for 1990 was 2.50. The importance of changes in educational attainment in contributing to this difference may be seen by considering the hypothetical fertility levels in each case if the educational attainment levels had been reversed. That is, given the mean levels of fertility by age and educational attainment jointly that prevailed in 1975, women aged 15-49 would have had an average number of children ever born of 2.71 if the education distribution within each age group that existed in 1990 had been present also in 1975. This decline represents just under half the actual difference.

Conversely, given the mean levels of fertility by age and educational attainment jointly that existed in 1990, women aged 15-49 would have had an average number of children ever born of 2.81 if the education distribution that was present in 1975 had prevailed also in 1990. In this case, the difference in educational attainment accounts for about 80 percent of the observed difference in the mean number of children ever born. While these figures span a broad range, they highlight the fact that the increased educational attainment that took place between 1975 and 1990 had a major impact in reducing overall fertility in Kinshasa.[12]

The steady growth from 1955 to 1990 in the percentage of women aged 20-49 with at least some secondary schooling is shown in figure 4.4. Data for 1975, 1984, and 1990 are especially of interest. Consider first the two years that mark the beginning and end points of the span during which fertility declined. In 1975, among women aged 20-34—who typically provide the largest share of the total number of births—secondary education was still unusual. That is, only about 45 percent of those aged 20-24, fewer than 30 percent of 25-29-year-olds, and not much more than 15 percent of those aged 30-34 had been to secondary school. By contrast, the corresponding figures for 1990 were over 80 percent, nearly 70 percent, and over 60 percent, respectively.

Increased penetration of women with secondary education into age groups that contribute substantially to overall fertility is, thus, temporally closely associated with the observed decline in fertility. In this regard, consider the data for 1984: for two of the three age groups, the majority of women had reached the secondary level of education, and, for the third (oldest) group, there is a substantial minority with secondary schooling. Hence, this provides some indirect evidence—given the argument being made here that growth in secondary education is a key factor fueling fertility decline—that (contrary to published

---

[12] It should be noted that the 1975 and 1990 samples also differed a bit with respect to their age distributions. In 1975, there were proportionately more women over age 35 (22 percent vs. only 14 percent in 1990) and fewer women in the age groups from age 20 to age 34 (50 percent vs. 61 percent). This difference contributes to the overall observed difference in average number of children ever born.

Fig. 4.4 Percentage of women with secondary schooling or higher by age group, 1955-1990

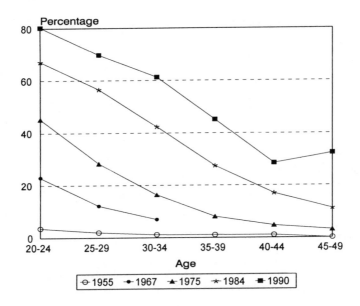

Sources: 1955-1984: table 2.1; 1990: calculated from survey data.

Note: For 1967, the oldest age group is 30 and above.

data from the census) the actual level of fertility in 1984 was probably intermediate with respect to the levels observed in 1975 and 1990.

A final descriptive table, meant to set the stage for the multivariate analyses in the following section, shows the educational attainment of the female population of reproductive age by ethnic group for the six principal groups in Kinshasa in 1975 and 1990 (table 4.5). Primarily because the data here include young women age 15-19, and also because women over age 49 are excluded, the overall levels of educational attainment for 1975 are higher than those reported in table 2.1 above, which covered women ages 20 and over.

The largest group in 1975 consisted of women with primary schooling. The balance of the women were almost equally divided between those with secondary education and those with no schooling, with the secondary-schooling group being heavily weighted toward the low end of the distribution. With respect to differences by ethnic group, it is clear from looking both at the percentages with no schooling and at the percentages with secondary schooling that, in 1975, the Kwilu-Kwango women had the lowest educational attainment and Luba women the highest level. The other four groups had very similar distributions of educational attainment, in between the two extreme groups.

Table 4.5 Educational Attainment of the Different Ethnic Groups, 1975 and 1990 (percentage distributions)

Ethnic Group	No Schooling	Primary	Secondary 1-2	3-4	5-6	University	Total
			1975				
Bakongo North	26	39	20	12	3	0.4	100
Bakongo South	27	38	20	12	3	0.3	100
Kwilu-Kwango	38	42	12	6	2	0.2	100
Mongo	25	42	19	10	3	0.7	100
Ubangi	25	42	19	11	3	0.5	100
Luba+	15	42	22	15	5	0.9	100
Total	30	40	17	10	3	0.4	100
			1990				
Bakongo North	6	26	17	28	17	6	100
Bakongo South	5	19	30	33	10	3	100
Kwilu-Kwango	9	36	22	21	9	3	100
Mongo	8	22	24	26	10	9	100
Ubangi	6	19	24	31	14	6	100
Luba+	1	17	22	33	19	8	100
Total	6	26	24	27	12	5	100

Note: The overall totals for each year include women from other ethnic groups. Their inclusion has very little impact on the overall distributions. Totals for 1990 include in the primary category a small number of women (1 percent of the overall total) who had taken apprenticeship or vocational courses. Universe: Women aged 15-49.

By 1990, reflecting the continuation of the long-term increase in women's educational attainment documented in chapter 2, the overall educational level of women of reproductive age had risen considerably. More than two-thirds of the women had attained at least a secondary school education, and only a small proportion had never been to school. In comparison with 1975, when the median woman had only 5 years of primary school education, by 1990 the median corresponded to 2 years of secondary schooling. Further, the three highest schooling levels—those associated with distinctly lower fertility—had increased in importance from being only 13 percent of the total in 1975 to constituting 44 percent of the total in 1990.

The ethnic differences apparent in 1975, at least at the extremes, persisted up through 1990: Kwilu-Kwango women had the highest proportion with no schooling and the lowest proportion with postprimary education, while for Luba women the reverse was true. Among the other four groups, some slight differentiation not apparent in 1975 had emerged. Bakongo North and Ubangi women were relatively well educated, with above-average percentages in the three highest education categories. Bakongo South women were underrepresented at both the low and the high ends of the schooling distribution, while Mongo women had the highest percentage with university education but for other categories they were typically at or below the overall average.[13]

The evidence on fertility by educational attainment presented earlier in this chapter suggests that these differences in education by ethnic group should have consequences for observed ethnic group differences in fertility. This is the issue to which we now turn.

Ethnicity, Education, and Fertility: Multivariate Analyses

In order to examine the associations between ethnicity, education, and fertility more closely, we have carried out multivariate analyses that control for these and other variables relevant to fertility behavior. The analyses begin with an examination of the data for 1975, and the approach here is to present these analyses in a stepwise fashion.

Table 4.6 reports results of estimated ordinary least squares regressions for 1975, in which the number of children ever born is the dependent variable. In the first equation in the table, this dependent variable is regressed on age, age squared, and a set of dummy variables identifying the six major ethnic groups in Kinshasa plus two additional groups: a small category of women from other ethnic groups in the country and those from other African countries.[14]

The coefficients of age and age squared imply that the number of children ever born increases with age, but at a decreasing rate. Controlling for age, the fertility of both groups of Bakongo women was no different from that of Kwilu-Kwango women. The contrast between this result and the difference in general fertility rates for 1975 reported in table 4.1 above (in which Kwilu-Kwango women had distinctly higher fertility than did Bakongo women) reflects two factors: the different measures of fertility being used and age differences among the three groups. With respect to the first factor, the general fertility rates refer only to the period from 1970 to 1974, while children ever born measures fertility behavior over a longer time period. As shown in table 4.1, in the mid-1950s the fertility of Bakongo women was high relative to that of other ethnic groups. This higher past fertility was reflected in the numbers of children

---

[13] Calculation of mean and median levels of schooling, based on single-year schooling distributions, shows the Luba group to be at the top and the Kwilu-Kwango women to be at the bottom by both measures. As far as the other four groups are concerned, the ranking by mean education puts the Ubangi women first, followed by the Bakongo North, Bakongo South, and Mongo groups, in that order; the ranking by median education puts the Bakongo North group highest among these four, followed by the Ubangi, Bakongo South, and Mongo groups, in that order. Mean schooling of the Luba women was just over 9 years, while for the Kwilu-Kwango women the corresponding figure was 6.6 years. Mean values for the other four groups fell within a narrow range, from 7.9 to 8.1 years.

[14] At that time, the six major groups represented approximately 86 percent of the population of women in Kinshasa aged 15-49. Foreigners (mostly Angolans) represented nearly 12 percent of the city's population (Houyoux and Kinavwuidi 1986), and the balance consisted of individuals from ethnic groups much more distant from Kinshasa. The discussion of ethnicity in the text focuses primarily on the six major groups.

Chapter 4

Table 4.6 Regression Analyses of Children Ever Born, 1975 (ordinary least squares regression coefficients)

Variable	All Women		Married Women	
	(1)	(2)	(3)	(4)
Age	.5888**	.6108**	.6630**	.6723**
Age squared	-.0058**	-.0062**	-.0068**	-.0069**
Ethnic group				
Bakongo North	.046	.104**	.280**	.284**
Bakongo South	.001	.061*	.198**	.211**
Kwilu-Kwango	—	—	—	—
Mongo	-.114**	-.063	.125*	.115*
Ubangi	-.166**	-.123**	.076	.081
Luba+	.198**	.288**	.585**	.600**
Other tribes	-.127+	-.049	.193+	.213*
Non-Congo	-.082*	-.039	.038	.067
Schooling level				
None	—	-.307**	—	-.295**
Primary	—	—	—	—
Secondary 1-2	—	-.299**	—	-.157**
Secondary 3-4	—	-.760**	—	-.469**
Secondary 5-6	—	-1.450**	—	-1.004**
University	—	-2.144**	—	-1.866**
Constant	-8.225	-8.283	-9.312	-9.302
R^2/adjusted R^2	.617/.617	.629/.629	.494/.494	.500/.499
F-ratio	6,205.1	4,199.1	2,313.5	1,520.9

Note: Mean number of children ever born equals 2.89 for all women and 4.16 for married women. Sample sizes are 34,719 and 21,352, respectively.

** Significant at the .01 level.
* Significant at the .05 level.
+ Significant at the .10 level.

ever born (among older women) as of 1975 but did not influence the general fertility rate.[15]

Age differences between the Kwilu-Kwango women and the two Bakongo groups are also a factor here. More specifically, the highest age-specific fertility rates for Kinshasa women in the early 1970s were for ages 20-34, and, while 56 percent of the Kwilu-Kwango group were in this age range, the corresponding figures for Bakongo North and South women were 51 and 49 percent, respectively. Hence, the Kwilu-Kwango women had an age distribution more conducive to producing births, given their total number. This age distribution effect is reflected in the general fertility rates but not in the regression equation because the latter controls for age.

[15] Among all women aged 15-49, the mean number of children ever born was 2.90 for Bakongo North women and 2.91 for Bakongo South women, compared to 2.94 for Kwilu-Kwango women. Among those aged 35 and above, the corresponding means for 5-year age groups are higher for each of the Bakongo groups than for the Kwilu-Kwango women, while, among women below age 30, those from Kwilu-Kwango have the highest fertility among these three ethnic groups.

For the other three major ethnic groups, the differences in numbers of children ever born likewise reflect a combination of recent fertility behavior and the differences that had existed in the past. Thus, relative to those from Kwilu-Kwango, Mongo and Ubangi women had significantly lower fertility, but the differences are fairly small, representing 4-6 percent of the mean level. Luba women had the highest level of fertility once age is taken into consideration, with a coefficient equal to about 7 percent of the average number of children ever born. The small number of women from other tribes had relatively low fertility, as did non-Congolese women.

Equation (2) in table 4.6 adds controls for educational attainment. These controls reveal the familiar "inverted-U" pattern of differences by schooling, with the highest fertility being that of women with primary-level education. Other things equal, women with no schooling report about the same number of children ever born as do those with 1-2 years of secondary education. This contrasts with the 1975 fertility rates by schooling reported in table 4.2 above, which showed distinctly higher fertility for women with no schooling. Since those rates were based on fertility over the past 5 years, the regression results are suggestive of some underreporting of lifetime fertility among women with no schooling. The progressively more negative coefficients as schooling increases beyond the lower secondary level are consistent with the evidence presented earlier. Of particular note is that, compared to the magnitudes of the differences by ethnic group seen in the previous equation, those by level of educational attainment are substantial, particularly those beginning with the group with 3-4 years of secondary schooling.

Once education is taken into account, the coefficients for the different ethnic groups all become a bit more positive: the previously insignificant positive coefficients for the two Bakongo groups are larger and now statistically significant, the negative coefficients for the Mongo and Ubangi groups as well as those for women from other tribes and those not from the Congo are all diminished in absolute value and for the most part insignificant, and the coefficient for Luba women has increased from just under 0.2 to almost 0.3. These changes in the estimated coefficients are a consequence of the fact that the different ethnic groups for which coefficients are estimated all have higher levels of schooling than does the reference group, Kwilu-Kwango women. That is, a good part of the relatively high fertility of Kwilu-Kwango women in equation (1) is due to their relatively low educational attainment; once education is taken into account (equation [2]), the Kwilu-Kwango women are no longer an especially high-fertility group.

Controlling for age and education, the maximum difference across ethnic groups is that between Luba and Ubangi women, amounting to just over 0.4, all else equal. This maximum figure is slightly larger than the differentials among women with no schooling, only primary schooling, or 1-2 years of secondary schooling; it is substantially smaller than the differences between women in these groups and those in the three highest educational attainment groups.

The latter two equations in table 4.6 are comparable to the first two but restricted to married women. The most notable feature of these equations as compared to their counterparts for all women is the disappearance of negative coefficients for ethnicity. That is, among married women in Kinshasa in 1975, controlling for age, those from the Kwilu-Kwango group had the *lowest* numbers of children ever born. With the exception of Ubangi women, the differences among the major groups are statistically significant, and the coefficients by ethnic group are distinctly larger than in the equations for all women. In particular, the magnitude of the coefficient for Luba women has become quite large, exceeding 14 percent of the average number of children born to married women. These results suggest that at least part of the observed (gross) ethnic differences in fertility reflects differences across ethnic groups in the incidence of marriage—that is, in the percentage of women who are married at various ages.

Indeed, examination of the proportions married by age and ethnic group reveals distinct differences across the groups, with Kwilu-Kwango women generally having the highest proportions married and Mongo and Ubangi women tending to have the lowest proportions married. The greater likelihood of Kwilu-Kwango women being married thus is an important factor contributing to their relatively high overall fertility level, and the lower proportions married of Mongo and Ubangi women are responsible in part for their low overall fertility.[16]

Controlling for the education of married women (equation [4]) has very little impact on the coefficients of the ethnic group variables. However, the estimated fertility differences by education group, particularly beyond the primary level, are clearly smaller among married women than among all women. This suggests that a key aspect of schooling influencing fertility is delaying marriage.[17] At the same time, substantial fertility differences by education exist among married women. Despite the smaller coefficients by education and the larger coefficients by ethnic group, it is still the case that the differentials by educational attainment for women in the three highest groups are quite substantial relative to differentials by ethnic group, apart from that for Luba women.

Analysis of data on fertility in 1990 parallel to that in table 4.6 for 1975 is found in the first four equations of table 4.7. Controlling only for age and ethnicity in the sample of all women aged 15-49 (equation [1]), there are statistically significant differences by ethnic group in the number of children ever born for all but Luba women. Consistent with the general fertility rates for

[16] This issue will be addressed further later in this chapter and in chapter 6.

[17] Analyses controlling for age at marriage or duration of marriage would have been helpful here but could not be carried out because the necessary data were not collected in the 1975 survey. Such analyses are undertaken below for 1990, and the impact of schooling on age at marriage will be examined directly in the following chapter.

Table 4.7 Regression Analyses of Children Ever Born, 1990 (weighted ordinary least squares regression coefficients)

Variable	All Women			Married Women		
	(1)	(2)	(3)	(4)	(5)	(6)
Age	.1866**	.2909**	.2254**	.3073**	.2387**	.2859**
Age squared	.0019**	-.0011	.0014+	-.0002	-.0029**	-.0033**
Ethnic group						
Bakongo North	-.416**	-.151	-.406*	-.139	-.019	.093
Bakongo South	-.341**	-.196*	-.390**	-.191+	-.106	-.025
Kwilu-Kwango	—	—	—	—	—	—
Mongo	-.290*	-.101	-.333+	-.069	-.040	.083
Ubangi	-.459**	-.245*	-.608**	-.353*	-.302*	-.187
Luba+	.076	.424**	.241	.638**	.422**	.633**
Other tribes	-.653**	-.204	-.677*	-.214	-.221	-.007
Non-Congo	-.540**	-.500**	-.612**	-.503*	-.452*	-.408*
Schooling level						
None	—	-.246+	—	-.193	—	-.170
Primary	—	—	—	—	—	—
Secondary 1-2	—	-.281**	—	-.265*	—	-.148
Secondary 3-4	—	-.793**	—	-.858**	—	-.546**
Secondary 5-6	—	-1.505**	—	-1.553**	—	-.919**
University	—	-2.202**	—	-2.409**	—	-1.505**
Other schooling	—	-1.135**	—	-1.052*	—	-.960*
Years married	—	—	—	—	.265**	.230**
Constant	-3.441	-4.279	-3.894	-4.411	-3.517	-3.869
R^2/adjusted R^2	.665/.663	.707/.705	.610/.608	.660/.657	.711/.709	.728/.725
F-ratio	506.3	368.2	264.7	196.2	373.8	253.5

Note: Mean number of children ever born equals 2.50 for all women and 3.23 for married women. Sample sizes are 2,309 and 1,533, respectively.

** Significant at the .01 level.
* Significant at the .05 level.
+ Significant at the .10 level.

1990 shown in table 4.1 above, Luba and Kwilu-Kwango women clearly have higher fertility than do those from the other four major groups, with the difference in the number of children ever born being on the order of 0.3 to almost 0.5, given age. The significant negative coefficients for the four groups represent differentials by ethnic group amounting to 12-18 percent of the average level of fertility. The differences for Congolese women from other tribes and for non-Congolese women are somewhat larger.

In comparing equation (1) with its counterpart from 1975 in table 4.6, it is apparent that the differences in number of children ever born (given age) between Kwilu-Kwango women and those from other groups have widened considerably for all the principal groups apart from the Luba. There are substantial significant negative coefficients for both groups of Bakongo women, and the low fertility of Ubangi women is especially marked in 1990.

When educational attainment is taken into consideration (equation [2]), the differences by ethnic group change dramatically and considerably more so

than in 1975. Each of the four statistically significant coefficients for the principal groups from equation (1) shrinks in absolute value, with those for Bakongo
North and Mongo women becoming insignificant. As was the case in 1975, net
of age and schooling, Luba women have the highest fertility, and Ubangi women have the lowest fertility among the major ethnic groups.[18] Bakongo women
went from having relatively high cumulative fertility net of age and schooling
in 1975 to having low levels in 1990. The pattern of differences by educational
attainment remains as it was in 1975, and, indeed, for the most part, the magnitudes of the estimated coefficients are quite similar for the two years.[19]

As was the case for 1975, the low levels of educational attainment in 1990
of Kwilu-Kwango women documented earlier in table 4.5 help explain why,
once schooling is controlled for in table 4.7, the estimated coefficients for the
ethnic groups increase in value (i.e., negative coefficients become less negative,
and the one positive coefficient—for the best-educated group—increases sharply). That is, a good deal of the lower fertility in equation (1) of Bakongo,
Mongo, and Ubangi women as compared to Kwilu-Kwango women simply reflects the fact that these groups of women are all better educated than are the
Kwilu-Kwango women. This is also the case for Congolese women in Kinshasa
who are from other tribes. Once educational attainment is explicitly taken into
consideration, the difference in fertility associated with ethnicity per se declines
substantially for all but the Luba women. Conversely, the insignificant difference for Luba women in equation (1) masks a significant ethnic difference net
of education since they have substantially more schooling than the Kwilu-
Kwango women do.

Equations (3) and (4) of table 4.7 repeat the analyses of equations (1) and
(2), but are restricted to married women. In contrast to the situation for 1975,
in which this sample restriction eliminated the negative coefficients and sharply
changed the magnitude and significance of the coefficients for virtually all the
ethnic groups, there is not much impact in 1990 of limiting the sample to married women, either with or without controlling for schooling. The changes of
note are that the negative coefficients for Ubangi women and the positive coefficients for Luba women both increase somewhat in absolute value. Also in
contrast to the results for 1975, limiting the sample to married women does not
reduce the (absolute) size of the coefficients for educational attainment.

Our more detailed questionnaire from 1990 allowed us to calculate the
duration of marriage on the basis of reported marital history, and equations (5)
and (6) in table 4.7 add controls for the duration of marriage. Not surprisingly,
given the low use of modern contraception (see Shapiro and Tambashe 1994a;
and chapter 7 below), this variable is a very highly significant predictor of

[18] Overall, non-Congolese women have the lowest fertility by far once schooling is taken
into consideration. This differential represents a substantial change compared to 1975, when the
corresponding coefficient was small and insignificant.

[19] The "other schooling" category consists of the relatively small number of women who had
taken apprenticeship or vocational courses.

the number of children ever born. In the absence of any control for schooling, addition of this variable results in a sharp reduction in the absolute value of the significant negative coefficients for the principal ethnic groups in equation (3), and three of the four become insignificant. The positive coefficient, for Luba women, increases and becomes statistically significant. A tendency for negative ethnic group coefficients to become less negative or even positive can be seen in comparing equations (4) and (6) as well, but it is not quite so pronounced. These results suggest that women from Kwilu-Kwango tend to marry earlier and stay married longer than women from other ethnic groups do.[20]

From equation (6), it is apparent that, once marital duration and schooling are taken into account, the only significant ethnic group coefficient is that for Luba women. That is, among women with comparable durations of marriage and educational attainment, fertility differentials by ethnic group are largely absent, with one notable exception. Further, controlling for marital duration reduces the absolute value of all the educational attainment coefficients, and only those for the three highest groups remain statistically significant. The smaller coefficients are indicative of delays in entry into marriage associated with schooling. At the same time, there are substantial differences in fertility behavior *within marriages of comparable duration* for women with at least 3 years of secondary education as compared to women with lower levels of schooling.

The multivariate analyses presented in tables 4.6 and 4.7 control by and large for only three variables: age; ethnicity; and education. However, research on fertility in the Congo and elsewhere has documented that there are a number of other factors that also influence fertility.[21] Tables 4A.1 and 4A.2 in the appendix to this chapter thus present estimates of fertility regressions with additional variables, for 1975 and 1990, respectively. These regressions include, in addition to ethnicity, education, and age, variables for employment status, migration status, and marital status. In brief, the estimates reported in the appendix demonstrate that these variables tend to be significant influences on fertility. At the same time, our findings regarding ethnicity and education are essentially unchanged once these additional variables are included in the analyses.

[20] Indeed, examination of proportions married in 1990 by age and ethnic group shows that Kwilu-Kwango and also Luba women tend to have especially high proportions married relative to the other four groups. For further details, see chapter 6.

[21] For studies on fertility in the Congo and/or Kinshasa, see Romaniuk (1967, 1968), Ngondo (1980), Sala-Diakanda (1980), Tabutin (1982), Tambashe (1984), and Shapiro and Tambashe (1997a, 1998). Evidence on the relation between women's employment and fertility is discussed by Lloyd (1991), Poirier et al. (1989), and Standing (1983). Socioeconomic factors influencing fertility are discussed by Muhuri et al. (1994) and by Tabutin (1997).

Summary and Conclusions

This chapter has provided a considerable body of evidence suggesting that, between 1955 and 1990, education replaced ethnicity as a key factor influencing fertility in Kinshasa. In 1955, ethnic group differences in fertility were quite substantial, while the vast majority of adult women had never been to school. By 1975, ethnic group differences in fertility had diminished considerably, thanks to major reductions in sterility, while substantial fertility differentials by educational attainment had emerged for women with at least 3 years of secondary education. These differentials were considerably larger than those among the ethnic groups. However, because women with this much schooling represented only 13 percent of the population of reproductive-age women, their relatively low fertility had a negligible impact on the overall level of fertility in the city.

By 1990, the substantial differentials by educational attainment were still in evidence and comparable to the magnitudes that had been apparent in 1975. But, in 1990, 44 percent of the women of reproductive age were in these relatively well-educated groups, and, hence, overall fertility showed a distinct drop as compared to 1975. Again, education group differences in fertility (for these relatively better-educated women) were substantially larger than were the differences by ethnic group. Fertility differences by ethnic group were wider in 1990 than in 1975, but this widening was in fact linked to differences across ethnic groups in levels of educational attainment.

One ethnic group stands out from the rest with respect to fertility behavior: the Luba. In 1975, and again in 1990, Luba women were characterized by both relatively high levels of educational attainment and relatively high fertility. We have not attempted to provide an explanation for this fertility difference; an in-depth ethnographic study is probably required to investigate the underlying reasons. However, it is worth noting that the greater fertility of Luba women is consistent with our 1990 data concerning desired fertility. Simple tabulation of desired fertility by ethnic group shows that Luba women have the highest desired fertility, by 0.2 children compared to the second-highest group, the Kwilu-Kwango women. Regression analysis of desired fertility, controlling as well for age and education, reveals a statistically significant coefficient for Luba women (as compared to Kwilu-Kwango women), with a value of +0.3.

The chapter also highlights the importance of marriage as a factor contributing to ethnic group differences in fertility and linked in part to fertility differentials by educational attainment. In 1975, and in 1990, Kwilu-Kwango women were more likely than women in other groups to be married, and this helps account for their higher overall fertility. Indeed, in 1975, among married women, those from Kwilu-Kwango had the *lowest* fertility. In comparable analyses for 1990, by contrast, married Kwilu-Kwango women had relatively high fertility, exceeded only by that of married Luba women. However, controlling for the duration of marriage in 1990 resulted in no significant differences by ethnicity per se, except for Luba women.

With respect to education, limiting the analysis to married women resulted in smaller fertility differentials by education group in 1975. This was not the case in 1990, but controlling for marital duration in 1990 did have a similar effect. Hence, this evidence suggests that part of the effect of education is to delay entry into marriage. This phenomenon and other issues pertaining to both entry into marriage and the importance for fertility of differences in marriage by ethnic group and by education group will be explored as part of the analyses in the following two chapters.

Finally, we also find evidence (presented in the appendix to this chapter) that other factors influence fertility. Employment status, migration status, and marital status all matter, to varying degrees, although the effects of the latter two in particular appear to be distinctly weaker in 1990 than they were in 1975. Regardless of these other factors, however, the conclusions described above concerning education and ethnicity still hold.

Appendix: Expanded Multivariate Analyses of Fertility

This appendix reports results of estimation of multivariate fertility regressions for 1975 and 1990 in which the number of children ever born is regressed on a woman's age, ethnic group, education group, and variables identifying three factors not previously considered in our analyses: employment status; migration status; and marital status. The additional variables used here are limited to those that can be generated for both 1975 and 1990. This facilitates comparison of results from the two years. Mean values of the variables used in the analyses of children ever born, both in the body of the chapter and in this appendix, are reported in table 4A.3 at the end of the appendix.

Inclusion of these variables serves a dual purpose: it allows us to ascertain the relation in 1975 and 1990 of each of these variables to fertility in Kinshasa, all else equal; and it permits determination of the robustness of the estimated differentials by ethnicity and education reported above. In each set of estimates, we report results for all women and for the subset of married women. Further, reflecting the importance of marital status for assessment of fertility differences by ethnicity and education, we report results both with and without controlling for marital status. For 1990, we also (as in table 4.7 above) report results for married women that control for marital duration.

The first equation in table 4A.1 documents that both employment status and migrant status were significantly related to fertility in 1975. Women who were self-employed (almost 9 percent of those aged 15-49) had slightly lower fertility than those who were not employed, all else equal, while the 4 percent of women who worked as employees had distinctly lower fertility, by almost 0.7 children. Migrants, who represented almost three-quarters of the women, had significantly higher fertility than did nonmigrants, by 0.2 children.

The coefficients of the different ethnic groups are quite similar to those in the counterpart equation (2) in table 4.6 above, not controlling for employment and migration status: there are moderate positive coefficients for the two Bakongo groups, negative coefficients for the Mongo and Ubangi women, and a more substantial positive coefficient for Luba women. The education coefficients are similar as well, although slightly smaller in absolute value from the early secondary level on, reflecting the positive association between schooling and the likelihood of being employed.[22]

The second equation in table 4A.1 adds controls for marital status. As suggested by much (but not all) previous research, women in polygamous unions had significantly lower fertility than those in monogamous unions (Romaniuk 1967; Ngondo 1980; Pebley and Mbugua 1989).[23] Those who were widowed, divorced, or separated as well as those who were never married had substantially lower fertility than did women in monogamous unions, all else equal. Inclusion of the variables representing marital status also brings about changes in a number of the other coefficients. The coefficients for the different ethnic groups all become more positive, reflecting the greater frequency of marriage among Kwilu-Kwango women. There are small declines in the absolute values of the coefficients of the education variables, suggesting (for those with at least some secondary schooling) that part of the effect of schooling on fertility is to delay marriage.

The coefficient for self-employed women has now become positive and significant, while that for employees remains negative and significant but is substantially diminished in absolute value. These changes indicate that employment status and marital status are correlated. Indeed, widowed, divorced, and separated women were most likely to be self-employed (23 percent) and at the same time most likely to be employees (12 percent), while those in polygamous unions also had a relatively high rate of self-employment (17 percent). Once marital status is explicitly controlled for, the fact that women in these low-fertility marital status groups are disproportionately likely to have been employed results in a distinct reduction in the (absolute value of the) negative employment status coefficients.

The migrant-nonmigrant differential disappears once marital status is included. This reflects the greater likelihood of migrants being in monogamous marriages as compared to women born in Kinshasa. That is, given age,

---

[22] More than one in six women with 3-4 years of secondary schooling worked as an employee in 1975, and, for those at the two highest education levels, the corresponding figure exceeded one in three. Chapter 11 will provide further evidence on the relations between education and employment.

[23] There are different suggestions offered in the literature to explain this result, including both lower exposure to the risk of pregnancy among women in polygamous unions owing to a lower frequency of intercourse and a greater tendency for subfecund women to be in polygamous unions (Romaniuk 1967; Pebley and Mbugua 1989).

Table 4A.1 Regression Analyses of Children Ever Born, 1975, Expanded Model (ordinary least squares regression coefficients)

	All Women		Married Women	
Variable	(1)	(2)	(3)	(4)
Age	.6054**	.4347**	.6716**	.6766**
Age squared	-.0061**	-.0036**	-.0069**	-.0070**
Ethnic group				
Bakongo North	.110**	.173**	.280**	.254**
Bakongo South	.099**	.140**	.223**	.212**
Kwilu-Kwango	—	—	—	—
Mongo	-.076*	.093*	.111*	.124*
Ubangi	-.124**	.023	.075	.052
Luba+	.255**	.333**	.580**	.576**
Other tribes	-.082	.011	.195*	.174+
Non-Congo	-.002	.043	.080+	.078+
Schooling level				
None	-.342**	-.315**	-.307**	- .277**
Primary	—	—	—	—
Secondary 1-2	-.250**	-.186**	-.122**	-.137**
Secondary 3-4	-.628**	-.516**	-.349**	-.360**
Secondary 5-6	-1.218**	-1.017**	-.778**	-.797**
University	-1.929**	-1.585**	-1.544**	-1.540**
Employment status				
Self-employed	-.089*	.102**	.021	.069
Employee	-.658**	- .379**	-.597**	-.572**
Not employed	—	—	—	—
Migrant	.208**	.027	.132**	.092*
Nonmigrant	—	—	—	—
Marital status				
Married—monog.	—	—	—	—
Married—polyg.	—	-.673**	—	-.703**
Wid., div., sep.	—	-1.276**	—	—
Never married	—	-1.159**	—	—
Constant	-8.347	-5.254	-9.398	-9.378
R^2/adjusted R^2	.632/.631	.656/.656	.501/.500	.507/.507
F-ratio	3,497.6	3,305.5	1,258.9	1,218.5

Note: Mean number of children ever born equals 2.89 for all women and 4.16 for married women. Sample sizes are 34,719 and 21,352, respectively.

** Significant at the .01 level.
* Significant at the .05 level.
+ Significant at the .10 level.

Kinshasa-born women were generally more likely to have been either never married, in a polygamous union (for those aged 25 and over), or widowed, divorced, or separated.

Equation (3), limited to married women, may be compared with both equation (1) for all women and equation (4) from table 4.6 (for married women). With respect first to the latter comparison, the addition of employment status and migrant status reveals that, among married women, employees have significantly lower fertility, by 0.6 children, and migrants have significantly higher fertility, but only by a little more than 0.1 children. The ethnic group co-efficients are very similar to those in the counterpart equation in table 4.6, while the education coefficients beginning at the lower secondary level are reduced in absolute value. Comparing the results for married women with those for all women (equations [3] and [1] of table 4A.1), the ethnic group coefficients all become more positive (as was seen in table 4.6), indicating that, among married women, those from Kwilu-Kwango have relatively low fertility, other things equal. Similarly, there is again a narrowing in the magnitude of differences by education. The fertility of self-employed married women is not significantly different from that of nonemployed women, while the differential for employees is maintained. Finally, there remains a migrant-nonmigrant dif-ferential among married women, but only about two-thirds the size of the corresponding differential among all women.

The final equation in the table documents that, among married women, those in polygamous unions have significantly lower fertility, other things equal. Controlling for this variable has little impact on the other coefficients in the equation, although the magnitude of the migrant-nonmigrant difference is reduced somewhat. This is a consequence of the lesser incidence of polygamy among married migrants as compared to nonmigrants.

Equations parallel to those in table 4A.1, but for 1990, are found in the first four columns of table 4A.2. The discussion here first focuses on comparing the effects in 1990 with those in 1975 of employment status, migration status, and marital status. In 1975, the estimated coefficients for self-employed women varied depending on whether marital status was included and on whether all women or only married women were considered. In 1990, however, when self-employment was more than three times as common (involving about 30 percent of the women aged 15-49), the fertility of self-employed women did not differ significantly from that of nonemployed women. By contrast, the fertility of em-ployees was consistently significantly lower than that of nonemployed women, as was the case in 1975, although the size of the difference was somewhat greater in 1990. A tendency for the fertility of migrants to be higher than that of nonmigrants was still evident in 1990, but the coefficients are generally considerably smaller than in 1975 and no longer significant. Differentials by marital status were present in 1990, as they were in 1975, but were only rough-ly about half or less of their earlier magnitude.

Comparison of the coefficients for the ethnic and educational attainment groups in equations (1), (3), and (5) of table 4A.2 with those in equations (2), (4), and (6) of table 4.7 shows that addition of the employment status and mi-grant status variables has little impact other than slightly reducing the absolute values of the education coefficients among women with relatively high levels of schooling. Controlling for marital status among all women (i.e., comparing equations [1] and [2] of table 4A.2) tends to reduce slightly the magnitude of the absolute value of the negative ethnic group coefficients and increase the one positive coefficient while showing only small changes and no systematic effect on the education group coefficients. Among married women, there is essentially no impact on the ethnicity and education coefficients of controlling for polygamy (i.e., comparing equations [5] and [6] of table 4A.2). In sum, then, the results presented earlier concerning ethnicity and education appear to be quite robust.

Table 4A.2 Regression Analyses of Children Ever Born, 1990, Expanded Model (weighted ordinary least squares regression coefficients)

Variable	All Women			Married Women		
	(1)	(2)	(3)	(4)	(5)	(6)
Age	.2924**	.2822**	.3012**	.3095**	.2893**	.2963**
Age squared	—	—	-.0001	-.0002	-.0033**	-.0033**
Ethnic group						
Bakongo North	-.139	-.093	-.115	-.111	.100	.103
Bakongo South	-.184*	-.140+	-.178	-.178	-.019	-.020
Kwilu-Kwango	—	—	—	—	—	—
Mongo	-.107	-.064	-.085	-.057	.076	.099
Ubangi	-.253*	-.200+	-.363*	-.359*	-.198	-.196
Luba+	.411**	.464**	.610**	.624**	.620**	.631**
Other tribes	-.167	-.138	-.187	-.146	.005	.039
Non-Congo	-.490**	-.461**	-.506*	-.490*	-.405*	-.391*
Schooling level						
None	-.268+	-.250+	-.210	-.184	-.179	-.158
Primary	—	—	—	—	—	—
Secondary 1-2	-.250**	-.273**	-.235+	-.233+	-.132	-.130
Secondary 3-4	-.733**	-.749**	-.794**	-.793**	-.515**	-.514**
Secondary 5-6	-1.389**	-1.443**	-1.430**	-1.447**	-.869**	-.884**
University	-2.018**	-2.015**	-2.183**	-2.201**	-1.408**	-1.425**
Other schooling	-1.044**	-1.002**	-.944*	-1.001*	-.911*	-.960*
Employment status						
Self-employed	.010	-.032	.031	.027	-.059	-.061
Employee	-.900**	-.867**	-.883**	-.869**	-.516**	-.505**
Not employed	—	—	—	—	—	—
Migrant status						
Migrant	.073	.063	.083	.080	.030	.027
Nonmigrant	—	—	—	—	—	—
Marital status						
Married—monog.	—	—	—	—	—	—
Married—polyg.	—	-.199+	—	-.301*	—	-.255*
Wid., div., sep.	—	-.671**	—	—	—	—
Never married	—	-.521**	—	—	—	—
Marital duration						
Years married	—	—	—	—	.227**	.226**
Constant	-4.375	-3.933	-4.414	-4.522	-3.950	-4.043
R^2/adjusted R^2	.711/.708	.718/.715	.664/.660	.666/.661	.729/.726	.730/.727
F-ratio	330.8	290.8	166.3	158.4	214.5	204.7

Note: Mean number of children ever born equals 2.50 for all women and 3.23 for married women. Sample sizes are 2,309 and 1,533, respectively.

** Significant at the .01 level.
* Significant at the .05 level.
+ Significant at the .10 level.

Table 4A.3 Mean Values of Variables in the Analyses of Children Ever Born

Variables	1975		1990	
	All	Married	All	Married
Age	26.7	30.0	25.6	27.5
Ethnic group				
Bakongo North	.099	.096	.076	.070
Bakongo South	.265	.255	.222	.212
Kwilu-Kwango	.244	.281	.369	.395
Mongo	.079	.068	.074	.071
Ubangi	.086	.075	.079	.074
Luba+	.092	.091	.111	.110
Other tribes	.019	.019	.019	.021
Non-Congo	.116	.115	.050	.047
Schooling level				
None	.297	.398	.063	.065
Primary	.398	.401	.249	.266
Secondary 1-2	.174	.108	.238	.221
Secondary 3-4	.100	.075	.274	.263
Secondary 5-6	.027	.016	.118	.134
University	.004	.002	.047	.043
Other schooling	.000	.000	.011	.008
Employment status				
Self-employed	.088	.101	.302	.361
Employee	.043	.026	.040	.044
Not employed	.869	.873	.658	.595
Migrant status				
Migrant	.743	.867	.472	.522
Nonmigrant	.257	.133	.528	.478
Marital status				
Married—monog.	.552	.897	.614	.855
Married—polyg.	.063	.103	.097	.145
Wid., div., sep.	.101	NA	.069	NA
Never married	.284	NA	.220	NA
Marital duration				
Years married	NA	NA	NA	9.64
Children ever born	2.89	4.16	2.50	3.23

Note: NA = not applicable or not available.

Chapter 5. Family Background and Early Life Course Transitions

The preceding chapter documented the importance of education, ethnicity, marriage, and other factors as influences on fertility. In this and the next chapter we turn to a closer examination of fertility behavior as of 1990, beginning with a focus on family background and its impact on early life course transitions. More specifically, this chapter examines the role of various family background factors in influencing the timing of three key life course events: age at entry into sexual activity; age at first union; and age at first birth.

Each of these events constitutes a significant milestone in a young woman's transition to adulthood. In addition, the timing of each is likely to have important consequences. Early onset of sexual activity raises the likelihood of experiencing adverse health outcomes. Early entry into marriage may well have detrimental effects on a young woman's socioeconomic attainment, particularly in a modernizing setting. Early childbearing is likewise often associated with constraints on achievement of educational and occupational goals and attainments as well as with health hazards to young mothers and their children. In addition, in a setting like Kinshasa where the prevalence of modern contraception is low, early onset of childbearing is likely to foreshadow high lifetime fertility.

There is a substantial literature on family background influences on the timing of these life course transitions. However, most of this literature is based on data from the United States and other industrialized countries. This chapter adds to that literature by providing evidence on some of the same issues but from an urban setting in sub-Saharan Africa, where families are distinctly different than in the industrialized West. In traditional African societies, for example, entry into marriage and the choice of a spouse are very much the affairs of extended families and clans, rather than simply individuals or the nuclear family. Hence, the characteristics of the nuclear family environment in which a woman grows up may be less pertinent to these life course transitions in an

African setting. In addition, high fertility means that the size of households in which children grow up is typically considerably larger than in Western settings, and the relatively high prevalence of child fostering in sub-Saharan Africa results in households that often include children from the extended family.

Several dimensions of family background are considered in the analyses: father's schooling; mother's schooling; parental survival status; family size; birth order; type of place where a woman grew up; her ethnic group; and her religious background. These factors are likely to influence a young woman's socioeconomic well-being while she is growing up, the options available to her to engage in various activities, her schooling and ultimate educational attainment, and her socialization, tastes, and attitudes. Consequently, there are multiple paths by which these family background factors will influence the likelihood that a young woman will initiate sexual activity, enter a union, and begin her reproductive career. Knowledge of the ways in which characteristics of the family environment influence the behavior of young women should permit a better understanding of the changes taking place in Kinshasa and likely to occur in the future with regard to sexuality, nuptiality, and fertility.

The following section provides a discussion of the transitions to be studied and a selective review of past research on family background effects on the timing of these life course transitions. This is followed by a discussion of methodological and data considerations pertinent to the empirical analyses. Empirical findings based on estimation of three models for each of the behaviors of interest are then presented and discussed. The empirical work first puts emphasis on the role of parental educational attainment, then focuses on the full set of family background characteristics, and finally considers the intervening effects of school enrollment. The chapter concludes with a summary of several key findings and a discussion of the implications of the analysis for the timing of these transitions and for future fertility.

Early Life Course Transitions and Family Background Influences

For women in sub-Saharan Africa, marriage is near universal and occurs at relatively young ages. Initiation of sexual activity also occurs early, often prior to marriage (Gage and Meekers 1994; Meekers 1994). Early sexual activity is typically unprotected, and the use of (modern) contraceptives is not common (Gage-Brandon and Meekers 1993; National Research Council 1993a, 1993b). In such an environment, age at first birth is a key determinant of a woman's ultimate level of fertility (Westoff 1992).

In addition, the younger a woman is when she begins having sexual intercourse, the sooner she is exposed to various reproductive health hazards. With limited access to family-planning information and services (especially condoms), sexually active adolescent women are exposed to a high likelihood of contracting sexually transmitted diseases (STDs). Small-scale studies done in

Kenya, for example, have revealed that 16-36 percent of youths had one or more STDs (Meheus 1992; Maggwa and Ngugi 1992). Further, early entry to sexual life also increases the risk of becoming pregnant. Through pregnancy, a young woman's sexual behavior may lead to induced abortion or to child-bearing and teenage marriage, which may exact a heavy toll on her educational and socioeconomic aspirations and accomplishments.

From a life course perspective, both marriage and childbearing are key milestones in the transition to adulthood (Bozon 1993; Hogan 1986). Yet early marriage and especially early motherhood may have adverse socioeconomic consequences for women. Where school regulations do not allow pregnant girls to stay in school, as is the case in most of sub-Saharan Africa (United Nations 1994; Meekers et al. 1995), the age at which a woman becomes pregnant and has her first birth is critical to her educational and occupational goals and at-tainments. Indeed, younger childbearers complete significantly less schooling than late initiators. As a result, young mothers are more likely to have little con-trol over resource allocation decisions within the household and to take on traditional roles that foster high fertility aspirations (Lloyd 1994). Further, the establishment of a family during the teenage years is likely to have an adverse effect on a young woman's prospects for participation in the labor market, her earnings potential, and her general economic well-being. Thus, early age at family formation sets in motion a cycle of disadvantages that tend to perpetuate high fertility and poverty.[1]

Early marriage and early childbearing are also associated with various adverse reproductive health hazards among young women and their children. Adolescent women face higher morbidity and mortality risks from childbearing than do those aged 20-34 (Harrison 1985; UNFPA 1989). In addition, the risks of morbidity and mortality among children are estimated to be higher among those born to women under age 20 than among those born to women aged 20 years and over (United Nations 1994). Spontaneous and unsafe abortions, anemia and high blood pressure, and labor complications that may lead to per-manent injury to or the death of the mother are reproductive health problems that are distinctly more prevalent among adolescent women. Studies in Cam-eroon, Nigeria, and Zimbabwe have found that 60-70 percent of abortion and/or obstetric complications are accounted for by teenagers (United Nations 1994). As indicated by selected studies carried out in Ethiopia, Kenya, and Nigeria, vesicovaginal fistula is also a common pathology among adolescent women:

---

[1] These considerations are particularly relevant in an urban setting like Kinshasa, where women's access to schooling is relatively high and substantial numbers of women are labor market participants. In rural areas of sub-Saharan Africa, by contrast, women's economic oppor-tunities are likely to be much more limited: labor markets are not well developed, and often women cannot own land. In these circumstances, women's reproductive capabilities tend to be highly valued, and early marriage and childbearing are not disadvantageous—on the contrary, they provide perhaps the most effective means for gaining social status.

40-60 percent of the victims of vesicovaginal fistula were found to be women under age 20, while 60-65 percent of the cases were found to occur at the first labor/delivery (United Nations 1994).

Early initiation of sexual activity, marriage, and childbearing thus appears to result in numerous adverse health, educational, social, and economic consequences. A number of studies, particularly in the United States, have looked at the impact of various family background characteristics on the timing of these early life course transitions. Most studies of the timing of entry into sexual life, marriage, and childbearing in sub-Saharan Africa have looked at the individual's current socioeconomic characteristics as the relevant influences (see, e.g., United Nations 1987, 1990; Westoff 1992; Meekers 1994; Tambashe 1984; Tambashe and Shapiro 1991; National Research Council 1993c). By and large, education has consistently been identified as the single most powerful factor determining the timing of these transitions. We turn now to a brief overview of relevant results from the body of research focused on family background characteristics.

With respect to the effects of parental educational attainment, young women with more-educated parents have been found to be less likely to experience sex at early ages (Carolina Population Center 1984). In comparison with the effect of mother's education, father's education has been shown to have less of an impact on the likelihood of early initiation of sexual activity (Carolina Population Center 1984). High levels of parents' educational attainment appear to negatively affect the probability of entering a union or having a birth at early ages (Kiernan and Diamond 1983; Michael and Tuma 1985; Lehrer 1985; Kahn and Anderson 1991). A study by Lehrer (1985) suggests that key family background variables positively influence children's schooling and hence, indirectly delay the formation of a family by either marriage or childbirth (see also Moore and Hofferth 1980).

Parents' education is likely to be linked to the economic status of a young woman's family of origin; hence, research findings on the impact of economic well-being may well reflect an important path by which parental education influences the timing of these transitions. A study by Bozon (1993) in France shows that females from well-off families tend to become sexually active at later ages. Adverse conditions in the family of origin have been found to lead to early entry into marriage and childbearing. In particular, the probability of an early transition to marriage or to motherhood has been shown to decline as the family's resources increase (Michael and Tuma 1985; Anderson and Hill 1983).

Living in a nonintact family, characterized as a family where one of the biological parents is not present, has been found to raise the likelihood of an early transition to sexual life (Newcomer and Udry 1987). Growing up in an intact family and having a small number of siblings, two key dimensions of the family background environment, both tend to delay the onset of marriage and childbearing (Moore and Hofferth 1980; Kiernan and Diamond 1983; Bachrach and Horne 1987; Hogan 1986; Michael and Tuma 1985; Lehrer 1985; Boult and Cunningham 1991). A study by Panzarine and Santelli (1987) indicated that sibling influences, lack of parental supervision, and poverty were all family structure features that place teenagers at high risk. Those from families in poverty or with larger numbers of siblings were more likely to begin sexual activity at an early age and, consequently, to have a teen pregnancy.

Children with more-religious parents tend to begin sexual experience at relatively later ages than those whose parents are less religious, with those from Protestant families more likely to begin having intercourse at earlier ages than their counterparts from Catholic families (Bachrach and Horne 1987). Studer and Thornton (1987) report findings from several previous studies documenting the importance of adolescents' religion and frequency of attendance at religious services. Both variables have been found to have a positive effect on age at first coitus and a negative effect on frequency of sexual activity (see also Bozon 1993).

Methodology and Data Considerations

The events under study in this chapter are initiation of sexual activity, entry into a first union (of at least 6 months' duration), and timing of the first birth. The data set includes women who have not yet experienced one or more of these events and others who have experienced these events at varying ages; both of these aspects must be taken into consideration. In order to account for the censoring effect associated with the fact that for some respondents the event has not yet taken place and the effect of the respondents' differential exposure to a particular risk studied, we perform a discrete-time event-history analysis, using logistic regression of a person-year data file (as described in Allison 1984). With this approach, each year that an individual is exposed to the risk of experiencing a particular event is treated as a separate observation.

More specifically, the person-year data file is generated by creating a separate record for each individual respondent for each year of age from a starting age (12 or 13) until either (i) the age at which the transition to a given state took place (if that age is less than or equal to the cutoff age),[2] (ii) the cutoff age (if the respondent is at least 1 year older than that cutoff age and

---

[2] The analyses of these events demarcating the early reproductive life cycle transitions use different starting and cutoff ages in the creation of the person-year data files. For the initiation of sexual activity we cover ages 12-25, while for the transition to first union or to motherhood we begin at age 13 and go through age 30. The lower cutoff age for analysis of first intercourse reflects the fact that by age 25 this phenomenon is essentially universal, as may be seen in figure 5.1 below. For the latter two events, there are individuals who did not experience them prior to age 25 but did so subsequently; we have chosen age 30 as a cutoff because absence of a first marriage as well as a first birth by that age is a very unusual occurrence in Kinshasa.

never made the transition to the state under study prior to her [cutoff age + 1]th birthday), or (iii) her current age -1 (if she is under the cutoff age and never made the transition to the state under study).[3]

In all cases, the dependent variable is dichotomous, equal to 1 if the respondent experienced the event under study at the age of a particular person-year observation and 0 otherwise.[4] The independent variables include both time-varying and fixed factors. Age as of the person-year observation and a dichotomous variable indicating whether the respondent had been enrolled in school in the year prior to the person-year observation are the time-varying variables.

A number of family background characteristics constitute the non-time-varying variables. These include a series of dichotomous variables for the respondent's father's and mother's level of schooling, the survival status of her parents at the time she was age 15, the size of her family of origin (as measured by the number of children with whom she resided at the onset of puberty), her birth order, the type of place in which she grew up through age 12 (in a major city, a small urban center, or a village), the type of place in which she resided during adolescence (ages 12-18), her ethnic group, and her initial religious affiliation. These latter variables are fixed for any individual respondent and do not vary over time. Additional time-invariant variables identify each woman's broad age cohort, to allow for trends in the behaviors analyzed independent of the other explanatory variables.

Since the dependent variables in the analyses are based on respondents' recall and reporting of key life course events, concerns about the validity of the data are warranted. It is difficult to assess the accuracy of the reports of age at first intercourse. Although it can be assumed that the first sexual experience may be a significant enough emotional event that a woman would not very easily forget when it happened (Bozon 1993), some women may have been embarrassed to report that first intercourse occurred as early as it did. That is, the proportion of those responding "don't know" to the question about age at

---

[3] Thus, e.g., consider the hypothetical case of a woman who was age 23 when interviewed and who experienced first intercourse at age 17, married at age 21, and had not yet had a child. She would contribute six observations to the data file for analysis of age at first intercourse (representing ages 12-17 inclusive) and nine observations to the data file for analysis of first marriage (ages 13-21 inclusive). In each of these cases, there are person-year observations for the individual for each year for which the event in question was not experienced and for the year in which the event was experienced. Beyond the age at which the event has been experienced, the individual is no longer included in the sample since by definition she is no longer at risk of experiencing the event for the first time. For first birth, the individual is right censored: she will contribute 10 observations to the data file for first birth, representing ages 13-22 inclusive (since she has not yet reached age 24, the observation for age 23 is truncated).

[4] Since, as indicated in the previous note, individuals are removed from the sample of observations once they have experienced the event in question, mean values of the dependent variables are low, and the mean age in each person-year data file is also low. The mean values are reported in table 5A.1.

first intercourse may reflect, not only some respondents' recall lapses, but also their reluctance to admit an early debut of sexual activity.[5] In explaining observed inconsistencies between age at first union and age at first intercourse, Blanc and Rutenberg (1990) have shown that age at first union, calculated from the date of first union, was more problematic than age at first intercourse, which was reported and recorded as an age. The data used here for these two variables reflect reported age, not date, of the event in question. While Blanc and Rutenberg (1991) call for caution in the analysis of individual-level data on the initiation of coitus, they conclude that aggregate measures are of greater validity. In any case, we have excluded from the analyses reported below all women whose information on age at (or, in the case of the first birth, date of) occurrence of the events under study is missing.

Empirical Findings

Figure 5.1 shows the cumulative proportions of women reporting having experienced first intercourse, a first union, and a first birth, by age. These events clearly tend to follow one another sequentially. By age 16, for example, 46 percent of women reported having had first intercourse, while nearly a third had entered a first union by that age, and only 16 percent had had a first birth. By age 20, the corresponding percentages for these events were 93, 75, and 62, respectively.

Early entry into sexual activity in Kinshasa may be compared to that of residents from urban areas of other countries in sub-Saharan Africa. Meekers (1994) analyzed data on age at first intercourse from Demographic and Health Surveys (DHS) carried out between 1986 and 1989 in seven countries in sub-Saharan Africa. In Kinshasa, 13 percent of women reported having had sexual intercourse prior to reaching age 15. This figure is comparable to those for women from urban areas in three of the countries studied by Meekers: Zimbabwe (11 percent), Burundi (13 percent), and Togo (15 percent). Urban women in three other countries (Ghana, Kenya, and Mali) had somewhat higher corresponding figures, ranging from 19 to 24 percent, while over 35 percent of urban women in Liberia reported having had intercourse prior to reaching age 15 (Meekers 1994, table A1, p. 62).

Tables 5.1-5.3 present the results of multivariate analyses of the timing of entry into sexual, marital, and reproductive life. There are three models in each table. The first model controls only for the individual's age, which is included in the analysis to account for biological maturation, and father's and mother's schooling. This initial model provides a useful baseline or reference point that focuses on parental schooling. In model 2, the additional family background variables are introduced: survival status of the respondent's parents when she

---

[5] These responses represented 10 percent of the women who had ever been sexually active. Older and lesser-educated women (those with no or only primary schooling) are disproportionately represented among these "don't know" responses.

Fig. 5.1 Age at first intercourse, first union, and first birth

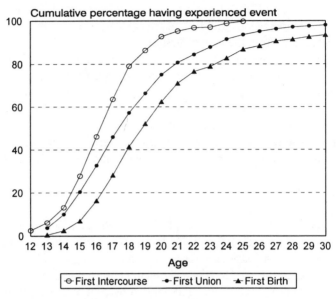

Note: Universe is women aged 15-49 at time of survey, 1990.

was age 15; number of coresident children at menarche; information on birth order; type of place where the respondent grew up; ethnic group; and religious background. The variables identifying the woman's broad age cohort are also included in model 2. School enrollment status is introduced in model 3. This allows us to examine the direct impact of schooling on the timing of these life course transitions; further, we are also able to ascertain the extent to which the family background environment influences the family formation process indirectly through schooling, as suggested by previous research (Lehrer 1985; Moore and Hofferth 1980).

Turning to the empirical results, the highly significant positive coefficients for age and negative coefficients for age squared in model 1 indicate that the likelihood of entry into sexual, marital, and reproductive life at any given year of age increases with age but at a decreasing rate. The turning point of the quadratic specification is just over 20 for the initiation of sexual activity and between 21 and 22 for the entry into marriage and motherhood. By the respective turning point age, more than 90 percent of the women report having experienced first intercourse, while over 80 percent have entered a first union, and more than 70 percent have had a first birth. Introduction of additional family background and cohort variables (model 2) and the school enrollment variable (model 3) leaves the coefficients of age and age squared largely unchanged.

Effects of Parental Educational Attainment: Model 1

Before examining the effects of parental educational attainment, it is necessary to consider the nature of the data on parental schooling. High proportions of respondents did not know the educational attainment of their parents. This was true for about 45 percent of the total observations for father's education in the data files and for roughly 25 percent of the observations for mother's education. However, respondents were also asked about the literacy of each of their parents, and this information was used where the parent's schooling level was not known. Hence, in such cases we have identified the parent as literate or illiterate. Presumably, those who were illiterate had little or no formal education. Those categorized as literate, representing almost 90 percent of the fathers whose education was not known and about two-thirds of the mothers, are most likely a more heterogeneous group. They may include, not only individuals with several years of primary education, some secondary education, or even higher education, but also those with little or no formal schooling who learned to read and write as adults.

In addition, for about 4-5 percent of fathers and mothers the respondents were unable to characterize parental educational attainment via conventional levels of schooling. These cases, which most likely represent parents with little or no formal schooling who took some sort of vocational training course or literacy training, are identified as "other" in the tables. The following discussion focuses on the conventional schooling levels plus the "not known—illiterate" group (described as *illiterate* for short). Ex ante, we expected coefficients for the illiterate group to be similar to those for individuals in the "no schooling" category.

Results from model 1 show a clear tendency for increased father's education to result in delayed transitions. More specifically, women whose fathers were illiterate had the greatest likelihood of early initiation of sexual life, while increases in father's education beyond the primary school level are associated with delays in the onset of sexual activity (table 5.1). Table 5.2 also reveals highly significant differences by father's education, showing earliest entry into a union by women whose fathers were illiterate or had no schooling and later entry for daughters of university-educated fathers (although first marriage transitions among daughters whose fathers had secondary school education are no different than among those whose fathers had only primary school education). A quite strong relation is evident with respect to the timing of the first birth: women whose fathers were illiterate or had no schooling were most likely to have a first birth, given their age, and the higher the level of the father's education, the later the onset of childbearing (table 5.3).

The relation in model 1 between mother's education and the respondent's early sexual, marital, and reproductive behaviors is somewhat different and

Table 5.1 Logistic Regression Analyses of Entry into Sexual Activity

	Models		
Variables	(1)	(2)	(3)
Respondent's age			
Age	2.210**	2.188**	2.216**
Age squared	-.0542**	-.0529**	-.0540**
Father's schooling			
None	-.016	-.123**	-.248**
Primary	—	—	—
Secondary	-.124**	-.106**	-.110**
University	-.288**	-.210**	-.197**
Other	-.178**	-.175**	-.174**
Not known—illiterate	.336**	.301**	.197**
Not known—literate	.122**	.106**	.070*
Mother's schooling			
None	.128**	.110**	.088**
Primary	—	—	—
Secondary +	-.083*	-.067+	-.037
Other	-.149**	-.079	-.030
Not known—illiterate	-.227**	-.262**	-.290**
Not known—literate	.130**	.179**	.145**
Parental survival status			
Father only deceased		-.150**	-.167**
Mother only deceased		-.203**	-.196**
Both deceased		.221**	.207*
Both alive		—	—
Number of coresident children at menarche			
0-3		.178**	.151**
4-6		—	—
7+		-.089**	-.049*
Birth order			
Oldest		-.167**	-.166**
Second oldest		.023	.020
Third through fifth		—	—
Sixth or higher		.049+	.076**
Residence to age 12			
Major city		—	—
Small urban center		-.067	-.099*
Village		.191**	.145**
Residence from age 12 to age 18			
Major city		—	—
Small urban center		-.224**	-.235**
Village		-.351**	-.407**
Ethnic group			
Bakongo North		-.365**	-.297**
Bakongo South		-.343**	-.313**
Kwilu-Kwango		—	—
Mongo		-.043	-.004
Ubangi		.008	.062+
Luba		-.579**	-.512**
Other tribes		-.717**	-.649**
Non-Congolese		-.379**	-.419**
Religious background			
Catholic		—	—
Protestant		.043+	.008
Kimbanguist		.011	-.060
Other specified religions		.155**	.068+
Other		-.049	-.026
Enrollment status			
Enrolled			-.533**
Not enrolled			—
Cohort			
Age 15-24 in 1990		—	—
Age 25-34 in 1990		-.034	-.078**
Age 35-49 in 1990		.238**	.161**
Parameters			
Constant	-22.712	-22.464	-22.140
Log likelihood	-39,929.7	-39,480.6	-39,219.8

Note: Sample size = 12,753; mean of dependent variable = .156.

** Significant at the .01 level.
* Significant at the .05 level.
+ Significant at the .10 level.

Table 5.2 Logistic Regression Analyses of Entry into Marriage

Variables	Models (1)	(2)	(3)
Respondent's age			
Age	1.123**	1.158**	1.170**
Age squared	-.0256**	-.0261**	-.0269**
Father's schooling			
None	.316**	.242**	.155**
Primary	—	—	—
Secondary	-.025	-.024	-.013
University	-.287**	-.291**	-.248**
Other	.185**	.211**	.243**
Not known—illiterate	.546**	.537**	.452**
Not known—literate	.236**	.237**	.206**
Mother's schooling			
None	.050+	-.006	-.029
Primary	—	—	—
Secondary +	.120**	.099*	.124**
Other	.052	.120*	.169**
Not known—illiterate	-.033	-.113**	-.122**
Not known—literate	.162**	.180**	.157**
Parental survival status			
Father only deceased		-.142**	-.143**
Mother only deceased		-.286**	-.290**
Both deceased		-.191**	-.245**
Both alive		—	—
Number of coresident children at menarche			
0-3		.191**	.145**
4-6		—	—
7+		-.173**	-.151**
Birth order			
Oldest		-.179**	-.188**
Second oldest		-.086**	-.114**
Third through fifth		—	—
Sixth or higher		-.031	-.014
Residence to age 12			
Major city		—	—
Small urban center		.088*	.090*
Village		.208**	.171**
Residence from age 12 to age 18			
Major city		—	—
Small urban center		-.334**	-.370**
Village		-.214**	-.238**
Ethnic group			
Bakongo North		-.169**	-.131**
Bakongo South		-.319**	-.307**
Kwilu-Kwango		—	—
Mongo		.040	.050
Ubangi		.066+	.119**
Luba		-.169**	-.101**
Other tribes		-.370**	-.315**
Non-Congolese		-.262**	-.264**
Religious background			
Catholic		—	—
Protestant		.162**	.125**
Kimbanguist		.065	.007
Other specified religions		.378**	.299**
Other		.167**	.180**
Enrollment status			
Enrolled		—	-.478**
Not enrolled		—	—
Cohort			
Age 15-24 in 1990		—	—
Age 25-34 in 1990		-.117**	-.154**
Age 35-49 in 1990		.271**	.214**
Parameters			
Constant	-13.474	-13.715	-13.266
Log likelihood	-43,419.8	-42,966.0	-42,702.5

Note: Sample size = 14,235; mean of dependent variable = .136.

** Significant at the .01 level.
* Significant at the .05 level.
+ Significant at the .10 level.

Chapter 5

Table 5.3 Logistic Regression Analyses of Entry into Motherhood

	Models		
Variables	(1)	(2)	(3)
Respondent's age			
Age	1.884**	1.947**	1.952**
Age squared	-.0438**	-.0451**	-.0461**
Father's schooling			
None	.252**	.125**	-.042
Primary	—	—	—
Secondary	-.309**	-.331**	-.302**
University	-.627**	-.593**	-.439**
Other	-.115*	-.100$^+$	-.110$^+$
Not known—illiterate	.336**	.346**	.156**
Not known—literate	.109**	.114**	.041
Mother's schooling			
None	.115**	.042	-.011
Primary	—	—	—
Secondary +	-.228**	-.055	-.010
Other	-.463**	-.483**	-.418**
Not known—illiterate	.064	-.053	-.066
Not known—literate	-.078*	-.035	-.058
Parental survival status			
Father only deceased		-.066$^+$	-.100*
Mother only deceased		-.377**	-.309**
Both deceased		-.042	-.156*
Both alive		—	—
Number of coresident children at menarche			
0-3		.192**	.138**
4-6		—	—
7+		-.131**	-.040
Birth order			
Oldest		-.022	-.018
Second oldest		.033	-.022
Third through fifth		—	—
Sixth or higher		.060*	.091**
Residence to age 12			
Major city		—	—
Small urban center		.115*	.151**
Village		.352**	.372**
Residence from age 12 to age 18			
Major city		—	—
Small urban center		-.378**	-.502**
Village		-.477**	-.664**
Ethnic Group			
Bakongo North		-.476**	-.372**
Bakongo South		-.488**	-.446**
Kwilu-Kwango		—	—
Mongo		-.093*	-.081$^+$
Ubangi		-.130**	-.037
Luba		-.191**	-.057
Other tribes		-.426**	-.352**
Non-Congolese		-.528**	-.569**
Religious background			
Catholic		—	—
Protestant		.302**	.240**
Kimbanguist		-.009	-.110*
Other specified religions		.524**	.370**
Other		.143*	.059
Enrollment status			
Enrolled		—	-.932**
Not enrolled		—	—
Cohort			
Age 15-24 in 1990		—	—
Age 25-34 in 1990		.181**	.082**
Age 35-49 in 1990		.770**	.590**
Parameters			
Constant	-21.421	-22.107	-21.175
Log likelihood	-34,770.1	-34,126.6	-33,292.9

Note: Sample size = 14,690; mean of dependent variable = .098.

** Significant at the .01 level.
* Significant at the .05 level.
+ Significant at the .10 level.

appears to be weaker.[6] Increases in mother's schooling are associated with delays in the onset of sexual activity and childbearing (although daughters of illiterate women have the lowest likelihood of initiating sexual behavior). This broadly parallels the results for father's education. However, differences by mother's schooling with respect to the timing of the first marriage unexpectedly show that, relative to daughters of women with primary schooling, those whose mothers had a secondary-level education or higher were more likely to enter into a first union at younger ages.

With respect to father's and mother's education, these results are generally consistent with findings from previous research in the United States (Carolina Population Center 1984; Kahn and Anderson 1991; Lehrer 1985; Michael and Tuma 1985), indicating that greater parental educational attainment lowers the probability of initiating sexual activity or becoming a mother at early ages. There is partial agreement (for father's but not mother's schooling) regarding entry into union.

The effects of parental educational attainment may be seen in figure 5.2, which shows the cumulative predicted probabilities by age from model 1 of a young woman having had a first birth, according to parents' education. It is evident that the likelihood of initiating childbearing at a young age is considerably lower for a young woman whose parents had both attained secondary education as compared to a woman whose parents had no schooling. For example, the predicted probability of a birth by age 16 is only 0.10 in the former case, compared to 0.22 in the latter. By age 18 the corresponding figures are 0.24 and 0.48, and by age 20 they are 0.43 and 0.73, respectively.

Effects of Additional Family Background and Cohort Variables: Model 2

In model 2 we add a host of additional family background characteristics as well as two cohort variables. The coefficients for the variables representing parental educational attainment are, by and large, quite robust with respect to inclusion of these additional factors. The one notable exception to this statement concerns the impact of mother's educational attainment on the timing of the first birth: the tendency for greater mother's schooling to be associated with delays in the onset of childbearing that was present in model 1 has disappeared in model 2.

The death of one or the other parent by the time a young woman has reached age 15 is associated with delays in entry into sexual life, marriage, and childbearing. This is more so the case regarding the consequences of loss of a mother than of a father on the timing of first union and especially first birth. Effects of death of a father are distinctly weaker for these two events. These

---

[6] The more limited categorization of mother's schooling reflects the more-restricted access of women to education, particularly prior to independence in 1960. More than half the observations in the data files for women who reported their mother's level of education indicated no schooling at all.

Fig. 5.2 Predicted probabilities of having had a first birth, by age and parental schooling

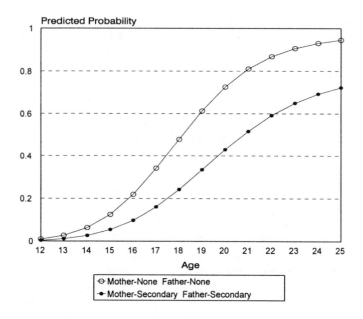

Note: Cumulative probabilities calculated from model 1.

results suggest that the death of one parent may result in young women being given additional household work burdens within their families of origin, such that their own transitions to adult life are delayed.[7]

By contrast, there are distinctly different consequences in the relatively small number of cases where both a young woman's parents are deceased by the time she reaches age 15. In this situation, it is likely that the young woman will have been fostered in to live with relatives in her extended family. Initiation of sexual activity begins significantly sooner, entry into marriage is delayed, and the timing of the onset of childbearing is not significantly different than for women with both parents alive.

Unlike the pattern that is evident from studies conducted in the United States, women in Kinshasa from smaller families do not tend to delay the key life course transitions that we are examining.[8] Quite the opposite: women from

---

[7] Dominique Meekers has pointed out to us that, often, marriage occurs only after bride-wealth payments are made to the father of the bride and that, in cases where a young woman's mother is deceased, her father may refuse to accept bride-wealth offers because he needs his daughter to do household work.

[8] Our use of the number of children with whom the respondent resided at menarche as a measure of size of family of origin reflects the context. Polygynous unions, divorce and remarriage, and child fostering all imply that a girl may grow up living with a different number of children than simply her maternal siblings. In addition, since size of family of origin changes over time and may change substantially in a high-fertility context, the ultimate size may be quite

small families show a relatively high likelihood of initiating each activity early as compared to women from medium-sized families, while these transitions are delayed among women from large families. It seems likely to us that later transitions reflect greater involvement in work at home. If this is indeed the case, this pattern of delayed transitions as family size increases is suggestive of increased parental demand for labor at home by girls and young women in larger families.

In addition to family size, birth order appears to influence the pace of these early life course transitions. There is a clear tendency for women who are the oldest children in their families to delay entry into sexual life and marriage, and delayed marriage is also apparent for daughters who are second born within their families. These effects likely are a consequence of the greater household responsibilities often assigned to elder daughters in African households. Later-born daughters, by contrast, show some evidence of initiating sexual activity and childbearing relatively early.

From model 2, women who spent all or most of their first 12 years of life in a village were significantly more likely to begin sexual life and become a spouse or a mother at earlier ages than were those who grew up in a major city (the overwhelming proportion of whom were originally from Kinshasa). The difference is particularly large regarding the onset of childbearing. Similar, albeit less-pronounced, differences are evident with respect to entry into union or motherhood by women who grew up in small urban centers. In marked contrast, those who spent all or most of their adolescence (ages 12-18) in a village or small urban center were significantly and substantially less likely to initiate each of these transitions, given their age. Taken together, these results suggest that migration is an important influence on the behaviors examined here. Migrants to Kinshasa who spent most of their preadolescent years in a village or small urban center tend generally to make these transitions sooner, other things equal, while women who migrated after adolescence (most of whom migrated soon after adolescence) typically experience delayed transitions.[9]

Ethnicity is clearly linked to variation in the timing of these life course transitions. Focusing on the six principal ethnic groups found in Kinshasa, it is apparent that initiation of sexual activity occurs relatively early for Ubangi, Kwilu-Kwango, and Mongo women, distinctly later for the two Bakongo groups, and latest for Luba women. Ubangi women are most likely to enter a union early, followed by Mongo and Kwilu-Kwango women. Entry into

different from what it was when the respondent initially was at risk for undergoing these various life course transitions. For example, a first-born woman with six siblings would not necessarily have had all those siblings at the time that she was first exposed to the risk of becoming sexually active.

[9] To determine the effect of migration after adolescence, one must sum the two corresponding coefficients (for before age 12 and for ages 12-18). When this is done, delayed initiation of sexual activity and later onset of childbearing are evident for postadolescent migrants from both villages and smaller urban centers. Entry into marriage is also delayed for such migrants from smaller urban centers but not for those from villages.

marriage is delayed somewhat for Luba women and Bakongo North women and especially so among Bakongo South women. With respect to the onset of child-bearing, Kwilu-Kwango women begin soonest, there are delays for Mongo, Ubangi, and Luba women, and the Bakongo North and Bakongo South groups show the lowest likelihood by far of initiating motherhood, other things equal.

Differences by religious background are modest with respect to initiation of sexual activity and more evident for entry into marriage and childbearing.[10] Relative to Catholics, the largest group, women from other religious groups apart from Kimbanguists show earlier transitions to first union and to child-bearing. The differences are largest among women from the "other specified religions" category, and there is also a relatively large difference for entry into motherhood by Protestant women.

Finally, the equations in model 2 also include variables identifying each woman's broad age cohort. The coefficients of these variables indicate the presence of trends in behavior not reflected in other variables included in the equation. Thus, among the oldest women in the data set, initiation of sexual activity occurred significantly sooner than was the case for the two younger groups of women. Other things equal, entry into union was earliest among the oldest of the three broad cohorts and latest among the middle group. Timing of the onset of childbearing was earliest by far for the oldest cohort and also some-what earlier for the middle group as compared to the youngest cohort. For the most part, then, there is a clear tendency toward increasing delays in these life course transitions as time goes by.

Controlling for School Enrollment: Model 3

The model 3 equations differ from those of model 2 in one respect only: a vari-able for school enrollment in the preceding year has been added. This variable has a highly significant negative coefficient for each of the events being stud-ied, with a particularly large coefficient for the onset of childbearing. These negative coefficients mean that being enrolled in school at age x is associated with a significantly lower likelihood of experiencing each event at age $x + 1$.

The impact of school enrollment in delaying these life course transitions is evident in figure 5.3, which shows the predicted probabilities of experi-encing each of the events, by age and enrollment status. There are clear differ-ences by enrollment status in the likelihood of initiating sexual activity, of entering into a first union, and of having a first birth. The magnitude of the dif-

---

[10] Women identified as Kimbanguist had been brought up in the church of that name found-ed in the Congo in 1925 by Simon Kimbangu. The "other specified religions" category includes a diverse collection of mostly Christian sects, some foreign (e.g., Jehovah's Witnesses) but most domestic. These women tended to have a high frequency of religious attendance, second only to the Kimbanguist women. The "other" category identifies a small residual group, consisting primarily of women who indicated affiliation with a religious group not specified in our question-naire, plus a small number of cases indicating no religion.

Fig. 5.3 Predicted probabilities of experiencing each event, by age and enrollment status

a. First intercourse

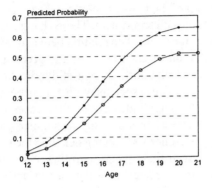

b. First union

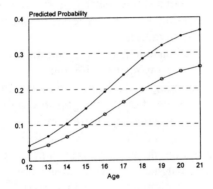

c. First birth

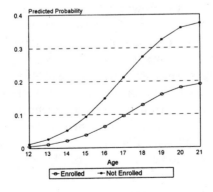

Note: Age-specific probabilities calculated from model 3.

ferences increases with age, and, holding age constant, the differences are greatest for entry into motherhood. Clearly, then, being enrolled in school is associated with significant and substantial delays in the timing of these life course transitions.

Once school enrollment status is included, there are changes in the coefficients of some but not all of the family background variables, reflecting the correlation of these variables with enrollment. These changes are most evident with regard to entry into motherhood. The relation between father's education and the likelihood of initiation of each event at any given age is weakened somewhat. For first union and first birth, there is still indication of a tendency for greater father's schooling to be associated with a reduced likelihood of experiencing the event, but the magnitudes of the differences have diminished (fairly substantially in the case of childbearing) as compared to model 2. For first intercourse, evidence of father's schooling delaying the event is distinctly weakened. In particular, given their school enrollment status, daughters of fathers with no schooling are *least* likely to initiate sexual activity, other things equal. Indeed, for all three transitions, controlling for school enrollment systematically reduces the magnitude of positive coefficients for women whose fathers were illiterate or had no schooling. This, in turn, reflects distinctly lower school enrollment of daughters of such fathers.

Hence, models 2 and 3 taken together suggest that an important part of the impact of father's education on delaying these life course transitions stems from the influence of father's schooling on the likelihood of daughter's enrollment in school. At the same time, even after allowing for this indirect effect of father's education via daughter's schooling, there remains evidence of direct negative effects for first marriage and first birth. Hence, there is a strong indication here of the presence of multiple paths by which a father's education level influences the timing of his daughter's life course transitions.

Controlling for school enrollment has little impact on the generally weak estimated effects of mother's education. The impact of parental survival status on the timing of these life course transitions is also largely unaffected by controlling for enrollment status. However, the consequences of having both parents deceased for the timing of the first birth do vary according to whether school enrollment is taken into account. In particular, controlling for enrollment status, a tendency for young women who have lost both parents to begin childbearing later emerges. Since these women are likely to have lower enrollment rates than are those with both parents alive,[11] the effect of enrollment in delaying childbearing means that model 2 masks a tendency for such women to enter motherhood later, given their enrollment status. It thus appears that support for a young woman's schooling by her extended family is an important influence on her propensity to begin her own family.

---

[11] Evidence presented in chapter 9 below suggests that children who have been fostered in tend to have lower school enrollment rates than do biological children of the household head, other things equal.

The effects of size of family of origin tend to diminish modestly once school enrollment is taken into consideration. This suggests that family size is positively related to school enrollment, as Chernichovsky (1985) found for Botswana. This issue will be examined directly in chapter 9. The timing of transitions by type of place in which the respondent spent her first 12 years is not systematically influenced by including enrollment, but differentials by residence in adolescence do tend to widen somewhat (reflecting lower enrollment rates in villages and smaller urban centers), particularly with respect to the onset of childbearing.

Reflecting the pattern of differences by ethnic group in educational attainment shown in chapter 4, there are systematic changes that occur in the coefficients by ethnic group once enrollment is included. The low schooling and hence low school enrollment of the Kwilu-Kwango reference group means that incorporating enrollment tends to reduce the absolute value of negative coefficients and increase the few positive coefficients. These effects are generally modest for first intercourse and first union, but they are more important for first birth, where significant coefficients in model 2 for Ubangi and Luba women have now become insignificant. That is, the apparent delayed entry into motherhood for these women as compared to Kwilu-Kwango women in model 2 in fact reflects primarily a school enrollment effect rather than an effect of ethnicity per se. Differentials by religious group tend for the most part to narrow a bit in going from model 2 to model 3.

Finally, there are changes in the coefficients of the cohort variables, reflecting the sharp secular increases in women's schooling. The oldest group remains as the cohort with the earliest transitions, other things equal, but controlling for their lower enrollment reduces the estimated cohort effects. For the middle group, a significant negative coefficient emerges for the onset of sexual activity, there is a slight increase in the absolute value of the negative coefficient for entry into marriage, and the positive coefficient for initiation of childbearing is reduced by more than half.

Discussion and Implications

The results reported here document the importance of family background in influencing the timing of early family formation behaviors in Kinshasa. Parental education, parental survival status, size of family of origin, birth order, type of place of residence in childhood, ethnicity, and religious background all appear to be features of the family environment that are associated with significant differentials in rates of transitions to adulthood.

By and large, differentials according to father's level of schooling were the most striking. Greater paternal education for the most part is significantly associated with delays in the timing of first intercourse, first marriage, and first birth. Father's education has been shown to affect the early family formation behavior of daughters both directly and indirectly through its effect on their schooling. That is, when school enrollment status is controlled for, the direct effects of father's education on transitions to family formation become less powerful, reflecting the influence of greater father's education in contributing to increased schooling of daughters.

Greater mother's schooling also tended to be associated with delays in the timing of these transitions, but with generally weaker effects as compared to those of father's education. The greater impact on the timing of marriage (and hence, ultimately, on the timing of the first birth) of father's schooling as compared to mother's education is presumably a reflection of greater paternal authority on nuptiality matters.[12] This greater paternal authority is, at least in part, a consequence of bride-wealth payments, typically made to the father. Maternal influences appear to be relatively unrelated to timing of daughters' entry into a conjugal union. In the context of traditional African family systems, it is indeed a matter of fact that mothers have relatively little say about when a daughter is to marry.

Also of note is the positive association between family size and the age at which these key life course transitions are initiated. In marked contrast to the situation in the United States, where girls and young women from small families are most likely to delay these activities, Kinshasa women from small families are least likely to do so, while those from large families have the highest likelihood of later transitions. These results, as well as several others relating to parental survival status and birth order, appear to reflect the effects of these different factors on the demands for the labor of young women in the household.

Further, we have documented that the timing of first intercourse, entry into marriage, and first birth tends to differ between migrants and those born in Kinshasa. The nature of these differences depends on the timing of migration in relation to adolescence: migrants who spent most of their preadolescent years in a village or small urban center tend to initiate these transitions sooner, while later migrants experience delayed transitions.

An additional important background characteristic is ethnic group. Broadly speaking, the Mongo, Ubangi, and Kwilu-Kwango women tend to experience each of the three events earliest. The two Bakongo groups, in contrast, have distinctly later onset of each event. Luba women are unique: they are most likely by far of the six major ethnic groups to delay entry into sexual life while being similar to the Bakongo women regarding timing of the first union and comparable to the Mongo, Ubangi, and Kwilu-Kwango women as regards the onset of childbearing.

Besides family background, school enrollment status has been shown to raise very significantly the likelihood of delayed transitions to adult life roles. This is quite consistent with other studies in sub-Saharan Africa indicating that

---

[12] We have shown elsewhere (Tambashe and Shapiro 1996) that, among women in Kinshasa, the timing of entry into marriage is a very highly significant predictor of the timing of the first birth. See also Westoff (1992).

literacy or education is very strongly linked to the timing of entry into sexual, marital, and reproductive life (Meekers 1994; Westoff 1992). As expected, school enrollment turned out to be an important path through which family background influences life course transitions.

In settings like Kinshasa, if use of modern contraception remains low, future fertility will be strongly influenced by changes in the starting patterns of family formation. The results reported in this chapter show that increases in parental educational attainment are likely to be instrumental in bringing about changes toward delayed age at entry into sexual, marital, and reproductive life. As noted in chapter 2, since independence in 1960 the Congo has been characterized by increasing levels of schooling for women and men, with each successive cohort having higher levels of educational attainment than preceding cohorts. This has been true, not only in Kinshasa, but elsewhere in the country as well (see, e.g., Shapiro and Tambashe 1997a, table 6; Institut National de la Statistique 1991a). These increases in schooling levels will contribute to delayed transitions to adulthood, and, in conjunction with the growing percentages of women reaching secondary school, they are likely to result in some further reductions in fertility.

In conclusion, it should be added that this chapter provides evidence on issues that have been studied extensively in the United States but much less so in sub-Saharan Africa, where families are distinctly different from those in the United States in several respects. Most notable in this regard is the difference in family structure: in sub-Saharan Africa the extended family and the clan are extremely important, while in the United States the nuclear family is the locus of decision making about family matters. Children in sub-Saharan Africa belong to the clan—they are not simply members of the nuclear family. In addition, reflecting sharply higher levels of fertility, African nuclear families are substantially larger than are those in the United States.

In the light of the differences in family structure, then, it is quite possible that nuclear family background influences on life course transitions would be very weak in sub-Saharan Africa, reflecting a major role for the extended family in influencing these decisions. However, the data analyzed here for the most part do not suggest the presence of such a dilution effect: we have provided evidence of important influences of nuclear family background on life course transitions among young women in Kinshasa, comparable in several respects to findings for such transitions in the United States. At the same time, the influence of family size in Kinshasa is opposite to that found in studies in the United States. This difference appears to reflect greater involvement in household work for girls and young women in Kinshasa and particularly so for those from larger families.

Appendix

Table 5A.1 Mean Values of Variables in the Analyses of First Intercourse, First Union, and First Birth

Variables	First Intercourse	First Union	First Birth
Respondent's age	14.75	16.26	16.57
Father's schooling			
None	.108	.113	.118
Primary	.181	.193	.176
Secondary	.171	.168	.160
University	.044	.040	.037
Other	.044	.042	.046
Not known—illiterate	.057	.054	.057
Not known—literate	.395	.390	.406
Mother's schooling			
None	.407	.439	.425
Primary	.170	.170	.165
Secondary +	.115	.098	.098
Other	.037	.039	.043
Not known—illiterate	.093	.085	.088
Not known—literate	.178	.169	.181
Parental survival status			
Father only deceased	.075	.071	.075
Mother only deceased	.045	.048	.047
Both deceased	.012	.014	.015
Both alive	.868	.867	.863
Number of coresident children at menarche			
0-3	.270	.259	.263
4-6	.467	.463	.460
7+	.263	.278	.277
Birth order			
Oldest	.229	.234	.234
Second oldest	.187	.197	.190
Third through fifth	.406	.395	.402
Sixth or higher	.178	.174	.174
Residence to age 12			
Major city	.758	.753	.748
Small urban center	.104	.104	.104
Village	.138	.143	.148
Residence from age 12 to age 18			
Major city	.802	.793	.786
Small urban center	.092	.096	.094
Village	.106	.111	.120
Ethnic group			
Bakongo North	.075	.078	.081
Bakongo South	.223	.237	.239
Kwilu-Kwango	.352	.347	.348
Mongo	.074	.073	.072
Ubangi	.079	.078	.075
Luba	.124	.113	.107
Other tribes	.025	.024	.026
Non-Congolese	.048	.050	.052
Religious background			
Catholic	.689	.691	.681
Protestant	.192	.195	.198
Kimbanguist	.038	.039	.042
Other specified religions	.055	.047	.049
Other	.026	.028	.030
Enrollment status			
Enrolled	.807	.740	.711
Not enrolled	.193	.260	.289
Cohort			
Age 15-24 in 1990	.489	.433	.460
Age 25-34 in 1990	.376	.438	.413
Age 35-49 in 1990	.135	.129	.127

Chapter 6. Proximate Determinants of Fertility

In chapter 4, we examined the relation between fertility and various socio-economic and cultural factors. The chapter focused on education and ethnicity and how they are related to fertility, but we also considered other factors such as employment status and migration status. All these variables may be thought of as background factors that influence fertility. These influences, in turn, are seen as operating through the demand for children, the supply of children, and the costs of contraception (Easterlin and Crimmins 1985).

The effects of these background factors on fertility are indirect, however. These variables typically operate through other factors that are more immediately linked to fertility behavior, in the sense that changing one of these other factors will result directly in a change in fertility, ceteris paribus. These other factors constitute the proximate determinants of fertility, and they are the focus of this chapter.

The following section gives an overview and discussion of the proximate determinants of fertility, the framework in which they are analyzed, and their relation to background characteristics. This is followed by formal analyses of the proximate determinants for women in Kinshasa as of 1990, analyses based on procedures first suggested by Bongaarts (1978) and used widely since (see, e.g., Bongaarts and Potter 1983; Bongaarts et al. 1984; Tambashe 1984; Jolly and Gribble 1993; Zulu 1998). Included with these analyses are comparisons with other populations in sub-Saharan Africa. The subsequent section of the chapter provides additional analyses of key proximate determinants: age at marriage; contraception; abortion; breastfeeding; and postpartum abstinence. Each analysis begins with a brief descriptive overview of the proximate determinant in question, with an emphasis on differences by educational attainment. Multivariate analyses are then presented and discussed; these analyses help identify the pathways or mechanisms by which education and other background characteristics influence fertility. The concluding substantive section of the chapter illustrates the compensating mechanisms of the proximate determinants as they relate to observed differences in fertility by ethnic group.

The Proximate Determinants Framework

In a classic article, Davis and Blake (1956) distinguished two sets of factors affecting fertility: background variables and intermediate variables. The background variables consisted of economic, social, cultural, psychological, and health factors. They were seen as influencing fertility, not directly, but rather indirectly, through their influence on the intermediate variables. These latter factors (now commonly known as *proximate determinants of fertility*) were seen as the direct influences on fertility behavior. As Bongaarts (1978,105-106) has noted: "The primary characteristic of an intermediate fertility variable is its direct influence on fertility. If an intermediate fertility variable, such as the prevalence of contraception, changes, then fertility necessarily changes also (assuming the other intermediate fertility variables remain constant), while this is not necessarily the case for an indirect determinant such as income or education. Consequently, fertility differences among populations and trends in fertility over time can always be traced to variations in one or more of the intermediate fertility variables."

Davis and Blake (1956) identified 11 intermediate fertility variables, which Bongaarts (1978) collapsed into eight factors grouped in three broad categories:

A.   Exposure factors
     1. Proportion married
B.   Deliberate marital fertility control factors
     2. Contraception
     3. Induced abortion
C.   Natural marital fertility factors
     4. Lactational infecundability
     5. Frequency of intercourse
     6. Sterility
     7. Spontaneous intrauterine mortality
     8. Duration of the fertile period.

In subsequent work, Bongaarts and Potter (1983) identified seven fundamental proximate determinants of fertility: marriage structure; use and effectiveness of contraception; induced abortion; postpartum infecundability; natural fecundability; spontaneous intrauterine mortality; and onset of sterility. Marriage, contraception, induced abortion, and postpartum infecundability have been found to have the greatest effects on fertility differentials and trends (Bongaarts and Potter 1983). However, as we saw for the Congo and Kinshasa in chapters 3 and 4, in sub-Saharan Africa sterility often plays an important role in helping account for fertility differentials (see Romaniuk 1967; Frank 1983). Natural fecundability and spontaneous intrauterine mortality are generally less important owing to limited variation across populations.

From among these proximate determinants, then, analyses for sub-Saharan Africa have tended to focus on four aspects: marriage (or union) patterns; contraception; postpartum infecundability; and sterility. The difficulty of obtaining reliable information on the prevalence of induced abortion has prevented this factor from being systematically analyzed in studies of African populations, despite evidence that abortion is increasingly common among urban women in particular (Coeytaux 1988; Shapiro and Tambashe 1994a), with associated health problems (Zulu 1998).

The conceptual framework considers these proximate determinants as factors that reduce fertility below its biological maximum. Traditionally in sub-Saharan Africa, for example, marriage has been early and near universal, contraception has been very limited, durations of breast-feeding and postpartum abstinence have been long (contributing to extended periods of postpartum infecundability), and sterility has been evident in certain subpopulations. Thus, while fertility is high, it is nonetheless well below its biological maximum, and prolonged periods of postpartum infecundability have typically been found to be the principal factor inhibiting higher levels of fertility (Bongaarts et al. 1984; Jolly and Gribble 1993).

By contrast, in Western industrial societies where fertility has moved to much lower levels, marriage tends to come later and is distinctly less than universal, the practice of contraception has been extensive, and induced abortion is often considerably more common. These proximate determinants thus play a major role in keeping fertility low, while short breast-feeding durations and very limited postpartum abstinence mean that these latter two factors do not play an important fertility-inhibiting role.

More generally, then, for each proximate determinant that is analyzed, an index is constructed that in principle can range from 0 to 1. The value of the index reflects the fertility-inhibiting magnitude of the proximate determinant in question: a value of 1 means that the factor does not inhibit fertility, while a value of 0 corresponds to complete limitation. The relation between observed fertility, the proximate determinants, and the theoretical maximum level of fertility is described by the following model:[1]

$TFR = C_m \times C_c \times C_i \times C_s \times TF$, where
TFR = the observed total fertility rate,
C_m = index of marriage or union patterns,
C_c = index of contraceptive use,
C_i = index of postpartum infecundability,

---

[1] Missing from the model is C_a, the index of induced abortion. While the information that we have on abortion is quite useful for examining the incidence of abortion, it is not sufficient to generate an index of abortion. Hence, as with other analyses of the proximate determinants in sub-Saharan Africa, abortion has not been considered here. However, later in this chapter we examine differences in the incidence of abortion according to key socioeconomic and cultural characteristics.

C_s = index of permanent sterility, and

TF = total fecundity rate, the theoretical maximum level of fertility.

The index of marriage or union patterns, C_m, seeks to measure the effect on fertility of the proportion of women in a sexual union. Two issues emerge in applying this formulation to data from Kinshasa and elsewhere in sub-Saharan Africa. First, complications may arise as a consequence of difficulties in defining marriage. As van de Walle (1993) has noted, entry into marriage is a process and not a single event in much of sub-Saharan Africa. In particular, women who do not consider themselves to be married may nonetheless be living in a fairly stable sexual union and hence regularly subject to the risk of becoming pregnant. It is thus most useful to consider C_m as covering, not simply women who describe themselves as married, but also those who are living in a stable sexual union. Here, then, we will treat "marriage" as equivalent to living in a stable union, unless noted otherwise.

The second issue is that a nontrivial amount of childbearing in sub-Saharan Africa occurs to women who describe themselves as single or never married and who are not living in a stable union. C_m is calculated as the ratio of the TFR to the number of children women would have if they entered a union at age 15, remained in a union until the end of their childbearing years, and during that span bore children at the prevailing (current) age-specific rates of women in union. This latter figure is the total marital fertility rate, or TMFR, so we have C_m = TFR/TMFR. When all women of reproductive age are married, the index has a value of 1, and it would be equal to 0 if no women of reproductive age were married.

As described, C_m is a good indicator of the fertility-inhibiting effects of marriage or union patterns when all births take place within unions. However, as just noted, in many parts of Africa childbearing outside unions is not at all uncommon. Jolly and Gribble (1993) have added a modification to the Bongaarts framework to take account of childbearing outside stable unions. They introduced a variable, M_o, to capture the effect on total fertility of births outside unions. M_o is a measure of births outside marriage, and it is calculated as the ratio of the actual total fertility rate to the hypothetical total fertility rate that would exist if there were no births outside unions.[2] Thus, a value of M_o of 1.2, for example, would indicate that the total fertility rate was 20 percent higher than it would have been if the fertility occurring outside unions had not in fact taken place.

Further, Jolly and Gribble also define C'_m as the ratio of the hypothetical total fertility rate that would exist if there were no births outside unions (TUFR) to the total marital fertility rate, TMFR. C'_m is called the *adjusted index of marriage*, and it shows the effect of the reported age pattern of unions, in the

---

[2] That is, this hypothetical fertility rate—what Jolly and Gribble call the TUFR, or total union fertility rate—is the sum of age-specific union fertility rates (ASUFRs), where ASUFR = marital births to women age i/mid-year population of women age i.

absence of births outside unions. Since the product of C'_m and M_o is C_m, then, as noted by Jolly and Gribble (1993, 73), "C_m is the combined result of the fertility-inhibiting effect of union pattern and the fertility-promoting effect of sexual relations outside union."

The index of contraceptive use, C_c, reflects both contraceptive prevalence among women in union and the use effectiveness of the different contraceptive methods used. Following Jolly and Gribble (1993), we have distinguished traditional from modern methods so as to assign a lower use-effectiveness value to traditional methods. The index of postpartum infecundability, C_i, is inversely related to the duration of postpartum infecundability, estimated as the mean number of months of postpartum amenorrhea or abstinence, whichever is longer. Finally, the index of permanent sterility is based on the presence of older, ever-married women who have never had any children. In Kinshasa, reported childlessness among women aged 40-49 was so low that the index effectively was equal to 1.0,[3] implying no fertility-inhibiting effect of permanent sterility.[4]

The Proximate Determinants of Fertility in Kinshasa: A Comparative Overview

Calculated values for Kinshasa of the two marriage indices, C_m and C'_m, and the indicator of fertility outside marriage, M_o, are shown for all women in union in the first row of table 6.1. These figures are based on births in the 3 years prior to the survey to women who were in union at the time of the survey.[5] The sensitivity of these measures to the definition of *marriage* or *union* is highlighted by the data in the second row of the table, which show the values for Kinshasa that result if one looks at self-described marital status rather than whether a woman was in a stable union.[6] For purposes of comparison with women elsewhere in sub-Saharan Africa, the remaining rows of the table show unweighted averages of these three indices, based on Demographic and Health

---

[3] As Larsen (1989) has noted, it is possible that childlessness is somewhat underreported because some women may not want to reveal that they have borne no children. For Kinshasa in 1990, we do not believe that such underreporting is very important.

[4] For a concise discussion of the derivation of the indices, including the formulas for the different indices, see Jolly and Gribble (1993, 103-106). See also Bongaarts and Potter (1983).

[5] Our use of a 3-year period to look at fertility differs slightly from the 4-year period used by Jolly and Gribble. However, whether one uses a 3-, 4-, or 5-year period with the Kinshasa data has little impact on the estimates. As Jolly and Gribble have noted (1993, 104), use of current marital status in conjunction with past fertility entails some compensating errors: some past fertility that took place outside marriage to women who were married at the time of the survey will incorrectly be counted as marital childbearing, while some births that took place to women previously married but no longer in union at the time of the survey will be treated as nonmarital childbearing.

[6] Self-described marital status reflects responses to a single question: what is your current marital status? All women in union include, not only those who described themselves as married in response to the single marital status question, but also those who indicated in response to subsequent questioning that they currently lived or cohabited with a man and had been doing so for at least 6 months.

Table 6.1 Indices of Marriage and Births outside Marriage and Total Fertility Rates, Kinshasa 1990, and Averages Calculated from Data Reported by Jolly and Gribble for 11 Countries in Sub-Saharan Africa

Data for	C_m	C'_m	M_o	TFR
Kinshasa—all women in union	.88	.82	1.07	5.7
Kinshasa—women self-described as married	.78	.64	1.21	
Average—all	.86	.78	1.10	6.4
Average—urban	.79	.68	1.18	5.1
Average—education = 8+	.74	.63	1.19	4.6

Sources: Kinshasa: calculated from survey data; Average—all: Jolly and Gribble (1993, table 3-3, p. 78); Average—urban: Jolly and Gribble (1993, table 3-5, pp. 90-91); Average—education = 8+: Jolly and Gribble (1993, table 3-6, pp. 92-94).

Note: Averages are unweighted averages for 11 of the 12 countries for which Jolly and Gribble (1993) provide data. Botswana, which had an inordinately high value of M_o (1.89) and a correspondingly low value of C'_m (0.46), has been excluded from the averages.

Surveys (DHS) data reported by Jolly and Gribble (1993) for 11 of 12 different populations, overall, for urban women, and for women with eight or more years of schooling.[7] The table also shows corresponding total fertility rates.

The indices for all women in union in Kinshasa are fairly close to the overall average figures from the DHS data. For both the conventional index of marriage, C_m, and the adjusted index of marriage, C'_m, the index values are slightly higher in Kinshasa, while fertility outside unions is a bit lower. If self-described marital status is used as the basis of calculation of the indices, the measure of fertility outside marriage/union rises considerably, and the indices of marriage patterns imply a distinctly more substantial fertility-limiting effect of marriage.[8]

Comparing Kinshasa to overall DHS data involves rural as well as urban women from the other countries, and, as shown in the last column of the table, the national populations clearly tend to have somewhat higher fertility rates.

[7] Jolly and Gribble report data for Botswana, Burundi, Ghana, Kenya, Liberia, Mali, Ondo State in Nigeria, Senegal, Northern Sudan, Togo, Uganda, and Zimbabwe. Botswana is an outlier with respect to values of M_o and C'_m, and, hence, has been excluded from the averages reported in the table. Also, the designation of 8 or more years of education is provided for each country except Northern Sudan, for which the group used is simply women with secondary or higher education.

[8] Overall, 73 percent of women aged 15-49 were in a stable union, defined operationally as being in a sexual union of at least 6 months' duration; about three-quarters of them, or 55 percent of the total number of women, described themselves as married in response to the initial question on marital status. The differences between these two measures were greatest for the two youngest groups of women, those aged 15-19 and 20-24. The fact that younger women are most likely to be in unions but not (yet) consider themselves as married is consistent with van de Walle's (1993) argument that, in much of sub-Saharan Africa, marriage is a process rather than a single event. The fertility of those who were in unions but did not describe themselves as married was distinctly lower than the fertility of self-described married women.

The fourth row of data in the table thus refers only to urban women in the various DHS countries. Relative to the corresponding national populations, their average fertility is lower by well over one child, and both indices of marriage are lower, while the indicator of fertility occurring outside unions is distinctly higher. Comparing the data from Kinshasa for all women in union to the data for the urban areas of the DHS countries shows the fertility-inhibiting effects of union patterns in Kinshasa (as reflected by both C_m and especially C'_m) to be distinctly weaker and births outside unions to be less common in Kinshasa. Interestingly, the differences are quite small if the comparison is made instead with women in Kinshasa who described themselves as married.

The last row of the table shows the indices for the highest education group, those with 8 or more years of schooling. The average fertility of these women is distinctly below that for Kinshasa, where such women represent 58 percent of all women in union aged 15-49. As expected, the indices of marriage patterns are both lower for this group than for all urban women, and they are also lower than the figures for all women in union in Kinshasa (but somewhat similar to the figures for women self-described as married).

Table 6.2 shows data for Kinshasa and for the countries covered by Jolly and Gribble for the remaining proximate determinants analyzed here.[9] Contraception in Kinshasa has a greater fertility-inhibiting effect than does contraception in the DHS countries overall. The effect is comparable to that for all urban women and not as strong as that for the best-educated women. It reflects a high prevalence of traditional contraception.[10] Comparison with Kenya, a country experiencing rapid fertility transition on a national basis, is instructive. Jolly and Gribble (1993) report a value of C_c for Kenya from the 1989 DHS of 0.80, slightly lower than that for Kinshasa. At that time, the TFR for Kenya was estimated at 6.6. In 1993, another DHS survey yielded a value of C_c that had fallen to 0.71 (Zulu 1998), while the TFR had declined to 5.5.

The average duration of breast-feeding in Kinshasa of 16-17 months (Shapiro and Tambashe 1997a) is primarily responsible for postpartum infecundability being the proximate determinant in the city with the lowest (i.e., most fertility-inhibiting) value. At the same time, the shorter duration of breast-feeding in Kinshasa as compared to the national populations, where the simple average is 20 months (Jolly and Gribble 1993, table 3-2, p. 74), results in a weaker fertility-inhibiting effect. In comparison with the urban and better-educated women, Kinshasa women have essentially the same level of the index of postpartum infecundability. Finally, as mentioned above, permanent sterility does not appear to have any impact at all.

---

[9] Data for Botswana are included in table 6.2, because the country is not an outlier on these measures. The averages are largely unaffected by whether or not Botswana is included.

[10] As noted above, our calculations are comparable to those of Jolly and Gribble, in that a relatively low use-effectiveness value is given to traditional methods. Contraception and abortion in Kinshasa will be explored more fully later in this chapter and in the following chapter.

Table 6.2 Indices of Contraception, Postpartum Infecundability, and Sterility, Kinshasa 1990, and Averages Calculated from Data Reported by Jolly and Gribble for 12 Countries in Sub-Saharan Africa

Data for	C_c	C_i	C_s
Kinshasa	.82	.65	1.00
Average—all	.91	.57	1.00
Average—urban	.83	.64	0.99
Average—education = 8+	.75	.66	1.02

Sources: Kinshasa: calculated from survey data; Average—all: Jolly and Gribble (1993, table 3-3, p. 78); Average—urban: Jolly and Gribble (1993, table 3-5, pp. 90-91); Average—education = 8+: Jolly and Gribble (1993, table 3-6, pp. 92-94).

Note: Averages are unweighted averages for the 12 countries for which Jolly and Gribble (1993) provide data.

The effects of the different proximate determinants in inhibiting fertility and their relation to various fertility measures are shown in figure 6.1. Overall, the total fecundity rate is estimated at just over 12.1. This is a bit below the lower bound of 13 suggested by Bongaarts and Potter (1983) but comparable to the averages calculated from Jolly and Gribble (1993, 90-94) of 12.5 for urban women and 12.6 for women with 8 or more years of schooling. Similar to results found elsewhere in sub-Saharan Africa (Jolly and Gribble 1993), the single most important proximate determinant reducing fertility below its potential maximum level is postpartum infecundability resulting from extended durations of breast-feeding. In the absence of this factor, the model suggests that there would be more than four additional births per woman.

Somewhat in contrast to the situation in most of the rest of Africa, contraception plays the second most important role in Kinshasa, reducing fertility by about 1.4 births. As noted above, this is a consequence of a fairly high prevalence of traditional methods of contraception. Union patterns, which were the second-ranked proximate determinant overall in Jolly and Gribble's survey, reduce fertility by less than 0.8 births and, hence, rank as the third factor in Kinshasa.

Proximate Determinants: A More Detailed Examination

In this section we look at five proximate determinants: age at marriage; contraception; abortion; breast-feeding; and postpartum abstinence. In each case, there is a brief initial descriptive overview, with emphasis on differences according to educational attainment. We then present results of multivariate analyses. The multivariate analyses begin with a short-form equation, which controls for age as a key basic demographic variable and for educational attainment. A long-form equation then incorporates consideration of other

Fig. 6.1 Fertility-inhibiting effects of the proximate determinants and various measures of fertility

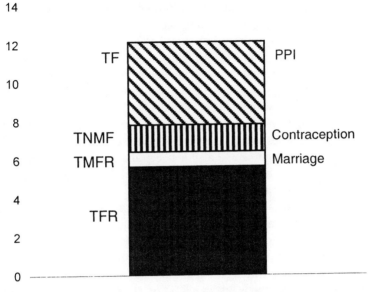

Note: PPI = postpartum infecundability; TF = total fecundity rate; TNMF = total natural marital fertility rate; TMFR = total marital fertility rate; and TFR = total fertility rate.

socioeconomic and cultural factors seen as likely influences on the behavior in question, including employment status, ethnicity, migration status, economic status, religion, and marital status.[11]

Age at First Marriage

The timing of entry into a first union that lasted for at least 6 months is the focus of interest here.[12] A descriptive look at age at first marriage was provided earlier in figure 5.1. From that figure, it is clear that nearly half the women had entered a first marriage prior to age 18. Median age at first union (measured for women age 25 and over at the time of the survey) varies systematically with educational attainment, rising from 16.9 for those with no schooling or only primary schooling to 17.6 for those with 1 or 2 years of secondary schooling, 18.8 for those with 3-4 years of secondary schooling, and 20.9 and 23.6 for those with upper-level secondary and university education, respectively.

[11] In the case of age at first marriage, which is analyzed using an event-history approach, school enrollment status rather than completed education is the education variable used. In addition, reflecting the relatively early onset of this event, a slightly different and more limited set of explanatory variables is used.

[12] *First union* and *first marriage* will be used interchangeably here to refer to this phenomenon.

Table 6.3 provides multivariate analyses of age at first marriage, using the same event-history approach with a person-year data file that was used in chapter 5. These analyses are similar to those in chapter 5, except that they do not take into consideration family background characteristics pertaining to parental schooling and survival status, family size, and birth order.[13] The dependent variable (entry into a first union) is dichotomous, equal to 1 if the individual married at the age of a particular person-year observation, and 0 otherwise. The independent variables include both time-varying and non-time-varying variables. Age as of the person-year observation and a dichotomous variable representing whether the respondent had been enrolled in school in the year prior to the person-year observation constitute the time-varying variables. Dichotomous variables representing the different ethnic groups, type of place of residence prior to age 12 and also between the ages of 12 and 18, and the respondent's religious background constitute the variables that are fixed for any individual respondent and do not vary over time.

Age at first marriage is analyzed initially simply as a function of women's age and enrollment status. The results of this analysis are shown in the first equation reported in table 6.3. Age is a very powerful variable in the equation, with a significant quadratic specification. The likelihood that a young woman will enter a union rises with age, but at a decreasing rate. The turning point of the quadratic specification is just in excess of 21 years. Given age, enrollment status is also very highly significant: women enrolled in school in the year prior to the time of the observation have a substantially lower probability of entering a first union as compared to those not enrolled in school.

The second equation in table 6.3 adds variables for ethnic group, type of place of residence in childhood and adolescence, and religion. Inclusion of these variables has a negligible impact on the estimated effects of age and school enrollment. There are significant differences with respect to ethnicity that parallel those already seen in chapter 5. Among the six principal ethnic groups in Kinshasa, all else—including school enrollment—equal, the Ubangi women are most likely to enter a union early, followed by Kwilu-Kwango and Mongo women, and then Luba women. Bakongo women, and especially those from the area south of the Congo River, show the greatest propensity to delay entry into marriage.

Women whose early childhood was spent in a small urban center or village were significantly more likely to enter a union early as compared to those who grew up in Kinshasa, all else equal. At the same time, those who spent their adolescence (ages 12-18) in a small urban center or village had significantly later entry into marriage. As in chapter 5, these results highlight the importance of migration and the timing of migration. Women who spent

---

[13] Exclusion of these family background characteristics here facilitates comparison with results for other proximate determinants reported below. The results for other variables (age, school enrollment, ethnicity, and religion) are largely unaffected by the exclusion of these variables.

Table 6.3 Logistic Regression Analyses of Entry into Marriage (weighted logistic regressions)

Variables	Models (1)	(2)
Respondent's age		
Age	1.127**	1.139**
Age squared	-.0265**	-.0266**
Enrollment status		
Enrolled	-.545**	-.530**
Not enrolled	—	—
Ethnic group		
Bakongo North		-.126**
Bakongo South		-.289**
Kwilu-Kwango		—
Mongo		-.039
Ubangi		.104**
Luba		-.074*
Other tribes		-.266**
Non-Congolese		-.182**
Residence to age 12		
Major city		—
Small urban center		.131**
Village		.213**
Residence from age 12 to 18		
Major city		—
Small urban center		-.387**
Village		-.190**
Religious background		
Catholic		—
Protestant		.093**
Kimbanguist		.070
Other specified religions		.285**
Other		.148**
Parameters		
Constant	-12.701	-12.811
Log likelihood	-43,235.8	-43,051.1

Note: Sample size = 14,235; mean of dependent variable = .136.

** Significant at the .01 level.
* Significant at the .05 level.
+ Significant at the .10 level.

their childhood in smaller places but then migrated to Kinshasa by age 12 tend to have the earliest entry into unions, while postadolescent migrants from small urban centers were most likely to experience delayed entry.

The likelihood of entry into marriage varies significantly by religious background, with differences comparable to those reported in chapter 5. All religious denominations show a greater likelihood of entering a first marriage more precociously than Catholics, with the differences being significant for all but the Kimbanguist women and greatest for those from the more traditional "other specified religions" group.

Contraceptive Use

Contraceptive prevalence is fairly high in Kinshasa, exceeding 53 percent of women in union who were not pregnant at the time of the survey. For the most part, however, reported contraceptive use pertains to traditional methods (primarily rhythm, secondarily withdrawal); prevalence of modern contraceptives among these women is limited to only 8 percent, with condoms being the principal modern method used, followed by oral contraceptives.[14] These results are broadly similar to those found in previous studies done in Kinshasa (Bakutuvwidi et al. 1985, 1991; Tambashe 1984). However, the level of contraceptive use that we find is slightly higher than that reported in these earlier studies, suggesting that there is increasing demand for contraception over time.

Differences in contraceptive practice by schooling show a clear tendency for increased contraceptive use and increased use of modern contraception as educational attainment rises. However, these increases, particularly with respect to modern contraception, are fairly modest. Just over a third of women with no schooling report using any method of contraception, and the figure rises to 60 percent for women with 3-4 years of secondary schooling and to 73 percent among those with university education. The percentage of women using modern contraception rose from 3 for those with no schooling to 11 for those with upper-level secondary schooling and 16 among university women.

Multivariate analyses of contraceptive use by nonpregnant women in union are shown in table 6.4. The first two equations refer to the use of any method, while the latter two are confined to the use of modern contraception. In each pair of equations, the first equation controls only for age and educational attainment, while the second equation includes other explanatory variables, consisting of employment status, ethnic group, religion, migration status, enrollment status at the time of the survey, economic status,[15] and marital status/stability.

Focusing first on schooling, it is apparent from table 6.4 that there is a clear tendency for increased educational attainment to be associated with a significantly greater likelihood of using any contraceptive method, all else equal. Controlling for ethnicity, religion, migrant status, and other factors reduces the

[14] The survey questionnaire provided DHS-type data on knowledge and practice of contraception. The pill, injection, IUD, female as well as male sterilization, condoms, and vaginals were the modern methods of contraception covered by the survey, while rhythm, withdrawal, and periodic abstinence were the traditional methods.

[15] Economic status is measured by a crude index counting the number of working household durable goods (e.g., hot plate, stove, refrigerator, fan, television, radio, etc.) in the respondent's household. The mean value of the index for women in the survey was 2.4.

Table 6.4 Analysis of Current Contraceptive Use (weighted logistic regressions)

Variable	Any Method $\hat{\beta}$	Any Method $\hat{\beta}$	Modern Method $\hat{\beta}$	Modern Method $\hat{\beta}$
Age at survey				
Age	.087**	.130**	.168**	.169**
Age squared	-.00181**	-.00254**	-.00198**	-.00201**
Schooling level				
None	-.218**	-.286**	-.775**	-.685**
Primary	—	—	—	—
Secondary 1-2	.451**	.411**	.611**	.491**
Secondary 3-4	.642**	.577**	.629**	.457**
Secondary 5-6	.729**	.540**	.743**	.525**
University	1.208**	.829**	1.179**	.943**
Other schooling	.049	-.116	.699*	.732*
Employment status				
Not employed	—	—	—	—
Self-employed	—	.196**	—	.015
Employee	—	.466**	—	.038
Religion				
Catholic	—	—	—	—
Protestant	—	.270**	—	.244**
Kimbanguist	—	.454**	—	.104
Other religion	—	.290**	—	.222**
No religion	—	-.621**	—	-.499[+]
Migration status				
Nonmigrant	—	—	—	—
Migrant	—	.007	—	-.288**
Ethnic group				
Bakongo North	—	.027	—	-.463**
Bakongo South	—	-.185**	—	-.163[+]
Kwilu Kwango	—	—	—	—
Mongo	—	-.179*	—	.044
Ubangi	—	-.190*	—	.229[+]
Luba	—	.141*	—	-.174
Other tribes	—	-.239[+]	—	.476**
Non-Congolese	—	-.160[+]	—	-.360*
Enrollment status				
Enrolled	—	.754**	—	-.322*
Not enrolled	—	—	—	—
Economic status				
Economic index	—	.046**	—	.075**
Marital status/stability				
Ever married stable	—	—	—	—
Married more than once	—	-.475**	—	-.216**
Parameters				
Constant	-1.183	-1.917	-5.950	-5.865
Log likelihood	-8,924.5	-8,725.1	-3,706.8	-3,657.5

Note: Sample size = 1,465. Mean of dependent variable = .535 for any method and .083 for modern method. Universe: Women aged 15-49 in union and not pregnant at time of survey.

** Significant at the .01 level, two-tailed test.
* Significant at the .05 level, two-tailed test.
[+] Significant at the .10 level, two-tailed test.

estimated schooling coefficients somewhat, but the basic pattern remains. Schooling is also highly significantly related to the use of modern contraceptives, with university-level women showing by far the greatest likelihood of use and those with no schooling the least likelihood.[16]

Age is significantly related to contraceptive use. The nonlinear relations are for the most part negative with respect to any contraception and positive with regard to modern contraception. That is, all else equal, older women are less likely than younger women to use any method of contraception but more likely to use modern contraception.[17] This differential may be due to differences in type of method used as a consequence of different motivations for contraception: modern methods may be used most heavily by women who seek to limit their childbearing, while the more widely used traditional methods may often be practiced for purposes of spacing. This issue will be pursued further in the following chapter.

Both self-employed women and those who work as employees have significantly higher probabilities of contraceptive use than do women who are not employed, with the likelihood of using any method of contraception being greatest for employees. These differentials do not carry over to the use of modern contraception, however: differences by employment status in the use of modern contraception are not statistically significant.

A number of other factors appear to be highly significant in determining the probability of using contraception, but there are often variations depending on whether one considers any method of contraception or modern contraception. For example, consider ethnic group differences. Ubangi, Bakongo South, and Mongo women are least likely among the principal ethnic groups to use any method of contraception, all else equal. With respect to the use of modern contraception, however, use appears to be highest among Ubangi women, while both groups of Bakongo women (and especially the North group) show a clear aversion as compared to other ethnic groups.

Protestant and Kimbanguist women as well as those from other religions all have somewhat higher contraceptive prevalence than Catholics, and, except for the Kimbanguist women, these differences by religious group persist with respect to use of modern contraceptives. Women with no religious affiliation report considerably lower contraceptive use, overall and for modern methods. Use of any contraception by migrants is no different than that by nonmigrants; however, there is significantly lower use of modern contraception by migrants.

[16] An exception to the pattern of monotonic increases associated with higher levels of schooling is evident for modern contraception in the expanded (second) equation: women with 3-4 years of secondary schooling have unexpectedly slightly lower use of modern contraception, ceteris paribus, than those with 1-2 years (but significantly higher use than women with only primary education).

[17] More precisely, the turning points of the quadratic specifications of age in the two equations for use of any contraceptive method are at 24.0 and 25.6 years, while for use of modern contraception the turning points are at 42.4 and 42.0 years, respectively. Thus, the greater use of modern contraception among older women referred to in the text does not appear to apply among women in their mid- and later 40s.

Women enrolled in school are significantly more likely to use any method of contraception than those not in school, but they are significantly less likely to use modern contraception. Increased economic status is associated with a greater likelihood of both overall and modern contraceptive use. Relative to ever-married women in stable unions (i.e., those still in their first union), married women in a second or higher-order union are less likely to use any method and somewhat less likely to use modern contraception.

Abortion

Data on abortion were gathered as an incidental part of the pregnancy histories that were collected. Approximately 15 percent of ever-pregnant women reported having had an abortion. As with contraception, the incidence of abortion rises with education, but the differences are much sharper. While only about 4 percent of women with no schooling report having had an abortion, this figure rises to 30 percent and above for women with upper-level secondary and university education.[18]

Logistic regression analyses of the incidence of abortion among ever-pregnant women who were in union at the time of the survey are shown in table 6.5. Controlling for age, there are quite substantial and highly significant differences by educational attainment in the incidence of abortion. The likelihood of a woman having had an abortion rises steadily as schooling increases, with a particularly sharp jump from mid-level to upper-level secondary schooling. Controlling for educational attainment, the likelihood of having had an abortion increases with age up through the late 30s and declines thereafter.

Differences by employment status are not significant for either self-employed women or those working in the modern sector.[19] The additional vari-

[18] As noted by Coeytaux (1988) and by Barreto et al. (1992), survey research on abortion may suffer from underreporting. In view of this possibility, our estimates of the incidence of abortion should be regarded as suggestive rather than definitive, and there is a good chance that they understate the true extent of induced abortion. At the same time, several factors suggest to us that reporting bias may be fairly modest. First, although induced abortion is illegal in Kinshasa, the prospects of legal sanctions in cases of abortion are effectively nil. Further, the data on abortion were gathered as an incidental part of the pregnancy history rather than in response to direct questions about abortion. Although we did not use the randomized response technique, we were surprised during the fieldwork at the willingness of respondents to provide information on induced abortion. Hence, Kinshasa appears to correspond to the situation described by Baretto et al. (1992, 163), where "induced abortion may be illegal but socially acceptable and discussed openly." Finally, while it could be argued that the observed differences by schooling level just noted reflect in part a greater willingness by better-educated women to acknowledge having had an abortion, it is worth noting that, in tabular data, holding schooling constant, women employed in the modern sector report a sharply higher incidence of abortion. This difference seems unlikely to reflect simply greater willingness to acknowledge abortion. On balance, then, we believe that our data on the reported incidence of abortion provide useful information for purposes of understanding abortion and contraceptive behavior in Kinshasa.

[19] Comparable analyses not limited to women in union indicate a significantly higher incidence of abortion among women employed in the modern sector. This suggests that nonmarried women working in the modern sector are especially likely to have had an abortion.

ables included in the long-form equation in the table—ethnic group, religion, migration status, economic status, and marital status—are all significantly related to abortion. Mongo and Ubangi women stand out as being especially likely to have had an abortion, and this is also true of women with no religious affiliation. Protestant women, those affiliated with more fundamentalist sects, and those who had migrated to Kinshasa all had a distinctly low incidence of abortion, all else equal.

Perhaps as a consequence of the resources required to pay for the procedure, women of higher economic status are more likely to have had an abortion. Finally, women in unions who had experienced marital disruption report a significantly higher incidence of abortion as compared to married women in their first union.

Breast-Feeding and Postpartum Abstinence

Data on postpartum practices were obtained for all births to a respondent since July 1984. For the last birth, information was sought on current status with respect to breast-feeding, postpartum amenorrhea, and sexual abstinence. In this subsection, the unit of analysis is the child rather than the mother. On average, children born in Kinshasa are breast-fed for 16-17.5 months, depending on whether the mean duration is calculated using births during the past 24 months or those from the past 36 months, respectively.[20]

There is clear evidence of an inverse association between educational attainment and the duration of breast-feeding. Among those with no schooling, average duration (measured using births during the past 36 months) is over 19 months, compared to 18 for those with primary education, roughly 17 for women with secondary schooling, and about 14 for those with university education.

Multivariate analyses of the likelihood of breast-feeding by children of women in union, using weighted logistic regression analyses, are provided in

[20] The calculated mean durations are generally slightly higher when based on births occurring during the past 36 months. In this regard, it is worth noting that the prevalence-incidence estimator that we use provides unbiased estimates of the mean if the number of births in each month is constant throughout the reference period. It has been shown that, in retrospective surveys like ours, this assumption of uniformity of births is often violated simply because, on average, there are half as many births in the month of interview as in all other months (Goldman et al. 1984). In order to account for this problem, we doubled the weighting of the births that took place in the month of interview. For other ways of properly handling this problem, see Grummer-Strawn and Trussell (1990).

For other evidence as illustrated from World Fertility Surveys (WFS) and DHS data, see Ferry and Smith (1983) and Grummer-Strawn and Trussell (1990). Increases in the prevalence-incidence mean as the reference period increases are related to inaccuracy in birth dating. In settings where dating of events may at times be poor, a disproportionate number of births tend to be pushed forward (thereby underestimating in each case the duration elapsed since the birth of the child). This inflates the incidence component of the estimator and leads to a downward bias in calculated mean durations.

Table 6.5 Analysis of Incidence of Abortion (weighted logistic regressions)

Variable	$\hat{\beta}$	$\hat{\beta}$
Age at survey		
Age	.117**	.123**
Age squared	-.0016**	-.0018**
Schooling level		
None	-.801**	-.597**
Primary	—	—
Secondary 1-2	.611**	.345**
Secondary 3-4	.860**	.568**
Secondary 5-6	1.601**	1.394**
University	1.893**	1.454**
Other schooling	.963**	.824**
Employment status		
Not employed	—	—
Self-employed	—	-.011
Employee	—	.043
Religion		
Catholic	—	—
Protestant	—	-.590**
Kimbanguist	—	.172
Other religion	—	-.522**
No religion	—	.310+
Migration status		
Nonmigrant	—	—
Migrant	—	-.403**
Ethnic group		
Bakongo North	—	.168
Bakongo South	—	.058
Kwilu Kwango	—	—
Mongo	—	.844**
Ubangi	—	.712**
Luba	—	.184*
Other tribes	—	.047
Non-Congolese	—	.135
Economic status		
Economic index	—	.090**
Marital status/stability		
Ever married stable	—	—
Married more than once	—	.807**
Parameters		
Constant	-4.429	-4.490
Log likelihood	-5,420.6	-5,110.7

Note: Sample size = 1,508; mean of dependent variable = .146. Universe: Women aged 15-49 in union at the time of the survey who have ever been pregnant.

** Significant at the .01 level, two-tailed test.
* Significant at the .05 level, two-tailed test.
+ Significant at the .10 level, two-tailed test.

the first two columns of table 6.6. These results are restricted to births occur-
ing during the 36 months preceding the survey. The dependent variable (practice of breast-feeding) is dichotomous, equal to 1 if the child is still being
breast-fed at the time of the survey and 0 otherwise. We regress breast-feeding
on the child's age and on the mother's schooling in the first equation, while in
the second equation there are additional control variables representing mother's
age, employment status, ethnic group, religion, migration status, economic status, and marital status.

Overall, just under half the children born in the 3 years prior to the survey
were still being breast-fed at the time of the survey. By far the single most
significant variable in determining the likelihood of breast-feeding is the child's
age, and the probability of being breast-fed declines at an accelerating rate as
the child ages. In addition to the negative influence of the child's age on breast-
feeding, there are highly significant differences by educational attainment for
children whose mothers have gone beyond the primary school level. These
children are less likely to be breast-fed, ceteris paribus, and the differences are
distinctly large among children whose mothers have reached or gone beyond
upper-level secondary school. At the same time, and contrary to our expectations, there is a weakly significant coefficient indicating that children of
mothers with no schooling have somewhat shorter durations of breast-feeding
as compared to those whose mothers have been to primary school. When the
additional explanatory variables are added, the differences by education above
the primary school level narrow somewhat but remain for the most part
(although women with 3-4 years of secondary education no longer differ from
those with primary schooling only).

There are no significant differences in breast-feeding behavior with respect to employment status, and mother's age is also not a relevant factor, all
else equal. There are, however, several significant differences by ethnic group,
with Ubangi and Kwilu-Kwango women most likely to be breast-feeding and
Mongo and especially Luba women least likely to be breast-feeding. Differences by religion are for the most part modest, and no migrant-nonmigrant
differential is evident. Economic status is highly significantly negatively related
to this behavior: economically better-off mothers were less likely to be breast-
feeding. This may well reflect more ready access of these women to substitutes
for mother's milk. Breast-feeding durations were also significantly shorter for
women in a second or higher-order union.

The overall average duration of postpartum abstinence, derived by the prevalence-incidence ratio method from the current status of abstinence for births
during the last 36 months, is 8.6 months. This is very close to the unweighted
mean of 8.8 months from Jolly and Gribble (1993, table 3-2, p. 74), although
it should be noted that there is considerable variation around that mean (from
2.4 to 22.7 months). Differences in abstinence durations by educational
attainment are evident, particularly at the extremes: whereas the average

Table 6.6 Analysis of Breast-Feeding and Postpartum Abstinence (weighted logistic regressions)

Variable	Breast-feeding		Abstinence	
Child's age				
Months	-.140**	-.141**	-.338**	-.344**
Age squared	-.0036**	-.0039**	.0054**	.0054**
Schooling level				
None	-.234$^+$	-.353**	.675**	.649**
Primary	—	—	—	—
Secondary 1-2	-.361**	-.269**	-.102	-.087
Secondary 3-4	-.216**	-.052	.089	.229**
Secondary 5-6	-.778**	-.614**	-.540**	-.434**
University	-.976**	-.775**	-1.408**	-1.122**
Other schooling	-2.279**	-2.227**	-1.673$^+$	-1.641$^+$
Employment				
Status				
Not employed	—	—	—	—
Self-employed	—	.022	—	-.167**
Employee	—	.060	—	.060
Mother's age				
Years	—	.005	—	-.015*
Religion				
Catholic	—	—	—	—
Protestant	—	-.150$^+$	—	-.604**
Kimbanguist	—	.086	—	.123
Other religion	—	.082	—	-.481**
No religion	—	-.398*	—	-.559**
Migration status				
Nonmigrant	—	—	—	—
Migrant	—	-.066	—	.133*
Ethnic group				
Bakongo North	—	-.286*	—	-.473**
Bakongo South	—	-.177$^+$	—	.185*
Kwilu Kwango	—	—	—	—
Mongo	—	-.381**	—	.007
Ubangi	—	.214	—	.442**
Luba	—	-.753**	—	.031
Other tribes	—	-1.242**	—	-1.975**
Non-Congolese	—	.037	—	1.177**
Economic status				
Economic index	—	-.056**	—	-.095**
Marital status/stability				
Ever married stable	—	—	—	—
Married more than once	—	-.696**	—	.069
Parameters				
Constant	3.547	3.879	1.855	2.559
Log likelihood	-3672.2	-3562.7	-3956.6	-3804.7

Note: Sample size = 1,108; mean of dependent variable = .486 for breast-feeding and .240 for abstinence. Universe: Births occurring in the 36 months prior to the survey to women who were in union at the time of the survey.

** Significant at the .01 level, two-tailed test.
* Significant at the .05 level, two-tailed test.
$^+$ Significant at the .10 level, two-tailed test.

duration of abstinence among women with no schooling was over 13 months, this figure fell to about 8.5 months for women with primary and with lower-level secondary education and to only a little more than 4 months for university-educated women.

Multivariate analyses of postpartum abstinence, restricted to women in unions who were mothers of children born in the 36 months preceding the survey, are shown in the latter two columns of table 6.6. As in the case of breast-feeding, the dependent variable is dichotomous, equal to 1 if the child's mother is still practicing postpartum abstinence at the time of the survey and 0 otherwise. The two equations parallel those used to analyze breast-feeding behavior.

Just under one-quarter of mothers of children born in the 36 months preceding the survey were still practicing postpartum abstinence at the time of the survey. As with breast-feeding, age of the child (i.e., duration since the birth) is the single most important variable influencing the prevalence of abstinence. Women with no schooling are significantly more likely by a considerable margin to practice abstinence than are those with primary schooling, while those with upper-level secondary schooling and especially those with university education are distinctly less likely to be doing so, all else equal. In between, there are no significant differences among women with primary and 1-2 and 3-4 years of secondary education in the first equation; and in the second equation there is an unexpected positive coefficient (longer abstinence duration) for women with 3-4 years of secondary education.

Self-employed women have a significantly lower propensity than non-employed women to engage in abstinence (although the magnitude of the coefficient is modest), while the difference is not significant for those working as employees. All else equal, abstinence is less prevalent among older women. As with most of the other proximate determinants, there are some substantial differences by ethnic group, with abstinence durations being particularly long for Ubangi women, relatively long for Bakongo South women, and comparatively short for Bakongo North women.

In addition, there are highly significant differences in abstinence behavior by religion, migration status, and economic status. Protestant women, those from the "other religions" group, and those with no religious affiliation all report relatively short abstinence durations, as compared to Catholics. Migrants to Kinshasa had somewhat longer abstinence durations than Kinshasa natives. Finally, greater economic well-being was associated with shorter abstinence durations.

Ethnic Fertility Differences and the Compensating Mechanisms of the Proximate Determinants

At the outset of the chapter we noted that multivariate analyses of the proximate determinants allow one to identify the mechanisms by which various characteristics influence fertility. Here we provide an illustration, focusing on ethnicity. In chapter 4, we saw evidence of significant differences in fertility by ethnic group. Controlling for age and education, Ubangi and Bakongo South women have significantly lower numbers of children ever born than do those from the Kwilu-Kwango reference group, with the differences on the order of 0.2 children, all else equal, while Luba women have sharply higher fertility, by 0.4 children (table 4.7, equation [2]). Controlling for factors other than marital status (table 4A.2, equation [1]) results in little change in these coefficients. Controlling for marital status (table 4A.2, equation [2]), the coefficients for Bakongo South and Ubangi women become smaller in absolute value and only weakly significant. By contrast, the coefficient for Luba women rises to almost 0.5. In sum, then, Luba women stand out quite clearly as the high-fertility group, all else equal, while there is some indication of slightly lower fertility for Ubangi and Bakongo South women.

In the preceding section we saw that, frequently, there are significant differences by ethnic group with respect to the proximate determinants. These results concerning the behavior of the different ethnic groups with respect to the various proximate determinants, as well as with regard to overall fertility, are summarized in table 6.7. Here we provide a synthesis of these results for each of the groups in an effort to ascertain the links between the proximate determinants and the observed differences in fertility.[21]

The relatively low fertility of the Ubangi women occurs despite a tendency toward early entry into marriage.[22] Somewhat greater use of modern contraception and distinctly longer spells of postpartum abstinence appear to contribute to the lower fertility of these women, and a high incidence of induced abortion undoubtedly contributes to the difference as well. Those in the other group with low fertility—the Bakongo South women—have comparatively short durations of breast-feeding and a relatively low use of modern contraception, which by themselves would result in higher fertility, all else equal. For this group, however, there are longer durations of postpartum abstinence contributing to lower fertility. Most notable, however, is the tendency of these women to marry latest by far among the six major ethnic groups.

The fertility of Bakongo North women, as well as that of Mongo women, does not differ significantly from the fertility of women from Kwilu-Kwango, controlling for age, education, and other factors besides marital status. However, there are quite distinct paths leading to this absence of an overall difference. The Bakongo North women show delayed entry to marriage compared to the Kwilu-Kwango women, but this is largely offset by a distinctly lower incidence of use of modern contraception and shorter durations of breast-feeding

[21] More specifically, for each of the groups other than the Kwilu-Kwango reference group we describe how that group's behaviors with respect to the proximate determinants help account for its relative level of fertility, controlling for age, education, and other factors apart from marital status.

[22] This tendency is offset in part by relatively low proportions married at higher ages. The combination of early entry into marriage and low proportions married at higher ages is the consequence of a relatively high incidence of divorce among Ubangi women.

Chapter 6

Table 6.7 Significant Coefficients of Variables Identifying the Different Ethnic Groups, for Children Ever Born and Proximate Determinants of Fertility, Controlling for Age and Other Factors

Ethnic Group	Children Ever Born	Age at Marriage	Modern Contraception	Abortion	Breast-feeding	Postpartum Abstinence
Bakongo North	ns	-.13**	-.46**	ns	-.29*	-.47**
Bakongo South	-.18*	-.29**	-.16$^+$	ns	-.18$^+$	.19*
Kwilu-Kwango	—	—	—	—	—	—
Mongo	ns	ns	ns	.84**	-.38**	ns
Ubangi	-.25*	.10**	.23$^+$	.71**	ns	.44**
Luba+	.41**	-.07*	ns	.18*	-.75**	ns

Sources: Children ever born: table 4A.2, equation 1; Age at marriage: table 6.3, equation 2; Modern contraception: table 6.4, equation 4; Abortion: table 6.5, equation 2; Breast-feeding: table 6.6, equation 2; Postpartum abstinence: table 6.6, equation 4.

Note: The abbreviation "ns" signifies that the coefficient was not statistically significant.
** Significant at the .01 level.
* Significant at the .05 level.
$^+$ Significant at the .10 level.

and postpartum abstinence. The Mongo women exhibit significantly shorter breast-feeding durations, but this is compensated for by a substantially higher incidence of abortion.

The high-fertility group is the Luba women. They tend to be a little older than Kwilu-Kwango women on entry into marriage and also to have a slightly higher incidence of abortion. Offsetting these fertility-reducing effects are substantially shorter durations of breast-feeding and low divorce rates that translate into the highest proportions married from age 30 on for any ethnic group.

Overall, then, what is evident from this comparison is that, despite the numerous significant differences by ethnic group in fertility-relevant behavior, these differences often serve to offset or compensate for one another. Hence, with the notable exception of the Luba women, there are not strong and substantial differences by ethnic group in actual childbearing behavior.

Summary and Conclusions

We use the Bongaarts framework to analyze the proximate determinants of fertility in Kinshasa and compare our findings to those from elsewhere in sub-Saharan Africa. Consistent with Jolly and Gribble's (1993) previous research based on DHS data, we find that postpartum infecundability resulting from extended periods of breast-feeding is the single most important factor reducing fertility below its biological maximum. Contraception ranks second in Kinshasa, reflecting a fairly high prevalence of use of traditional methods, while union patterns are the third-ranked proximate determinant. These results are slightly different from those of Jolly and Gribble (1993), who found union patterns to be the second-ranked fertility-inhibiting proximate determinant. The indices of marriage and births outside marriage for Kinshasa are comparable to the average values for the national populations examined by Jolly and Gribble. The indices of marriage for Kinshasa are distinctly higher than the average of the comparable indices for urban DHS data, indicating less of an impact of union patterns on fertility for Kinshasa as compared to elsewhere. Relative to its role in national populations, contraception in Kinshasa has a greater fertility-inhibiting effect, and postpartum infecundability has a weaker effect, while, relative to urban areas in the DHS, Kinshasa has almost the same index values.

Descriptive and multivariate analyses demonstrate that education, ethnicity, age, and a number of other factors tend to be significantly associated with the various proximate determinants. As indicated by our examination of ethnicity and the proximate determinants, however, these different effects often have offsetting consequences for fertility.

Chapter 7. Contraception and Abortion:
A Closer Look

This chapter takes a closer look at contraception and abortion in Kinshasa. As shown in chapter 4, fertility is lowest in the city for women with high levels of education (upper-level secondary and university), and this is especially so for those well-educated women who were employed in the modern sector of the economy. Yet, as described in the previous chapter, the prevalence of modern contraception is low, and, while it is highest among the best-educated women, it still does not reach particularly high levels even for them. At the same time, the incidence of abortion is quite high among these well-educated women, and it is also high among women employed in the modern sector (Shapiro and Tambashe 1994a).

In short, women with high levels of education and particularly those employed in the modern sector are in the vanguard of the fertility transition that the city is experiencing, yet their lower fertility is not strongly linked to higher use of effective contraception. Rather, it appears that their lower fertility is more closely related to greater recourse to abortion to limit fertility. In this chapter, we attempt to shed light on these phenomena, and we explore contraceptive behavior and the incidence of abortion more extensively than was done in chapter 6.

We begin with a detailed descriptive overview of contraceptive behavior and abortion. This includes information on method mix and comparisons of ever use and current use of contraception. Data on contraceptive use elsewhere in urban sub-Saharan Africa are provided for comparative purposes. Bivariate associations for several key variables of interest (age, ethnicity, employment status, and economic well-being as well as education) are also shown. Predicted probabilities of contraceptive use by age and education, based on multivariate analyses of contraceptive behavior, are illustrated to highlight the phenomena that we wish to examine more closely.

The legal and institutional setting is then described, and this is followed

by a look at unmet need for contraception. We differentiate between unmet
need for limiting and unmet need for spacing. The last substantive section of
the chapter looks at women's attitudes toward various modern methods, and the
concluding section considers prospects for and constraints on increased contraceptive use in the future.

Contraception and Abortion: A Descriptive Overview

Contraceptive prevalence, overall and by method, is shown in table 7.1. A little
more than half the women in union who were not pregnant at the time of the
survey were using contraception, with about 45 percent of contraceptive users
practicing rhythm and almost 30 percent practicing withdrawal. Modern methods, with just over 8 percent prevalence, are used by fewer than one in six women practicing contraception. The condom is the most widely used modern
method, accounting for 40 percent of modern contraceptive use and about 6
percent of overall contraceptive use.

Comparative data on contraceptive prevalence in urban areas and a number of large cities in sub-Saharan Africa, gleaned from various Demographic
and Health Surveys (DHS) reports, is shown in table 7.2.[1] The highest levels
of contraceptive prevalence, both overall and with respect to modern contraception, tend to be in Southern and East Africa. Compared to other urban areas
in West and Central Africa, Kinshasa has the highest reported prevalence of
contraception overall. However, especially given its high overall prevalence,
there is a rather low prevalence of modern contraception.

While Kinshasa shows the greatest disparity between overall and modern
contraceptive use, there are urban areas and large cities in several other West
and Central African countries where practice of any method of contraception
is reasonably common but modern contraceptive use is still fairly low. This is
most notably the case for Lomé and for other urban areas as well in Togo, for
Douala and Yaoundé as well as for urban areas in general in Cameroon, and for
the Greater Accra region in Ghana in the initial DHS survey. Further, in those
countries where more than one DHS survey has been carried out, and especially
those in West Africa, the data indicate that the proportion of overall contraceptive use represented by modern contraception is rising over time.

Information on past and current use of contraception by schooling level
in Kinshasa is shown in table 7.3. Nearly 80 percent of nonpregnant women in
union reported having ever used any method of contraception, although only
about a third of these ever users had practiced modern contraception. The
proportion of ever users having used modern contraception tends to rise with
increasing educational attainment. As of the time of the survey, any method of
contraception was practiced by about two-thirds of ever users, while modern

[1] The DHS contraceptive prevalence rates shown in the table include pregnant women in
the universe. For purposes of comparison, we note that the corresponding figures for Kinshasa in
1990 were 48.1 and 7.3 percent, for any method and modern methods, respectively.

Table 7.1 Current Contraceptive Use by Specific Method (percentage distributions, weighted estimates)

Contraceptive prevalence	53.5
Modern methods	8.3
Pill	1.7
IUD	0.4
Injection	1.2
Vaginals	1.0
Condom	3.3
Female sterilization	0.6
Male sterilization	0.0
Traditional methods	45.2
Withdrawal	15.2
Rhythm	24.2
Postpartum abstinence	4.5
Other methods	1.4
Not currently using	46.5
Total	100.0

Note: Universe is women in union not pregnant at the time of the survey; sample size = 1,465.

contraception was engaged in by almost one-third of those who had ever used modern contraception. There is a clear tendency evident in the table for overall and modern contraceptive use to rise as schooling level increases. In addition, the proportion of women currently using contraception relative to those who have ever used contraception rises as one moves from the no-schooling group up to the secondary-schooling level and above. This suggests that greater educational attainment is associated with a lower likelihood of contraceptive discontinuation.

As noted in the last chapter, the pattern of these results is broadly similar to what has been found in a number of other studies done in Kinshasa (Bakutuvwidi et al. 1985, 1991; Tambashe 1984). However, the level of current contraceptive use that we find is somewhat higher than that reported in these earlier studies, reflecting growth over time in the demand for contraception. For example, the data on contraceptive prevalence reported by Bakutuvwidi et al. (1991, 125), adjusted for their inclusion of pregnant women, suggest that overall contraceptive prevalence in Kinshasa was 41.0 percent of nonpregnant women in union in 1982 and had risen to 44.9 percent by 1988. The corresponding figures for modern contraception were 5.1 and 7.8 percent, respectively. This growth in demand for contraception parallels what has been occurring elsewhere in urban sub-Saharan Africa, as may be seen by examining the data in table 7.2 for urban areas and cities in countries with two or more DHS surveys.

Table 7.2 Contraceptive Prevalence, Urban Africa (from various DHS reports)

Country—Subgroup	Year	Any Method	Modern Method
Benin—urban	1996	19.0	5.8
Botswana—urban[a]	1988	38.8	38.2
Burkina Faso—urban	1993	26.0	17.1
Ouagadougou		30.6	19.9
Burkina Faso—urban	1998	29.4	20.1
Ouagadougou		32.2	22.5
Burundi—urban	1987	25.5	14.0
Cameroon—urban	1991	24.9	7.1
Yaoundé, Douala		38.6	12.1
Cameroon—urban	1998	34.6	13.1
Yaoundé, Douala		39.4	14.1
Central African Republic—	1994-1995		
Bangui		24.0	9.0
other cities		14.7	3.9
Chad—urban	1996-1997	9.4	4.2
N'Djamena		11.8	6.7
Côte d'Ivoire—Abidjan	1994	23.4	9.6
urban		19.3	8.0
Eritrea—urban	1995	19.3	14.5
Asmara		25.5	19.6
Ghana—urban	1988	19.6	8.1
Greater Accra (region)		27.2	10.6
Ghana—urban	1993	30.6	15.8
Greater Accra (region)		36.8	18.0
Ghana—urban	1998	30.4	17.4
Greater Accra (region)		32.2	17.4
Guinea—urban	1992	6.2	3.4
Conakry (region)		9.2	3.9
Guinea—urban	1999	13.9	9.5
Conakry (region)		13.1	7.6
Kenya—urban	1989	30.5	25.5
Nairobi (province)		33.5	27.9
Kenya—urban	1993	43.4	37.9
Nairobi (province)		45.4	37.8
Kenya—urban	1998	49.6	41.0
Nairobi (province)		56.3	46.8
Liberia—urban	1986	11.6	9.7
Malawi—urban	1992	22.9	17.2
Malawi—urban	1996	36.0	28.7
Mali—urban	1987	11.4	4.7
Bamako (region)		16.4	6.0
Mali—urban	1995-1996	16.2	11.6
Bamako (region)		23.4	16.4
Mozambique—urban	1997	17.7	16.6
Maputo		30.3	28.5
Namibia—urban	1992	47.8	46.6
Niger—Niamey	1992	20.8	17.3
other cities		14.1	8.6

Niger—Niamey	1998	26.1	21.3
other cities		22.9	18.6
Nigeria—urban	1990	14.8	9.6
Nigeria—urban	1999	23.4	15.7
Ondo State, Nigeria—urban	1986	8.9	5.4
Rwanda—urban	1992	28.4	19.7
Senegal—urban	1986	14.2	6.7
Senegal—urban	1992-1993	16.1	11.8
Senegal—urban	1997	23.8	19.3
Sudan, northern—urban	1989-1990	17.0	11.3
Khartoum		22.1	15.8
Tanzania—Dar es Salaam	1991-1992	15.7	10.9
other urban-mainland		18.7	15.1
Tanzania[a] —Dar es Salaam	1996	30.8	23.9
other urban-mainland		28.2	23.6
Tanzania[a] —urban	1999	33.0	28.9
Togo—Lomé	1988	31.1	6.9
other cities		34.2	6.0
Togo—Lomé	1998	25.2	10.7
other cities		29.0	9.9
Uganda—urban	1988-1989	18.0	12.2
Kampala (region)		24.6	17.9
Uganda—urban	1995	34.5	28.1
Kampala (region)		40.5	34.9
Zambia—urban	1992	20.8	15.3
Lusaka (province)		24.2	17.6
Zambia—urban	1996	33.3	23.6
Lusaka (province)		35.3	27.4
Zimbabwe—urban	1988	51.7	48.8
Harare/Chitungwiza		51.5	48.0
Zimbabwe—urban	1994	57.6	53.9
Harare		61.6	57.7
Zimbabwe—urban	1999	63.1	61.8
Harare		63.5	62.9

Source: Demographic and Health Surveys, various country reports.

Note: Universe is women in unions (unless otherwise noted).

[a] Data are for all women.

Compared to the findings for 1988, the increased contraceptive prevalence that we estimate for 1990 largely reflects a higher use of rhythm. The slightly increased prevalence of modern methods has been associated with some change in the method mix: there has been a distinct increase in the use of condoms, offset in part by reduced pill use and, to a lesser degree, reduced use of injections (see Bakutuvwidi et al. 1991, 106).

At the same time, there is clearly a good deal of experimentation and discontinuation among the minority of women who have tried modern methods

Table 7.3 Contraceptive Use by Educational Attainment (percentages, weighted estimates)

			Schooling Group				
			Secondary				
Contraceptive Use Category	None	Primary	1-2	3-4	5-6	University	Total
Ever used							
Any method	59	71	85	82	87	99	79
Modern method	14	24	27	26	33	41	26
Currently using							
Any method	35	42	56	60	63	73	53
Modern method	3	6	9	9	11	16	8
Ever users currently using							
Any method	57	60	64	72	71	74	66
Modern method	5	9	10	11	11	16	10
Ever used modern method							
Currently using							
Any method	59	50	60	62	70	77	61
Modern method	22	26	29	33	29	38	30
Current users using a							
modern method	9	14	16	15	17	22	16

Note: Universe is women in union not pregnant at the time of the survey.

of contraception. That is, fully 70 percent of the women who had ever used modern contraception were not doing so at the time of the survey. Indeed, only just over 60 percent of ever users of modern contraception were practicing any method of contraception at all, suggestive of some combination of weak demand and problems in service delivery with modern methods. The extent of discontinuation of modern contraception appears to decline somewhat as schooling increases, as reflected by the fact that the proportion of ever users of modern methods who were current users of such methods generally rises with educational attainment. Similarly, there is some increase in the use effectiveness of contraception as schooling increases, in that the share of current users practicing modern contraception tends to rise with greater educational attainment. However, the effect is modest: only among university-educated women do users of modern contraception represent as many as 20 percent of total contraceptive users.

Contraceptive use by age group, employment status, economic status, and ethnic group is shown in table 7.4. Overall, current contraceptive use is very low among the oldest women in the sample, and otherwise contraceptive prevalence is a bit lower among women aged 30-44 as compared to their younger counterparts. The relatively high prevalence among women under age 30 suggests that contraception for purposes of spacing births is fairly common.

Table 7.4 Contraceptive Use by Age, Employment Status, Economic Status, and Ethnic Group (weighted estimates)

Background Variables	Percentage Ever Used		Percentage Currently Using		Percentage of Current Users Using Modern Method
	Any Method	Modern Method	Any Method	Modern Method	
Respondent's age					
15-19	80	14	58	6	11
20-24	82	21	56	6	10
25-29	82	26	58	9	15
30-34	77	32	52	10	18
35-39	76	40	48	14	29
40-44	74	37	44	12	27
45-49	58	23	12	2	16
Employment status					
Not employed	79	25	52	8	15
Self-employed	78	27	54	9	16
Employee	93	43	65	14	21
Economic index score					
0	70	16	44	5	11
1	79	21	54	5	10
2-3	80	29	56	10	18
4-5	88	42	62	14	22
6+	89	33	62	11	1
Ethnic group					
Bakongo North	87	32	56	6	11
Bakongo South	81	26	53	8	16
Kwilu-Kwango	77	20	52	7	14
Mongo	76	41	51	9	18
Ubangi	78	32	50	11	23
Luba	83	26	61	9	15
Other tribes	79	47	53	15	29
Non-Congolese	78	31	52	6	12

Note: Universe is women in union not pregnant at the time of the survey.

Further, there is a decline with age in the use of traditional methods of contraception and an increase with age in use of modern methods.[2] As a consequence, there is a distinct increase with age in the effectiveness of contraceptive methods utilized. Further, there is relatively high use of modern contraception among women aged 30-44. Given the secular trend in educational attainment, this foreshadows increased demand for modern contraception in the future.

Contraception by self-employed women is almost the same as that among nonemployed women. Those in the modern sector tend to have higher contraceptive prevalence and a slightly higher use of modern contraception among

[2] Use of traditional methods is given by the difference between the figures for any method and for modern method. This falls from close to half among those aged 15-29 to roughly a third or less for those aged 35-44.

contraceptive users. These differences are largely a consequence of the greater educational attainment of these women.

Economic status shows a clear positive correlation with contraception, with both ever use and current use rising as the value of the index increases. Women in the lowest economic category (representing close to 30 percent of the sample) manifest particularly low contraceptive prevalence. In addition, use of modern contraception is greatest for the two highest economic groups (representing nearly 30 percent of the sample, with the highest category accounting for 12 percent).

Differences by ethnic group in contraceptive prevalence and ever use are for the most part quite modest. At the same time, it is apparent that Luba women have relatively high contraceptive prevalence for use of any method and that Ubangi women and those from other tribes show distinctly greater use of modern contraception than do other groups.

The reported incidence of abortion by schooling and employment status is given in table 7.5. Overall, 15 percent of the ever-pregnant women in the sample reported having had an abortion. Bakutuvwidi et al. (1991, 119) found an incidence of abortion among all women aged 15-49 of just under 10 percent. Among all women aged 15-49 in our 1990 data set, 12 percent indicated that they had had an abortion. Further, Bakutuvwidi et al. (1991, 118) stated that the 1982 Contraceptive Prevalence Survey in Kinshasa found an incidence of abortion of just over 9 percent among women in unions aged 13-49.[3] In sum, then, there appears to be a slight upward trend over time in the percentage of women who have had an abortion.

Consistent with the findings of Bakutuvwidi et al. (1991, 120) for all women, there is a sharp tendency for the incidence of abortion to rise with increased schooling. This is particularly so in moving from mid-level to upper-level secondary school, where the percentage having had an abortion nearly doubles, going from 17 to 30. There are also substantial differences by employment status in experience with abortion, with women in the modern sector showing a considerably higher incidence of abortion than either self-employed or nonemployed women. While this partially reflects the relatively high educational attainment of women working as employees (see chapter 11 below), it is also true for the most part within schooling groups (especially for the secondary-level women) as well as overall. These sharp differentials in

---

[3] It is interesting to note that restricting the sample examined by marital status has very little impact on the overall reported incidence of abortion. This is because women not in union consist of two groups with very different incidences of abortion: never-married women, whose reported incidence is relatively low, and previously married women, whose incidence of abortion is relatively high. For example, the reported incidence from 1988 for these two groups is 6.6 and 15.6 percent, respectively, while for women in union the corresponding figure is 10.5 percent (Bakutuvwidi et al. 1991, 120). Likewise, in our 1990 data set, the incidence of abortion among all ever-pregnant women is just over 15 percent, while among all ever-pregnant women in union at the time of the survey the figure is just under 15 percent.

Table 7.5 Reported Incidence of Induced Abortion by Schooling and by Employment Status (weighted estimates of percentage of women reporting having had an abortion)

Education	Not Employed	Self-Employed	Employees	All Women
None	3	6	a	4
Primary	8	12	14	10
Secondary 1-2	11	16	29	13
Secondary 3-4	17	17	24	17
Secondary 5-6	34	18	33	30
University	31	34	37	33
All women	15	14	31	15

Note: Universe is ever-pregnant women; sample size = 1,725.
*Fewer than five sample cases in cell.

experience with abortion contrast with the relatively modest differences by employment status in use of modern contraception.

Table 7.6 shows the incidence of reporting of abortion by age, economic status, and ethnic group. Age differences are fairly modest, for the most part. Caldwell et al. (1992) have suggested that young women seeking to delay the onset of childbearing (and, perhaps, remain enrolled in school) may constitute an important component of the demand for fertility control and, hence, presumably, abortion. However, the fact that the highest incidence of abortion occurs among women aged 25-39 and that the incidence is 10 percent or higher among women over age 40 suggests that abortion among young women accounts for only a portion of the overall incidence of abortion.[4] Higher economic status is associated with a progressively higher reported incidence of abortion, being approximately three times greater for the two highest categories than for the lowest category. Some differences by ethnic group are also readily apparent, with roughly twice as many Mongo and Ubangi women having had at least one abortion as compared to the incidence among Bakongo and Kwilu-Kwango women.

To supplement the bivariate relations that have just been reviewed, figures 7.1 and 7.2 show predicted probabilities of contraceptive use by age and education, based on the equations reported in table 6.4 above. Figure 7.1 shows predicted probabilities of modern contraceptive use, by age and educational attainment, for the two highest education groups and also for women with primary schooling. Overall, these predicted probabilities are low. Modern

[4] Survey results on attitudes toward abortion were reported by Bakutuvwidi et al. (1991, 118). These results indicate that, while very high proportions of women expressed unfavorable attitudes toward abortion under various circumstances, the highest proportion favorable (19 percent) was expressed for situations where the pregnancy threatened the health of the prospective mother. By contrast, only 6 percent of respondents were favorable to abortion when the pregnancy would have adverse consequences for the schooling of the mother.

Table 7.6 Incidence of Induced Abortion by Age, Economic Status, and Ethnic Group (weighted estimates)

Background Variables	Percentage Reporting Having Had an Abortion
Respondent's age	
15-19	13
20-24	15
25-29	17
30-34	16
35-39	17
40-44	10
45-49	12
Economic index score	
0	8
1	13
2-3	17
4-5	22
6+	27
Ethnic group	
Bakongo North	14
Bakongo South	13
Kwilu-Kwango	11
Mongo	26
Ubangi	28
Luba	18
Other tribes	16
Non-Congolese	16

Note: Universe is ever-pregnant women; sample size = 1,725.

contraceptive prevalence of 30 percent is reached only for the university-educated women and only from age 35 on.

As noted above, the tendency for modern contraceptive use to increase with age is accompanied by reduced use of traditional contraception as women get older. Consequently, as shown by the predicted probabilities in figure 7.2, the proportion of overall contraceptive use that is represented by modern use tends to rise steadily with age, for all education groups. For the higher ages in particular, these predicted probabilities are distinctly greater than the actual figures by age shown in table 7.4 above, because they control for the level of educational attainment. That is, the actual figures are dampened at higher ages because older women have lower levels of schooling relative to younger women and this lesser schooling translates into lower contraceptive use. The secular trend in educational attainment in conjunction with these predicted probabilities foreshadows important increases in demand for modern contraception.

Fig. 7.1 Predicted probabilities of modern contraceptive use, by age and education

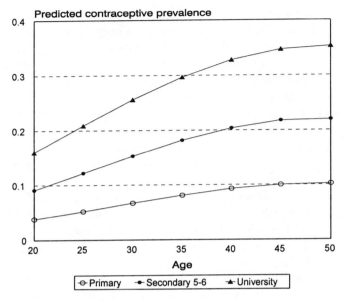

Note: From table 6.4, equation (3).

Fig. 7.2 Predicted probabilities of modern relative to total contraceptive use, by age and education

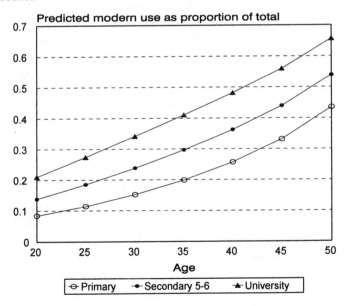

Note: From table 6.4, equations (1) and (3).

The Institutional and Legal Setting: Family Planning and Abortion in Kinshasa

In its 1993 study of contraceptive use in sub-Saharan Africa, the National Research Council (1993b) characterized the Congo as a country with consistently weak support for the national family-planning program. In 1972, President Mobutu enunciated the government's policy with respect to family planning as being one of *naissances désirables* (desirable births). Emphasis was on the desirability of birth spacing to promote maternal and child health. There was no demographic objective attached to the policy, and, indeed, the government was generally favorable to rapid population growth.[5] Pursuant to establishment of the policy, a clinic offering contraceptive services was established at Mama Yemo Hospital in Kinshasa in 1973, directly under the authority of the Office of the President.

Subsequently, three organizations were active in providing family-planning services in the Congo, primarily being involved in the distribution of contraceptives through clinics and hospitals and in the promotion of responsible parenthood. These organizations were the Projet des Services des Naissances Désirables (PSND), a government maternal and child health/family-planning organization, the Association Congolaise de Bien-Etre Familial (ACBEF), a nongovernment organization and International Planned Parenthood Federation affiliate, and Santé Rurale (SANRU), a primary health care program implemented and operated by the Eglise du Christ au Congo. With assistance from external donors, PSND was active throughout the country from the early 1980s on, principally in urban areas where 165 service delivery points had been established (Fisher et al. 1991). In an effort to reach rural residents, PSND sought to integrate its activities with those of SANRU. With 64 service delivery points, ACBEF also concentrated its activities primarily in urban areas (mostly in Kinshasa and in provincial capital cities), activities that consisted largely of the distribution of contraceptives and information, education, and communication efforts in the field of family planning. SANRU established approximately 300 service delivery points in rural areas, although, since many of these facilities did not report on their family-planning activities, the extent to which services were available and used is not well-known (Fisher et al. 1991).

In efforts to promote the use of condoms as part of the campaign against HIV/AIDS, the Social Marketing Project (a project funded by the U.S. Agency for International Development) was very active in the distribution of subsidized condoms and pills until late 1991. In a period of less than 5 years, condom sales increased tremendously. With such promising short-term results, the social marketing strategy appeared likely to contribute significantly to efforts aimed at promoting birth spacing. Unfortunately, however, owing to political in-

---

[5] Frequently in the past, government officials have argued that the vast size of the country and low population density mean that the country is underpopulated. Difficulties in providing adequate health and education services in response to rapid population growth, as well as difficulties in expanding other types of infrastructure in rapidly growing urban areas in particular, tend to be ignored by those who make this argument.

stability and civil disorder beginning in late 1991 (discussed in chapter 1), all external donor assistance to the country was withdrawn. Consequently, the social marketing project and the three organizations active in family-planning service delivery (whose program activities heavily depended on external assistance) saw the level of their activities considerably reduced or halted.

Over the course of the ensuing decade, this situation did not change very much. Family planning has never regained the priority that it previously had with donors, and external donor activity has remained very limited since the early 1990s. Condom distribution through social marketing activities has continued, but quantities declined precipitously initially. There has been a partial recovery during the past 3 years, but condom distribution in 2001 was still substantially lower (by more than one-third) than it had been 10 years earlier (John Loftin, personal communication, 2002).

Even before the crisis that began in the early 1990s, a situation analysis of the country's family-planning program revealed that the level of family-planning activity at medical outlets was typically very low (Fisher et al. 1991). The median number of new and continuing clients per month at a service delivery point was only 7.5, or fewer than one client every 2 working days in a month. About two-thirds of family-planning clients used contraception for birth-spacing purposes, whereas only 25 percent used contraception for purposes of limiting births.[6] Despite this low overall level of family-planning activity at service delivery points, both our own survey (Tambashe and Shapiro 1991) and earlier Contraceptive Prevalence Surveys in 1982 and 1988 (Bakutuvwidi et al. 1985, 1991) show a high level of knowledge in Kinshasa of modern as well as traditional methods of birth control. More than 90 percent of women know at least one method of contraception.

While abortion is not a contraceptive method, it is often cited as a family-planning method and, indeed, was the most frequently cited method in the most recent Contraceptive Prevalence Survey in Kinshasa (Bakutuvwidi et al. 1991). According to the Congolese penal code, abortion for reasons other than to save the life of the mother is illegal. However, a decree establishing a code of medical ethics allows therapeutic abortion:

> The conflict in the legal status of abortion is clarified by legal interpretation which reportedly considers abortion to be legal not only to save the life of the pregnant woman but also when there is serious danger to her physical or mental health. Based on this interpretation, it is also possible to perform an abortion for foetal impairment when there is the likelihood that the child will be born with a serious and incurable disease. Moreover, it is reported that in practice abortion is also

---

[6] Westoff and Ochoa (1991) report similar figures from DHS data for most sub-Saharan African countries, except Kenya.

tolerated when the family's socioeconomic conditions are inadequate to support another child.

Nevertheless, considerable numbers of clandestine abortions, especially among urban adolescents and single women, take place. . . . A majority of the patients hospitalized from complications following induced abortion are young, single urban residents. (United Nations 1995a, 185)

A Family Health International study also showed that abortion was a quite common practice in urban centers: the 60 clinicians who were surveyed at 10 health centers in Kinshasa and in Bukavu and Matadi (capital cities of the South Kivu and Bas-Congo Provinces, respectively) indicated they treated on average 3.3 women with abortion complications during a typical duty shift (Bongwele et al. 1986). The study showed that women admitted at these centers with complications following induced abortion were typically young, unmarried, and nulliparous. This finding, similar to those from other studies in Africa (see, e.g., Bongwele et al. 1986; Caldwell et al. 1992), indicates that abortion is often used by sexually active young women to delay the onset of childbearing and marriage.

Unmet Need for Contraception

The concept of unmet need for contraception has received considerable attention in the family-planning literature in recent years (Bongaarts 1991; Westoff and Ochoa 1991; Bongaarts and Bruce 1995; Westoff and Bankole 1995; Becker 1999). This concept emerged after surveys of contraceptive knowledge, attitudes, and practices documented discrepancies between the fertility intentions of women and their contraceptive behavior. Operationally, unmet need for contraception has typically been defined as existing when fecund women who are married or living in union state either that they do not want to have any more children or that they want to space their next birth while at the same time indicating that they are not presently using any method of contraception. There is considerable discussion in the literature concerning details of this approach, covering issues such as whether it is desirable to ignore women not in union, whether some adjustment should be made for women using inefficient methods, and whether women currently pregnant whose pregnancy was not wanted should be included (see, e.g., Dixon-Mueller and Germain 1992; DeGraff and de Silva 1996).

Here, reflecting the constraints of the available data, we focus on a fairly simple operational definition of *unmet need*. Our analyses are restricted to women in union who are at risk of becoming pregnant (i.e., not currently pregnant and neither postpartum amenorrheic nor postpartum abstaining). Those who indicated that they did not want to have any further children were counted as having a need for contraception for purposes of limiting their fertility, while those who stated that they did not wish to have a child now but did want to have one later were counted as having a need for contraception for spacing purposes.[7]

Table 7.7 shows the need for contraception for spacing and limiting, overall by broad age group and also by schooling and broad age group jointly. In total, 70 percent of women in union susceptible to becoming pregnant indicated a desire for either spacing or limiting their fertility. Three-quarters of this contraceptive need is for spacing; about one in six women in union at risk of becoming pregnant indicated a desire for no additional children. Need for contraception for spacing and limiting follows opposite tendencies with respect to age. The desire for spacing is very high among women under age 30, falls to about one in three women among those in their 30s, and drops sharply for older women. By contrast, demand for limiting fertility is negligible prior to age 30 and characterizes a quarter of the women in their 30s, and no further child-bearing is the desire of more than three-quarters of the women in their 40s. These contrasting patterns by age are evident as well within each schooling group.

The contraceptive behavior of women with need for contraception for either spacing or limiting is shown in the top panel of table 7.8. Somewhat unexpectedly, women with need for contraception for spacing have a higher level of contraceptive use overall (74 percent) than do women with need for contraception for limiting (57 percent). However, use of modern contraception is twice as great in total among those with need for limiting as compared to those with need for spacing. The bottom panel of the table shows unmet contraceptive need among all women in union and at risk of becoming pregnant. These unmet need figures reflect the contraceptive use patterns of those in contraceptive need and their proportions in the totals. There is unmet need for contraception for roughly one in five women. Two-thirds of this is unmet need for spacing, while the other third is unmet need for limiting.

Perhaps the most glaring figure from the table is the one showing that more than half the married women in their 40s are not using contraception, despite desiring to have no more children. This suggests that these older women should be a prime group to be targeted in efforts to extend the scope of modern contraceptive use in Kinshasa.

[7] Often, as in the DHS surveys, women are asked how long they wish to wait prior to the birth of their next child. This permits use of a fixed window in determination of need for spacing—e.g., women who wish to wait at least 2 years may be considered as having a need for spacing. Our questionnaire, by contrast, did not specify a time horizon; it simply asked women whether they wanted a child now and, if not, if they wanted one later. Hence, our measure of contraceptive need for spacing should be taken as a rough indicator and is not comparable to measures that use a fixed window.

Table 7.7 Need for Contraception for Spacing and Limiting, by Age Group and by Educational Attainment and Age Group

	Age Group			
Need	15-29	30-39	40-49	Total
Spacing	71	32	5	53
Limiting	3	25	77	17
Total	74	57	82	70
By educational attainment				
None				
Spacing	24	39	0	19
Limiting	8	9	94	42
Primary				
Spacing	62	24	8	36
Limiting	5	31	66	27
Secondary 1-2				
Spacing	71	29	2	57
Limiting	3	22	81	11
Secondary 3-4				
Spacing	79	37	1	64
Limiting	2	27	85	13
Secondary 5-6				
Spacing	69	41	8	61
Limiting	3	26	84	10
University				
Spacing	79	40	15	67
Limiting	5	17	56	9

Note: Need for contraception for spacing was defined as existing when a woman indicated that she did not presently wish to have a(nother) child but did wish to have one subsequently. Need for contraception for limiting was defined as existing for women who indicated that they did not wish to have any further children. Universe: Nonpregnant women in union who were not amenorrheic nor abstaining.

Attitudes toward Contraception

Women were asked about their intentions to use contraception in the future. Somewhat under half the women with unmet need for contraception at the time of the survey (42 percent) indicated an intention to use contraception in the future to avoid getting pregnant or to space births. Among these women, just over a third expressed a desire to use some type of modern contraception, with injection, spermicides, and oral contraceptives being the most popular methods cited. By comparison, 43 percent of the women opted for traditional methods (the remainder were undecided as to method).

At the same time, over 70 percent of the women indicated that they would never use one or more specific modern methods. Oral contraceptives were by far the method most disliked, followed by the IUD and female sterilization. When asked about the reasons for their distaste for these methods, more than 60 percent of the women who indicated an aversion to modern methods cited

Table 7.8 Contraceptive Use and Unmet Need by Women with Need for Contraception, by Type of Contraceptive Need and Age Group

Type of Need/	Age Group			
Contraceptive Use	15-29	30-39	40-49	Total

A. Contraceptive Use by Women with Need for Contraception, by Type of Need and Type of Contraception Used (percentages practicing contraception)

Spacing				
Any method	74	77	10	74
Modern method	9	16	0	10
Limiting				
Any method	84	72	34	57
Modern method	31	25	13	20

B. Percentage of Women with Unmet Need for Contraception, by Type of Need

Spacing	18	7	4	14
Limiting	1	7	51	7
Total	19	14	55	21

Note: Universe: Part A, nonpregnant women in union who were not amenorrheic or abstaining and indicated a desire to either limit or delay their fertility; part B, all nonpregnant women in union who were not amenorrheic or abstaining.

harmful effects, and nearly another 20 percent indicated irreversibility of the method. There is good reason to believe that these figures reflect poor information held by these women. The high proportion citing adverse effects of modern contraceptives seems out of line with actual experience. Among women who had used modern contraceptives during the 5 years preceding the 1990 survey, roughly a third were still using the method in question, and only 16 percent indicated that they had dropped a particular modern method because of harmful effects. A similar imbalance between perceptions of the harmfulness of modern contraception and actual experience was evident in the 1988 Contraceptive Prevalence Survey in Kinshasa (Bakutuvwidi et al. 1991). Further, sterilization was the only irreversible method included in the survey, but, while 20 percent of the women cited irreversibility as the reason for disliking modern methods, well under 20 percent of the women cited sterilization as a method that they would never use. It would appear that there is considerable scope for improving information flows to prospective users of modern contraception.

Conclusion

There is a clear trend toward increased prevalence of contraceptive use in Kinshasa, and, indeed, the overall prevalence is high. At the same time, use of modern contraception remains low. Data for other urban centers in sub-Saharan Africa suggest that we can expect continued increases in the demand for

152 Chapter 7

contraception in Kinshasa, consistent as well with the increasing educational attainment of the female population, particularly at older ages in the reproductive span. Further, it seems likely that—as has occurred during the ongoing fertility transition in Kenya (African Population Policy Research Center 1998, chaps. 4 and 5) and elsewhere in sub-Saharan Africa—the mix of contraceptive methods used will shift over time toward increased relative (as well as absolute) use of modern methods.

While strengthening of the demand for effective contraception seems quite likely, this chapter has identified several constraints on increased use of modern contraceptives. There is a substantial degree of unmet need for effective contraception among older women who wish to limit their fertility. This unmet need is associated with negative attitudes that exaggerate the adverse effects of modern contraceptives.

Further, providers of contraceptive services in Kinshasa and elsewhere in the Congo undoubtedly were set back considerably by the protracted political and economic crisis (and associated withdrawal of foreign donor support) that began in the early 1990s. They will require substantial assistance if they are to meet the anticipated increased demand. Only if such assistance is forthcoming does it appear likely that effective contraception will supplant abortion as a principal means of fertility control in Kinshasa.

Chapter 8. Secondary Education and Fertility Decline

In the preceding chapters, we've provided evidence of fertility decline in Kinshasa since 1975, most notably among women with secondary education. This chapter focuses on how and why education and in particular secondary education is so important to fertility decline. In part, this entails a recapitulation of evidence presented in the preceding several chapters. At the same time, some additional factors and evidence relevant to the impact of secondary education on fertility are also introduced here.

The substance of the chapter begins with a presentation and discussion of the Easterlin framework for fertility analysis. This conceptual framework provides a basis for understanding the different pathways by which women's educational attainment may influence fertility behavior. We shall see that, from the perspective of the Easterlin framework, there are numerous such pathways, not all of which may be readily observed and identified empirically. At the same time, however, there are several observable factors that will be relevant considerations and for which empirical evidence is available, either from our own data set on Kinshasa or from other studies or data sources. These factors include the timing of marriage and of the onset of childbearing, the use of contraception and abortion, durations of breast-feeding and postpartum abstinence, infant and child mortality, and women's aspirations for the education of their children and desired fertility. For each factor, we consider how its relation to women's educational attainment may have implications for fertility behavior.

The subsequent section of the chapter, then, reviews evidence pertaining to each of these factors. Data from Kinshasa and from elsewhere in sub-Saharan Africa are examined. In some cases for Kinshasa this evidence has already been presented (e.g., delayed marriage and childbearing were considered in chapter 5, while proximate determinants of fertility were discussed in chapter 6, and two of the proximate determinants, contraception and abortion, were the focus of additional analyses in chapter 7). In one case, the relation between perinatal mortality and mother's education, we draw on prior research done in Kinshasa.[1] We also present data from Kinshasa illuminating how women's aspirations for their children's education as well as their desired fertility are linked to their own educational attainment. In addition, for most of these factors we review evidence on their relation to women's education from the Demographic and Health Surveys (DHSs) that have been carried out elsewhere in sub-Saharan Africa.

The evidence and analyses are consistent both for Kinshasa and for numerous other countries in the region. In brief, they show that increased women's schooling—especially at the secondary level—is related to various proximate determinants of fertility and to the demand for children, the supply of children, and motivation for and costs of fertility regulation so as to result in decreased fertility.

The Easterlin Framework for Fertility Analysis

In a seminal work published in 1975 entitled "An Economic Framework for Fertility Analysis," Richard Easterlin set forth a very ambitious conceptual framework meant to serve as a tool for studying fertility behavior. Easterlin's approach was ambitious both because it was designed so as to integrate approaches to the study of fertility from a variety of disciplines and because it sought to serve as a framework flexible enough to be relevant to a wide range of circumstances, past and present. More specifically with regard to this latter point, Easterlin saw his framework as one, not only applicable to analysis of fertility transition in developing countries, but also relevant to contemporary industrial societies and to societies that had not yet undergone fertility transition (Easterlin 1975).[2]

In brief, the Easterlin model emphasizes three broad categories through which the "basic determinants" of fertility operate and that influence the proximate determinants of fertility. These three categories are the demand for children (the number of surviving children that parents would want if fertility regulation were costless), the supply of children (the number of surviving children that parents would have if they did not deliberately limit fertility), and the costs (subjective and objective) of fertility regulation (Easterlin and Crimmins 1985, 14-18).

The basic determinants of fertility (described in chapter 6 as background

[1] *Perinatal mortality* refers to the risk of stillbirth (a baby is born dead) or of early neonatal mortality (a baby is born alive but dies within 7 days of birth). We are not aware of any studies for Kinshasa of infant and child mortality, but later in the chapter we examine evidence on infant and child mortality from other places in sub-Saharan Africa.

[2] Easterlin's framework is also described in several subsequent publications of his, but one of the best restatements may be found in Easterlin and Crimmins (1985). In this work, we first encountered this framework in passing at the outset of chapter 6 on the proximate determinants of fertility. As will be evident shortly, the reason for its mention there is the prominent place of the proximate determinants in the Easterlin framework.

factors that influence fertility) include underlying socioeconomic conditions, or what Easterlin and Crimmins describe as "modernization variables," such as education, urbanization, and modern-sector employment, as well as cultural factors, such as ethnicity and religion, and other determinants, such as genetic factors (Easterlin and Crimmins 1985, 13). These basic determinants influence fertility through their impact on the demand for children, the supply of children, and/or the costs of fertility regulation.

The Easterlin framework has a strong economic orientation, but, as noted above, it was designed to be compatible with approaches to understanding fertility from other disciplines. In particular, it has served as the point of departure for a National Academy of Sciences panel focusing on the determinants of fertility in developing countries (Bulatao et al. 1983, chap. 1), and it is compatible with literature focused on women's status and fertility (see, e.g., Mason 1984; Kritz et al. 1992). The Easterlin framework has also been used by Cochrane (1979) in her analyses of the relation between fertility and education.

Consider the implications of the Easterlin model with respect to the influence of women's education on fertility. Acquisition of schooling results in changes to an individual, in that schooling provides (or may provide) literacy, job skills, enhanced productivity in nonmarket activities (e.g., child care), new values, new information, and potential for innovation. The extent to which education brings about each of these changes will vary with both the amount of schooling and the particular change being considered. For example, the difference between 2 and 4 years of primary-level education may be critical with respect to the acquisition of literacy but not necessarily as important with regard to learning skills that are highly valued in the labor market. In any case, these changes associated with increasing educational attainment influence the opportunities open to an individual, the attitudes and information possessed by the individual, and the individual's behavior, and these influences are likely to lead to changes in fertility. Figure 8.1 (from Cochrane 1979, 29) shows the changes directly associated with an individual's acquisition of education.

In the context of the Easterlin approach to fertility, there are several factors that influence the potential supply of children, including (among others) the probability of marriage, wife's age at marriage, health, duration of breastfeeding, taboos on sexual activity, and infant and child mortality. Each of these factors, in turn, is likely to be influenced by a woman's educational attainment. With respect to number of children demanded (often approximated by desired family size), attitudes regarding ideal family size, perceived benefits of children, perceived costs of children, and the prospective ability to pay for the costs of children are all relevant factors that are likely to be influenced by a woman's schooling.

156   Chapter 8

Fig. 8.1 Multiple effects of individual education

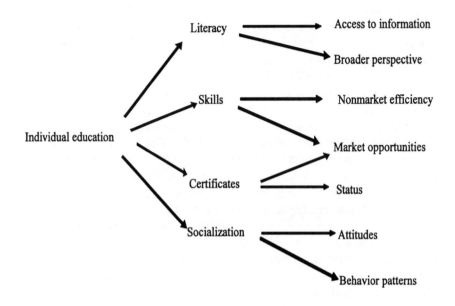

Source: Cochran (1979, 29).

The motivation for fertility control exists when the potential supply of children exceeds the number demanded. If (as we argue below) greater mother's schooling contributes to lower infant and child mortality and shorter durations of breast-feeding and postpartum abstinence, then supply is increased;[3] if greater mother's education tends also to reduce the number of children demanded, this further enhances the likelihood of supply exceeding demand. In these circumstances, then, increased women's education will be associated with a greater motivation for using contraception. In this situation, use of contraception is not automatic, as it will depend on the perceived costs (psychological as well as monetary) of contraception. In particular, attitudes toward fertility regulation, knowledge of contraception, and communication between husband and wife on these issues are relevant in this context.

It is, thus, apparent that there are numerous mechanisms through which education may influence fertility. We turn now to consider these mechanisms within the context of Kinshasa and in sub-Saharan Africa more generally.

[3] Reduced infant and child mortality means that a higher proportion of births will survive to adulthood, while shorter durations of postpartum abstinence increase a woman's exposure to the risk of becoming pregnant. Breast-feeding tends to prolong periods of postpartum amenorrhea, so (as noted in chapter 6) reduced durations of breast-feeding shorten periods of postpartum infecundability, and this also tends to increase a woman's likelihood of becoming pregnant.

Evidence on Education and Fertility Behavior

We begin with a review of the evidence presented in the preceding chapters pertaining to women's education and the proximate determinants of fertility as well as evidence on the timing of the onset of childbearing. In addition, we provide supplementary analyses for Kinshasa on a number of the points discussed, including how mother's education is related to perinatal mortality, aspirations for children's education, and desired fertility. We also examine a number of the relations under consideration using data from each of the 27 countries in sub-Saharan Africa where DHS surveys have been carried out.[4]

In chapter 5 we saw that enrollment in school was strongly associated with delays in the onset of sexual activity, marriage, and childbearing. The event-history analyses of the timing of these events were not able to examine the impact of the level of schooling.[5] However, even when these events (and especially first marriage and first birth) occur relatively early, they are most likely to occur at ages when women who are enrolled will have at least reached lower-level secondary school.[6] Hence, the evidence of a strong impact of school enrollment in delaying these events suggests that attainment of secondary education, in particular, is an important factor contributing to the overall effect on fertility of reaching and progressing through secondary school.

Direct evidence on the bivariate relation between educational attainment and the age at onset of sexual activity shows a positive effect of the former on the latter. Among women in Kinshasa aged 25 and over, the median age at first intercourse is 16 for those in the three lowest schooling groups and increases to 17, 18, and 19, respectively, for the three highest educational attainment groups. Data on age at first sexual activity from the DHS surveys indicates that,

[4] The figures reported below are based on a data set compiled from the most recent DHS reports for those countries in sub-Saharan Africa that had had at least one DHS survey (we did not consider countries usually classified as part of sub-Saharan Africa but not on the continent, such as Comoros and Madagascar, nor did we consider the 1989-1990 DHS that covered northern Sudan). For the variables of interest, we calculated simple unweighted means for three schooling groups: none; primary; and secondary and higher. In some cases the DHS reports provided more detailed educational categories (most commonly, incomplete primary was separated out from complete primary, but, in a few cases, data were given separately for women with secondary education and those with higher education). For these cases we calculated a weighted average for the education group in question, with the weights reflecting the relative proportions within the group of the two component subgroups.

[5] In order to assess the impact of level of schooling in the context of the event-history approach, we would need to know a woman's level of schooling for every year of her adolescence and early adulthood. This information was not available in our data set—we knew only each woman's highest level of schooling attained and the year she left school.

[6] In chapter 9, we note that more than half of 15-year-old female students in Kinshasa in 1990 were enrolled in either the first or the second year of secondary school (32 percent of enrolled females aged 15 were still in primary school, while about 15 percent had already gone beyond the second year of secondary school). As is evident from figure 5.1, by age 15, fewer than 30 percent of young women have experienced first intercourse, about 20 percent have entered a first union, and fewer than 10 percent have had a first birth.

on average, this age is 16 for women with no schooling, 17 for those with a primary education, and 19 for those with secondary or higher schooling.

In the same vein, when examining the relation between educational attainment and age at first marriage among women aged 25 and over in chapter 6, we saw that the median age at first union was systematically positively related to women's education. Women with no schooling or only primary schooling had a median age at first marriage of almost 17 years, compared to roughly 18 for those with only 1 or 2 years of secondary education, 19 for those with 3-4 years of secondary schooling, 21 for women with upper-level secondary education, and 24 for those with university education.

This tendency for secondary schooling or more to be associated with delays in the onset of marriage is apparent elsewhere as well, including both in earlier World Fertility Surveys (United Nations 1986) and in more recent Demographic and Health Surveys in sub-Saharan Africa. Information from DHS reports on median age at marriage by educational attainment shows that, overall, the (unweighted) average median age at first union was 17 for women with no schooling, 18 for those with primary-level education, and 21 for women with at least some secondary education.

Examination of our 1990 Kinshasa data on marital status shows that, especially among women aged 20-29, higher levels of educational attainment are associated with distinctly lower likelihoods that a woman will describe herself as married. For example, among women aged 25-29 with no, primary, or lower-level secondary schooling, between about 80 and 90 percent of each group is married, while the percentages fall to about 70-75 percent for those with mid- or upper-level secondary education and to less than half for university-educated women.

Analysis of the median age at first birth by educational attainment among women aged 25 and over reveals that this age is also positively related to schooling. It is 17 or 18 for the three lowest educational attainment groups, rising to 20 for those with 3-4 years of secondary schooling, 22 for those with upper-level secondary education, and 27 for women with university education. In a population where the use of modern contraception is low, these figures foreshadow differences in completed fertility. Data from the DHS surveys show a similar pattern: median age at first birth is just over 19 for women with no or only primary schooling and 21.5 for women with secondary or higher education.

Delayed onset of sexual activity, marriage, and childbearing as well as a lower likelihood of being married are factors linked to acquisition of secondary schooling that tend to reduce the supply of children. However, there are other factors related to women's educational attainment that have the effect of increasing supply.

The analyses of breast-feeding and postpartum abstinence in chapter 6 also find significant relations with educational attainment, albeit not quite as strong and consistent as those for the other proximate determinants.[7] Women with higher levels of education tend to have shorter durations of breast-feeding and shorter periods of postpartum abstinence. By making these better-educated women more susceptible to becoming pregnant following a birth, these differences, then, tend to increase the supply of children, all else equal, and, hence, increase the motivation for fertility control. Cochrane (1979) and the World Fertility Surveys (United Nations 1986) reported similar results, as do the DHS surveys. Overall, the DHS results indicate that, on average, the duration of postpartum insusceptibility declines from 18 months for women with no education, to 15 months for those with primary schooling, to 11 months for women with secondary or higher education.

An additional supply consideration is that based on the relation between women's educational attainment, on the one hand, and infant and child mortality, on the other.[8] In a study of perinatal mortality done in the nine largest obstetric units in Kinshasa during the early 1980s and covering almost 27,000 births, Nzita (1989) found that, among mothers in Kinshasa, increases in levels of educational attainment resulted in progressively lower mortality. Mothers with 4 or more years of secondary schooling experienced a level of perinatal mortality that was only 61 percent of the level of mortality experienced by mothers with no schooling and the perinatal mortality level of those with primary schooling was 88 percent of that of women who had not been to school (Nzita 1989, 36).

These findings for Kinshasa parallel similar findings of an inverse association between mother's education and infant and child mortality in a large number of different settings in sub-Saharan Africa as well as in other developing countries (see, e.g., Cleland and Van Ginneken 1988; Bicego and Boerma 1993; Agyei and Ssekamatte-Ssebuliba 2000). There is debate in the literature concerning the relative importance of different mechanisms of influence, which include differences in reproductive behavior (better-educated women are often less likely to engage in childbearing at relatively young and relatively old ages, at which the risk of infant and child mortality is greater) and differential use of health care services (which may occur for various reasons, including education-related differences in knowledge of and attitudes toward health care as well as differences in household economic well-being correlated with women's education). However, the empirical evidence indicating that better-educated mothers tend to experience distinctly lower infant and child mortality is quite strong.

Among the sub-Saharan countries covered by the DHS surveys, for example, the infant mortality rate averages 100, declining from 103 for women

[7] That is, as may be seen in table 6.6 above, there are some insignificant and anomalous coefficients for women with 1-2 or 3-4 years of secondary schooling. Only for upper-level secondary and university women are the relations clearly and consistently strongly negative.

[8] We have not carried out analyses of the relation between mother's education and infant and child mortality with our 1990 data because of the comparatively small sample sizes of infants and children for a number of the educational attainment groups in our data set.

with no schooling to 90 for those with primary schooling, and then falling more sharply to 61 for women with secondary and higher education. Similarly, under-5 mortality ranges from 184 to 153 to 97 across the same three education groups. The substantial decline in mortality of infants and children of women with secondary education evident in these data was observed as well in a multivariate analysis of DHS data from Uganda, prompting Agyei and Ssekamatte-Ssebuliba (2000, 240) to describe secondary education as a "threshold level" in considering the link between maternal education and infant and child mortality.

These findings imply that, all else equal, the supply of children will be greater for better-educated mothers and especially so for women with secondary education. This, in turn, as noted in the preceding section, translates into a greater motivation for these women to engage in fertility control. Consider now the link between women's schooling and the demand for children.

We begin by examining the relation between mother's education and aspirations for children's education. Table 8.1 shows data on the level of education desired for a hypothetical next child, according to the child's gender and the woman's educational attainment.[9] Relatively high proportions of women with little or no schooling did not specify desired education for children. As women's education increases, so does the likelihood that they will have specific aspirations for the schooling of their children. Further, it is apparent from the responses that increasing women's educational attainment is strongly positively associated with the amount of schooling that these women want their children to have. For example, the percentage of women desiring either a 5-year university degree or graduate training for their children rises steadily as one moves from lower to higher levels of women's educational attainment, with especially large increases in moving from low- to mid-level secondary schooling.

This is true with respect to both prospective daughters and sons, although clearly educational aspirations of women are higher for sons than for daughters: proportionately, almost twice as many women aspire to the highest two education levels shown for a son as for a daughter (58 percent vs. 31 percent). Conversely, a high school education is desired for proportionately twice as many daughters as sons. Given the notion of a quality-quantity trade-off (Becker and Lewis 1973), which suggests that the desire for greater levels of education for one's children will be associated with a higher cost of children and, hence, a desire for a reduced number of children, these data imply that better-educated women will desire fewer children.

Direct evidence on this point may be seen in table 8.2, which shows desired fertility according to the woman's educational attainment.[10] The table

---

[9] More specifically, the table shows the desired education given in response to the following questions: "If you were to have a girl (boy) now, up to what level would you like to see her (him) pursue her (his) schooling?"

[10] As in the Demographic and Health Surveys and other surveys about fertility preferences, we asked two different questions, according to whether the woman already had children. For women with no children ever born, the question asked was, "If you could choose exactly the

Table 8.1 Desired Education for Children, by Child's Gender and Woman's Educational Attainment (percentage distributions)

Desired Education Level	Woman's Educational Attainment						
	None	Primary	Sec. 1-2	Sec. 3-4	Sec. 5-6	Univ.	Total
A. For a Daughter							
High school	33	49	43	31	21	5	36
3-yr. univ.	15	14	18	24	27	24	20
5-yr. univ.	12	15	22	31	37	43	25
Grad. work	2	3	4	7	12	24	6
Don't know	38	19	14	7	4	5	13
Total	100	100	100	100	100	100	100
B. For a Son							
High school	22	31	26	10	3	2	18
3-yr. univ.	9	11	12	12	5	4	10
5-yr. univ.	27	32	39	50	60	48	43
Grad. work	2	7	9	21	25	44	15
Don't know	40	19	15	7	6	2	14
Total	100	100	100	100	100	100	100

Source: Calculated from our 1990 data.

reports responses that were numeric and excludes nonquantifiable responses such as "don't know" or "up to God." It is worth noting that the percentage of nonquantifiable responses is inversely related to educational attainment, falling from 34 percent for women with no schooling, to 17 percent for those with primary education, and to about 5 percent or less for women with mid-level secondary schooling or more.

The table shows percentage distributions across three size categories as well as the average number of children desired. These data are quite consistent with those presented in table 8.1 above (in terms of the quality-quantity trade-off concept), in that women's educational attainment is strongly inversely related to the desired number of children. The proportion of women desiring three or fewer children—clearly rather small families in the context of Kinshasa and, more generally, sub-Saharan Africa—is fairly low and rises only modestly as educational attainment increases. However, the percentage of women expressing a desire for four or five children—still relatively small families in Kinshasa, especially as compared to the size of the families of origin of these women—rises almost steadily as one moves across schooling groups. Conversely, the percentage desiring large families (six or more children) falls sharply, particularly in going from the no-schooling group to those with

number of children that you desire, how many children would you like to have in total?" For women who had children, however, the question asked was, "If you could start over at the time when you had no children and could choose exactly the number of children that you desire, how many children would you like to have in total?" This latter question is designed to minimize the impact of the actual number of children ever born on the woman's statement of the desired number.

162   Chapter 8

Table 8.2 Desired Fertility, by Educational Attainment (percentage distributions and means)

Desired No. of	Woman's Educational Attainment						
Children	None	Primary	Sec. 1-2	Sec. 3-4	Sec. 5-6	Univ.	Total
3 or less	16	14	18	21	21	23	18
4 or 5	33	47	54	58	57	65	53
6 or more	51	40	28	21	21	13	29
Total	100	100	100	100	100	100	100
Mean	5.9	5.6	4.9	4.7	4.6	4.4	5.0

Source: Calculated from our 1990 data.

primary schooling and then lower-level secondary education. The average number of children desired declines steadily in moving across the educational attainment groups, from nearly 6 for women with no schooling to about 4½ for those in the two highest educational attainment groups.

An inverse association between fertility preferences and women's education is also reported by Cochrane (1979) and may be found as well in the DHS data. Among women with no education, the average ideal number of children is 6.5, compared to 5.2 for women with primary schooling and 4.1 for women with secondary or higher education. These preferences are not very far from the total fertility rates (TFRs) by educational attainment from the DHS data. Among women with no schooling, the average TFR was 6.4, while it was 5.6 for women with a primary education and 3.8 for those with secondary or higher schooling.

Clearly, then, women with secondary education have a lower demand for numbers of children. As we have already seen, in conjunction with this lower demand there are several factors associated with women's schooling that point toward an increased supply of children. Within the Easterlin framework, increased supply and reduced demand imply greater motivation for fertility control. Consideration of both contraception and abortion and how they are related to women's educational attainment suggests that better-educated women indeed tend to have a greater excess of supply over demand than do their counterparts with less schooling.

In the multivariate analyses reported in table 6.4 above, contraceptive use, both with respect to any method and with respect to modern methods, was significantly related to educational attainment, all else equal. Overall, there is a strong tendency for contraceptive use to increase with educational attainment. This is readily shown by the bivariate relations given in table 7.3 above. Among women with no schooling, just over a third were current users of contraception (any method), while a little more than 40 percent of women with primary schooling were practicing contraception. By contrast, the percentage of contraceptive users among women with higher levels of schooling rose steadily as education increased, ranging from 56 percent for those with lower-level secondary schooling to 73 percent for women with university education. Current use of modern contraception was also positively related to educational attainment, although the variation was more modest, ranging from 5 percent for women with no schooling to 16 percent for those with a university education, and ranging only from 9 to 11 percent for those with intermediate levels of schooling.

Cochrane (1979) reported evidence of a positive association between women's educational attainment and contraceptive use, similar evidence was apparent from the World Fertility Surveys (United Nations 1986), and the DHS data also show this phenomenon. Current use of any contraceptive method in the DHS data averages 12 percent for women with no schooling, 20 percent for those with primary education, and 39 percent for those with secondary or higher schooling. The corresponding figures for use of modern contraception are 6, 12, and 27 percent, respectively. In both cases, then, there is substantial variation across groups, especially between better-educated women (the highest group) and those with comparatively little or no schooling (the two lower groups).

The modest differences in the practice of modern contraception by education group in Kinshasa clearly do not provide very much support for the impact of education on fertility via contraception since, while the direction is correct, the magnitude is small. However, it appears that differences by educational attainment in recourse to abortion are an important factor contributing to the observed fertility differentials (Shapiro and Tambashe 1994a). The multivariate analyses of abortion reported in chapter 6 reveal sharp differences by schooling level, particularly so for women with upper-level secondary and university education. The bivariate relations in table 7.5 above show the same phenomenon, with 30 percent and more of the women in the two highest educational attainment groups having had an abortion, compared to 10 percent or less for women with primary or no schooling and about 15 percent for those with 1-4 years of secondary education.

In sum, there are clear differences, both in Kinshasa and elsewhere in sub-Saharan Africa, in the extent of fertility control by women's educational attainment. These differences, along with the evidence on factors related to supply of and demand for children, are indicative of excess supply that increases with higher levels of women's schooling.

Summary and Conclusions

This chapter has pulled together and reviewed evidence from Kinshasa and elsewhere in sub-Saharan Africa on the factors contributing to the important impact of secondary education on fertility. Within the context of the Easterlin framework for fertility analysis, we have seen that various proximate determinants are related to women's educational attainment so as to imply lower fertility for women who have at least reached the secondary schooling level (as compared to women with no schooling or only a primary education), with fertility declining fairly sharply as schooling increases throughout the secondary level and beyond to the university level.

More specifically, women with secondary or higher education tend to initiate sexual activity later, tend to marry later, are less likely to be married, and tend to delay the onset of childbearing as compared to women with low or no schooling. These factors tend to reduce the supply of children. Other factors, however, tend to increase the supply of children. For example, better-educated women have shorter durations of breast-feeding and postpartum abstinence and, hence, shorter periods of postpartum infecundability. Further, previous research in Kinshasa has also documented a clear inverse relation between mother's education and early infant mortality. Within the Easterlin framework, this implies a greater supply of children to better-educated mothers, all else equal, and would be expected in turn to contribute to a greater propensity to control fertility. These and other findings reported in this chapter concord well with findings from the various DHS surveys done throughout sub-Saharan Africa, and they are also consistent with findings from earlier research as well as from research in other developing countries.

Direct evidence on educational aspirations for children and on desired fertility has also indicated that better-educated women are distinctly more likely to aspire to higher levels of education for their children and to desire fewer children, as compared to women with low levels of education. Indeed, a related aspect here is that women with little or no schooling are considerably more likely than those who have reached the secondary level of education not to have formulated aspirations for the education of their children or desires concerning their own fertility. That is, women with little or no schooling appear to be more likely to have a fatalistic approach to their children's education and their own fertility. In sharp contrast, women with secondary and higher education are much more likely to have formulated aspirations and desires in these areas that contribute to a willingness and desire to limit their own fertility.

Given increased supply of children and reduced demand among women with secondary and higher schooling, the implication in the Easterlin framework is that these women will have a greater motivation for fertility control. The evidence, both for Kinshasa and for elsewhere in sub-Saharan Africa, is consistent with this notion. These better-educated women are distinctly more likely to be contraceptive users and to be users of modern contraception. Among those in Kinshasa who have ever been pregnant, the better-educated women are also more likely to have had an abortion.

As noted earlier in chapter 3, in his formidable and exhaustive study of fertility in the Congo based on the massive survey done in the mid-1950s, Anatole Romaniuk argued that "the rather profound social transformations that the African city has been subjected to do not . . . seem to have notably affected the attitudes of urban dwellers with regard to procreation" (Romaniuk 1967, 324). While Romaniuk's assessment was an accurate one at that time, it is clear that in the three and a half decades following that survey, the attitudes and behaviors of women in Kinshasa with regard to procreation changed substantially. These changes, closely linked to women's acquisition of formal education and especially education at and beyond the secondary school level, have resulted in the onset of fertility transition in Kinshasa, and they foreshadow continuing declines in fertility.

Part III

Schooling, Extended-Family Solidarity,
Employment in the Formal
and Informal Sectors, and Migration

Chapter 9. Gender, Poverty, Family Structure, and Investments in Children's Education

This chapter examines gender differences in school enrollment and educational attainment in Kinshasa, with particular emphasis on the impact of poverty, household structure or composition, and economic well-being more generally on investments in children's education and differences by gender in such investments. Gender differences in resource allocation within the household and the links between conditions in the labor market and parental investments in children in low-income settings have been the subject of research by a number of economists (e.g., Rosenzweig and Schultz 1982; Pitt et al. 1990; Thomas 1990). Several years ago, a symposium on investments in women's human capital and development included papers (Parish and Willis 1993; Deolalikar 1993; Vijverberg 1993) that dealt with education and more specifically with gender differences in returns to schooling, educational attainment, and school enrollment. More recently, Lloyd and Blanc (1996) have examined data from seven countries in sub-Saharan Africa, analyzing factors influencing school enrollment, educational attainment, and gender differences in schooling, and Glick and Sahn (2000) have investigated gender differences in the determinants of several measures of schooling.

Educational attainment of the workforce is a very important factor contributing to economic growth (Mankiw et al.1992), and gender differences in schooling may be viewed as a key indicator of gender inequality. If economic growth and development tend to result in diminished gender differences in educational attainment, then the consequent reduction in gender inequality constitutes an additional benefit of growth and development over and above improvements in the material standard of living. Further, as we have seen in chapter 4, increased schooling of women, particularly secondary schooling, has been closely associated with declines in fertility in Kinshasa, and there is considerable literature indicating the importance of women's education for fertility both in sub-Saharan Africa and elsewhere in the developing world (see, e.g., Ainsworth et al. 1996; Muhuri et al. 1994).

A major factor influencing investments in children's education is the economic well-being of the household in which they reside (Schultz 1993). Sub-Saharan Africa is characterized by a considerable degree of interhousehold resource transfers (typically within the extended family) in support of children's education (as we shall see for Kinshasa in the following chapter) and also by a substantial amount of child fostering (Page 1989), often with a view to enhancing children's educational opportunities. Despite these influences, however, it is nonetheless the case that the economic well-being of the household in which a child resides is a strong determinant of educational investment in the child (Lloyd and Blanc 1996; Shapiro and Tambashe 1999b, 2001b). Opportunities for attending school as well as progress in school are especially likely to be more limited for children from poor households (Colclough with Lewin 1993; Lloyd and Blanc 1996).

In this context, both the direct costs of participation in school, in the form of school uniforms, supplies, and fees, and the opportunity costs are likely to loom large, especially for children from poor households. Indeed, given the chronic high levels of inflation characterizing the economy of Kinshasa, prices for goods and services (including in the public sector) are frequently set in hard currencies, generally the U.S. dollar or the Belgian franc. By contrast, wages and salaries are expressed in local currency and represent very little in real terms, even for top-level civil servants and private-sector employees. In addition, wages and salaries are not paid regularly, either to civil servants or to some private-sector employees. This makes it particularly difficult for households that are typically struggling for survival to cope with school costs, especially at the beginning of the school year (September), when expenses to send children back to school loom very large.[1]

In their examination of investments in children's education and gender differences in such investments, Lloyd and Blanc (1996, 266) note that "the resources of a child's residential household—in particular, the education of the household head and the household standard of living—are determining factors in explaining differences among children in . . . school outcomes." However, while some observers (e.g., Schultz 1993; Parish and Willis 1993) have suggested that greater economic well-being is associated with reduced gender inequality in human capital investments, this conclusion is by no means universal (cf. Deolalikar 1993; Lloyd and Blanc 1996; Shapiro and Tambashe 1999b).

Elsewhere, we have examined gender differences in school enrollment of

[1] While the monthly pay for a high-ranking civil servant or a university full professor is barely worth $50, the costs for sending a child back to school can easily be more than double that sum. Further, as noted by Sala-Diakanda (1997, 363 n. 5), salaries of those employed by the government frequently go unpaid for months at a time.

youths, and how those differences changed as one moved from very poor to relatively well-off households (Shapiro and Tambashe 1999b). Here, we extend our analyses to consider educational attainment as well. Following Lloyd and Blanc (1996), we examine the factors influencing whether children aged 10-14 have reached at least the fourth year of primary school. Achievement of grade level 4 has been identified by UNICEF (1993) as a key indicator of school progress for children and will presumably reflect age of entry to school and the rate of progress from grade to grade. In addition, we analyze factors influencing whether youths aged 15-19 have reached at least the third year of secondary school (ninth grade). This level marks the beginning of the last 4 years of secondary education in the Congolese education system, following a 2-year orientation cycle,[2] and, as we have seen in chapter 4, it is associated with significantly lower fertility among women in Kinshasa.

In this chapter, then, we address the question of how school enrollment and progress in school (grade-level attainment) are influenced by household economic well-being. In this context, we examine how (if at all) gender differences in these human capital investments in children vary with the household standard of living. Reflecting the importance of child fostering in urban sub-Saharan Africa, the analyses also assess the link between a school-age individual's relationship to the head of the household and educational attainment. In addition, we examine the effects of household composition or structure on the grade-level attainment of school-age youths, taking into consideration the number and ages of other youths in the household, who potentially compete for limited household resources.

The next section reviews some analytic issues and looks at results from relevant studies, with particular emphasis on the role of economic well-being on investments in children's education and on gender differences in such investments. Hypotheses and evidence pertaining to the effects on school enrollment and educational attainment of household size and composition are also reviewed. This is followed by a section laying out the methodology, including the basic empirical model to be estimated for examining children's educational attainment. The subsequent sections provide empirical findings, beginning with an overview of enrollment rates by age and gender among youths aged 6-25 and of enrollment status and grade-level attainment by age. We then look at multivariate logistic regressions analyzing the determinants of educational attainment among youths aged 10-14 and 15-19. The concluding section provides a summary and discussion of our results and points to the likely consequences of the persistent deterioration of the Congolese economy for investments in education in Kinshasa and in the country as a whole.

---

[2] Following the *cycle d'orientation*, which constitutes the beginning of secondary schooling in the Congo, continuing students are oriented (on the basis of their aptitude and performance) toward either a short (2-year) cycle for vocational education or a long (4-year) cycle focused either on more advanced technical (vocational) studies or on preparation for higher education.

Analytic Issues and Previous Empirical Work

Schooling is but one of three broad activities in which children in developing countries may engage: market work and home production are competing alternatives. Hence, as Skoufias (1994) and others have noted, adult and child market wage rates and opportunities as well as household demographic composition are likely to influence the time allocation of children among schooling, work at home, and work in the market.

There is good reason to expect that household income will be a significant determinant of children's schooling and educational attainment. If the schooling of children is regarded as a normal consumption good, then household income should be positively related to the demand for schooling. If, alternatively, emphasis is put on the investment aspects of schooling, it is still likely that higher parents' income will result in greater demand. In particular, Schultz (1993) notes that parents in low-income countries may underinvest in the schooling of their children, even when returns on the investment are good, owing to risk aversion and/or credit constraints; and he adds that both these factors are likely to be important among the poor. Hence, higher incomes will attenuate the effects of risk aversion and credit constraints on the demand for education. Parish and Willis (1993) note that credit constraints may lead to birth-order effects on educational investments in children, and they also discuss a "resource-dilution" perspective in which number of siblings and birth order may influence a child's opportunities for acquiring an education.

Consider now the question, How do gender differences in school participation and educational attainment vary by income level? In considering gender differences in the educational investments that parents make in their children, several contributing factors can be cited (Behrman et al. 1986; Parish and Willis 1993; Schultz 1993). Returns to education might be greater for males than for females, inducing parents to provide more schooling to their sons than to their daughters (Rosenzweig and Schultz 1982). In this regard, Schultz's (1993) observation that the increased human capital investment in women relative to men that has characterized experience in many countries during this century is concomitant with women's increased participation in the wage labor force (where more returns to investment in their education can be realized) is especially pertinent.

In addition to the influence of gender differences in the individual private returns to education, parents also might invest more heavily in sons than in daughters if they expect greater future flows of remittances from their male offspring. This factor is most likely to be relevant in patrilineal cultures where there are significant resource flows from children to parents and where a woman's family affiliation changes from that of her father to that of her husband when she marries. In reviewing this "lingering patriarchy" explanation for gender differences in schooling, Parish and Willis (1993, 866) argue that "the exploitation of daughters for family advantage is particularly strong when there are more sons in the family needing education in order to have the well-paid jobs that will allow them to support the parents well in old age."

Finally, parents might also invest more heavily in male offspring, independently of gender differences in returns to education or in expected remittances, if they value the economic success of their sons more highly than that of their daughters. This corresponds to what Behrman et al. (1986) describe as parents favoring boys.

Economic theory provides little guidance on the question of gender differences in educational investments. That is, as Deolalikar (1993) has pointed out in discussing his analysis of school enrollment of children, whether the process of intrahousehold resource allocation is viewed as the outcome of a constrained maximization of a unified household utility function or as the outcome of a bargaining process within the family, it results in a system of reduced-form demand equations for children's schooling, but, in the absence of restrictive assumptions (e.g., regarding preferences or education production functions), such an approach does not yield very many testable hypotheses.

Since theory provides no guidance on this question, it is useful to consider conjectures and evidence provided by different researchers. Schultz (1993, 695) raises the possibility that, independently of the magnitude of the private returns to investments in human capital, "as parents become wealthier, they may attach greater value to equalizing their investments in their daughters and sons." If this were indeed the case, there would be distinctly larger gender differentials in school enrollment and educational attainment among children from poor households than among children from financially well-off households.

Based on cross-country comparisons from 1950 to 1980, Schultz (1987) has found positive income elasticities and negative price elasticities of school enrollments and, further, these elasticities are larger in absolute value for female enrollment rates than for male enrollment rates. He has also observed greater responsiveness of female enrollment rates to changes in income and prices over time within countries (Schultz 1989). Given that male enrollment exceeds female enrollment at low incomes, these patterns are consistent with Schultz's conjecture that, as income increases, parents may put greater weight on equalizing investments in male and female children.

Parish and Willis (1993) emphasize that family investment decisions may be credit constrained, and they note in this context their expectation that gender differentials would be smaller the higher the parents' income and the smaller the number of children. On the basis of their empirical work on Taiwan, they conclude that "children's educational outcomes were highly dependent on economic security. . . . Families with low incomes chose more carefully who in the home got educated. . . . Among the most secure families, things were radically different. In this group, siblings essentially had no effect on educational opportunity" (Parish and Willis 1993, 885-886). This conclusion suggests the presence of an interaction between family economic well-being and household composition, with the latter influencing who enrolls in school in low-income households but not in high-income households. More generally, Parish and Willis (1993, 891), echoing Schultz's theme, argue on the basis of their research that "once families have the prospect of more income . . . sons and daughters begin to get more equal education."

The research by Schultz and by Parish and Willis cited above suggests that, by contributing to more rapid increases in school enrollment and educational attainment of females as compared to males, increased income will lead to a narrowing of gender differences as income increases. Consistent with this view, Sathar and Lloyd (1994) find evidence of such narrowing in primary schools in Pakistan, particularly in urban areas, and Glick and Sahn (2000) find that increases in household income lead to greater investments in girls' (but not boys') schooling in Conakry, Guinea. However, while Deolalikar's analysis of school enrollment in Indonesia finds that higher household (nonlabor) income significantly increases enrollment probabilities, it failed to detect any significant difference by gender in the effect of income on the likelihood of being enrolled in school.[3] Further, Lloyd and Blanc (1996) find that, in five of the seven African countries that they study, school enrollment of boys aged 6-14 is more responsive to an increased standard of living than is enrollment of girls and that, in four of the countries, educational attainment of boys is more strongly affected by household economic well-being than is that of girls. Our analyses of school enrollment in Kinshasa (Shapiro and Tambashe 1999b) indicate that gender differences are widest, not in the poorest segment of the population, but rather in the next-poorest group. Hence, there appears to be mixed evidence in the literature concerning the effects of income and household standard of living on gender differences in school enrollment and educational attainment.

In addition to income, greater education of the household head is also associated with increased schooling of youths. Lloyd and Blanc (1996), for example, find that increases in education of the household head are strongly associated with increased enrollment rates and educational attainment in the countries that they study. In some cases, the differences are modest, while, in others, they are substantial. However, there is no clear pattern of these education effects on gender differences in enrollment. In four countries, increased head's schooling raises enrollment of girls by more than that of boys, while, in three countries, the reverse is true; in only two countries is girls' educational attainment more sensitive than that of boys to greater education of the household head, while in the other five countries boys appear to benefit more than girls from being in a household with a relatively well-educated head.

Gender of the household head has also been found to be a relevant influ-

---

[3] In fact, Deolalikar's results suggest that the impact of income on school enrollment tends to be if anything higher for males than for females. For youths aged 18-23, he reports a positive coefficient on the male-income interaction term, with an asymptotic t-statistic of 1.6 (Deolalikar 1993, 927-928). For youths aged 15-17, the reported interaction coefficient is 0.000.

ence on investments in children's education. Lloyd and Blanc (1996) cite previous research documenting that female heads of households spend a larger percentage of the household budget on children than do male heads and note that female-headed households often tend to be disadvantaged economically. After controlling for the socioeconomic status of the household as well as other factors, the authors find that "children living in households headed by women are consistently more likely to be enrolled in school and to have completed grade four than children living in households headed by men" (Lloyd and Blanc 1996, 288). Further, their results indicate that gender differences in school investments in children tend to be smaller in female-headed households.

There is also evidence that household size and composition can influence the likelihood that any individual school-age member of the household is in school. This issue received considerable attention from Parish and Willis (1993), whose review of alternative hypotheses concerning how parents choose to invest in the education of their children highlights different possibilities concerning the effects of number of siblings and birth order. For example, their discussion of resource dilution suggests that large family size will tend to lower educational attainment for all children. At the same time, they note that, in many developing-country settings, "a large number of children in the family can lead not to universal resource dilution but to improved opportunities for the late born. Once they begin to work, early born children continue to send or bring resources back to the family. . . . [W]hen family obligations are strong, credit constraints help produce large inter-temporal transfers among siblings" (Parish and Willis 1993, 868-869). Simons (1994, 26) has argued that this sort of "sibling chain of educational assistance" is quite common in sub-Saharan Africa.[4]

More directly, Chernichovsky's study (1985) of schooling in Botswana found that the number of school-age children in a household was positively related to the likelihood of a child being enrolled in school. He interpreted this finding as reflecting reduced demand for the labor of any individual child at home when more children are available and, hence, a lower opportunity cost of schooling. His perspective emphasizes the importance of household demographic composition in influencing the demand for and supply of labor for home production activities.

Lloyd and Blanc (1996) find that the presence of very young children (ages 0-5) tends to be associated with lower school enrollment of youths aged 6-14 and less educational attainment of youths aged 10-14, presumably reflecting increased demand for child care, an activity often performed by school-age youths. At the same time, similar to Chernichovsky, they find that increased numbers of school-age children (ages 6-14) are consistently associated with higher enrollment rates of those aged 6-14, and they also find higher edu-

---

[4] A "sibling chain of educational assistance" may be seen as part of a broader phenomenon of an "inter- and intra-generational chain of solidarity." For a discussion of family solidarity, see chapter 10.

cational attainment in families with greater numbers of school-age youths. It should be noted, however, that the magnitudes of the estimated effects are often rather modest.

There is an additional aspect of household size and composition that has not been taken into consideration in these studies of educational attainment and school enrollment but that is especially pertinent in considering behavior in urban sub-Saharan Africa. This is the relationship of children to the head of the household. For the most part, the papers that have been discussed here implicitly treat the household as consisting of a nuclear family—parents and their own children.[5] However, there is a considerable degree of child fostering that takes place in Kinshasa (see chapter 10) as elsewhere in sub-Saharan Africa (Page 1989; Ainsworth 1992; McDaniel and Zulu 1996). Fostering of rural children to urban environments may provide them with greater and diversified opportunities for schooling as compared to what is available at home. Alternatively, child fostering may occur in response to a demand for child care and child labor more generally. In any case, the existence of fostering means that a significant proportion of school-age children in Kinshasa are not living with their parents and that parents are responsible for children other than their own (typically, children who are part of one parent or the other's extended family). For example, among youths aged 6-14 in Kinshasa, 22 percent were not children of the household head or the head's spouse; among those aged 15-19, the corresponding figure was 27 percent.[6]

In addition to a good deal of child fostering, Kinshasa is also characterized by a substantial degree of resource flows between and among households, again predominantly involving people who are members of the same extended family (Shapiro et al. 1995; chapter 10). Given such practices, questions of resource allocation to investments in human capital of children in the household become more complex since resources may come from outside the household to support the schooling of one or more children in the household. This support may be for children who are fostered in to the household, but it may also involve the kinds of intragenerational resource flows from older to younger siblings that have been emphasized by Parish and Willis (1993) and by Simons (1994).

As part of the analyses presented in this chapter, we examine how school-age individuals who are not children of the head of the household fare with regard to educational attainment. While such individuals may have available to them resources coming from outside the household, we expect that parents will value the economic success of their own offspring more highly than that of

---

[5] The notable exception is the paper by Lloyd and Blanc (1996), which reports results of analyses of school enrollment and educational attainment according to parents' survival status and discusses extended-family support networks as they relate to child fostering and children's schooling.

[6] By comparison, Lloyd and Blanc (1996) found that, in five of the seven countries that they examined, 27-28 percent of youths aged 6-14 were not living with a biological parent but that in Kenya the corresponding figure was 20 percent and in Namibia it was 51 percent.

other members of the extended family. On balance, then, we expect that not being a child of the head of the household will be associated with a lower likelihood of being enrolled in school and of reaching any given level of schooling.

Data and Methodology

Respondents to our 1990 survey provided information on the age, gender, school enrollment status, educational attainment, and relationship to the head of the household of all members of their household aged 6-25. These data allow one to examine the impact on school enrollment and educational attainment of age, gender, household characteristics (including the economic well-being of the household, the gender of the household head, and the age composition of children in the household), and relationship of the individual to the head of the household.[7]

Economic well-being (the household standard of living) is measured by the index that enumerates the number of working consumer durable goods in the respondent's household, and that was first introduced in the analyses in chapter 6.[8] The index in principle can range from 0 to 13, but over a quarter of school-age youths in Kinshasa are from households with a value of 0 on the index, and an additional 15 percent have a value of only 1. These two groups, representing 42 percent of Kinshasa's youths aged 6-25, are considered as the poverty groups in this chapter.[9]

The analysis of the data begins with an overview of school enrollment by age and gender for youths aged 6-25, then proceeds to look more closely at school enrollment and educational attainment by age and gender for children

---

[7] For analyses of the impact of these variables on enrollment status, see Shapiro and Tambashe (1999b).

[8] We would have liked to collect data on household incomes and wages, but, as these are very sensitive topics in Kinshasa, we were not able to do so. Among the goods enumerated in our economic index are radio, television, music system, refrigerator, freezer, hot plate, stove, fan, and air conditioner. We have also developed an alternate measure of economic well-being of the household, one based on characteristics of the home (roofing material, composition of walls and floors, fuel used for cooking, sanitary facilities, etc.). These two measures are very highly correlated, and, here, we have used the count of consumer durable goods as our economic index. As Hagenaars and Vos (1988) have noted, a measure of economic well-being based on ownership of commodities will tend to be biased downward for young households just starting out.

[9] Identifying the bottom 40 percent of the population with respect to ownership of consumer durables as the poor population is somewhat arbitrary, as Hagenaars and Vos (1988) have pointed out. This corresponds to the second of their three categories of definitions of *poverty*: having less than others in society. The notion of poverty frequently entails relative comparisons, and in view of the substantial decline in real incomes in Kinshasa extending over the past 40 years, it is plausible to suggest that 40 percent is too small for our "poverty groups." As a practical matter, our interest here is in the effects of differences in economic well-being and more specifically the consequences of relatively low levels of well-being, and the two groups that we have identified serve well for this purpose.

aged 6-19. Our analyses are similar to those of Lloyd and Blanc (1996) but cover a wider age range.[10] Following this descriptive overview, we estimate equations analyzing the educational attainment of youths. Separate equations are estimated for females and males, with a binary variable indicating whether a child has reached a particular grade level regressed on the child's age, relationship to the head of the household, and a set of household characteristics, including the economic index, a dummy variable identifying the gender of the household head, variables identifying the number and ages of other youths in the household,[11] and dummy variables identifying the principal religious and ethnic groups in the city.

We estimate equations separately for the 10-14 and the 15-19 age groups. In the first instance, the dependent variable equals 1 if the child has reached the fourth grade of primary school and 0 otherwise; in the latter case, the dependent variable equals 1 if the youth has reached the ninth grade (the third year of secondary school) and 0 otherwise. Given the oversampling of women in the modern sector and the fact that the dependent variable is dichotomous, we use weighted logistic regression.

Empirical Findings: Descriptive Overview

Enrollment Status and Educational Attainment by Age, Gender, and Economic Well-Being

There are distinct differences in 1990 school enrollment rates by age and gender, as shown in figure 9.1. While school regulations in the Congo permit children to begin school at age 6, it is clear that, in Kinshasa, many do not start until they are 7, 8, or 9. Peak enrollment is at age 9 among girls and age 11 among boys. Up through the age of 9, enrollment of girls is as high as or higher than that of boys. A clear gender difference in favor of boys emerges after age 10, and it becomes consistently large beyond age 15. Between ages 8 and 15 at least 9 out of 10 children in Kinshasa, females as well as males, were in school in 1990. Beyond age 15, however, enrollment rates drop relatively rapidly, and a gender difference in favor of males that appears to widen with age is clearly evident.

---

[10] Lloyd and Blanc (1996) focused their analyses on youths aged 6-14, and their examination of educational attainment looked at whether children aged 10-14 had completed the fourth grade of primary school. Since, in our data set, the education variable is highest grade attained, not completed, we look at whether those aged 10-14 had reached the fourth grade. In addition, in view of the relatively high levels of education in Kinshasa, we also examine the educational attainment of youths aged 15-19. For this group, the operational measure is whether these youths had reached the third year of secondary school (i.e., the ninth grade).

[11] Household composition is measured by three separate variables enumerating the number of youths aged 0-5, 6-14, and 15-25, respectively.

Fig. 9.1 School enrollment rates, by age and gender, ages 6-25

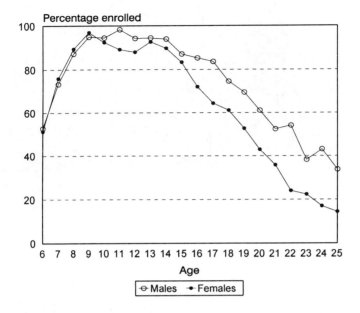

Figure 9.2 shows school enrollment and educational attainment by age, with enrolled students differentiated according to whether they are at the appropriate grade level for their age and nonenrolled students separated according to whether they had ever been enrolled in school.[12] Delayed entry is evident at the youngest ages by the presence of important percentages of never-enrolled youths. By age 9, near-universal exposure to schooling is a tangible reality, as the proportion of children never enrolled in school is minuscule. On the other hand, beginning at age 11, the proportion of children who have dropped out of school increases with age, with a sharp acceleration after age 14. Further, the proportion of children in Kinshasa who are in school but not enrolled at the appropriate grade level for their age increases from age 9 up through age 19. From age 13 on, students who are behind outnumber students at the appropriate grade level, and the gap increases as age rises. This tendency of children to lag

[12] Following Lloyd and Blanc (1996), but adjusting for the fact that our data refer to highest grade attained rather than highest grade completed, we have adopted procedures that provide conservative estimates of the proportion of children who are categorized as being behind grade level. In particular, children are classified as behind grade level if the grade they have reached is less than the grade they would have reached had they started school within 1 year of the recommended starting age (6) and attended continuously from that age on without repeating any grade. Note that, even in the absence of delayed entry or grade repetition, children in any given grade will be two different ages (e.g., some first graders will be 6 and others will be 7). Operationally, then, children are counted as being behind grade level if their current age - 6 is more than 1 year greater than their actual grade level. Hence, e.g., an 8-year-old in the first grade would be counted as being at the appropriate grade level, while a 9-year-old in the first grade would be classified as behind grade level.

Fig. 9.2 Children's school enrollment status and grade-level attainment by age

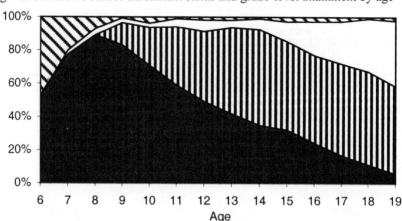

☒ Never enrolled

☐ Formerly enrolled, dropped out

▨ Currently enrolled, behind grade level for age

■ Currently enrolled, at appropriate grade level for age

behind their grade for age is a consequence of both delayed entry to school and grade repetition.[13]

These phenomena of delayed entry to school and relatively high rates of grade repetitions are similar to the situation described by Vijverberg (1993) for Côte d'Ivoire and also to that discussed by Lloyd and Blanc (1996) for Kenya, Cameroon, and Malawi. Ngom et al. (1999) report a similar pattern in terms of delayed enrollment for rural Ghana. As a consequence of delayed entry and grade repetition, there is considerable variability in Kinshasa in grade-level attainment within a single-year age cohort (i.e., an absence of age-grade normalization). For example, examination of our data for those age 15 shows that they may be enrolled in primary school (comprising six grades) or in the first or second year of secondary school (also comprising six grades). More specifically, the modal enrollment level for 15-year-olds was the first year of secondary school for both females and males, with one-fourth of males and more than 30 percent of females. Further, 23 percent of each gender were in the second year of secondary school. Among males, 37 percent of 15-year-olds were still in primary school, while the corresponding figure for females was 32 percent.

[13] We have produced gender-specific versions of figure 9.2. For the most part, gender differences are small: beyond the youngest ages, boys are slightly more likely than girls to be enrolled at the appropriate grade level and somewhat more likely to be enrolled but behind. Conversely, girls are more likely than boys to be dropouts, especially from age 14 on, and this gender difference widens as age increases.

Hence, the emergence of a distinct gender difference in enrollment rates beyond age 15 corresponds roughly to the early years of secondary school. In this regard, the results for Kinshasa are very similar to those reported by Deolalikar (1993) for Indonesia. Indeed, there are several similarities, including the slightly higher enrollment rates for girls among the very youngest children, the peak of enrollment rates at ages 9-12, and very high enrollment rates during primary school as well as emergence at the secondary school level of a distinct gender difference in enrollment rates that widens with age.

Table 9.1 provides an overview of the enrollment status and educational attainment of youths in Kinshasa, separately by age group and gender. Among those aged 6-9, the enrollment of girls slightly exceeds that of boys. Reflecting the phenomenon of delayed entry to school, enrollment rates are distinctly higher for those aged 10-14 than for those aged 6-9, with a modest difference among those aged 10-14 in favor of boys. For the oldest youths considered in the table, enrollment rates of males are down to essentially the same level as for boys aged 6-9, while enrollment rates of females are distinctly lower than those of their male counterparts as well as those of their younger counterparts. With respect to educational attainment, more than two-thirds of both boys and girls aged 10-14 had reached the fourth grade, with only a small gender difference in favor of boys. For those aged 15-19, distinctly lower proportions had reached the third year of secondary school, reflecting both grade repetitions and dropouts. In addition, there is a somewhat larger gender difference (as compared to the younger group) in favor of males.

Enrollment rates and educational attainment by age group, gender, and economic well-being are shown in table 9.2. For both boys and girls in all three age groups, there is a strong tendency for an increased household standard of living to be associated with higher enrollment rates and greater educational attainment. The range of differences in enrollment rates by economic well-being is relatively modest among those aged 10-14 but considerably larger (by a factor of 2-3) among those aged 6-9 and 15-19. The fact that, holding gender and economic well-being constant, enrollment rates of youths aged 10-14 are higher than those of children aged 6-9 indicates the importance of delayed entry to school in limiting enrollment rates of the younger group. In addition, however, the differences in enrollment rates across these two age groups are for the most part largest for those youths in the two poverty groups, suggesting that one impact of poverty is in delaying entry to school. Among the older youths, by contrast, the importance of the household standard of living as an influence on school enrollment emerges presumably because it is inversely associated with the propensity to drop out of school.

The absolute differences in educational attainment by economic well-being are generally larger than those in enrollment rates, especially among those aged 10-14, and the differences in attainment among youths aged 15-19 are modestly higher than those of their counterparts aged 10-14. In effect, then, the household standard of living appears to be of somewhat greater

Chapter 9

Table 9.1 Enrollment Status and Educational Attainment, by Age Group and Gender

	Percentage Enrolled		Educational Attainment[a]	
Age Group	Boys	Girls	Boys	Girls
6-9	80	81	—	—
10-14	95	91	70	68
15-19	81	68	41	35

[a] For those aged 10-14, figures show the percentage of those in the age group who have reached the fourth grade of primary school. For those aged 15-19, the figures indicate the percentages who have reached the third year of secondary school. Educational attainment was not examined for those in the youngest age group.

Table 9.2 Enrollment Status and Educational Attainment by Age Group, Gender, and Economic Well-Being

		Enrollment Status					Educational Attainment[a]				
		Index of Economic Well-Being					Index of Economic Well-Being				
Age Group	Gender	0	1	2-3	4-5	6+	0	1	2-3	4-5	6+
6-9	Boys	65	80	87	86	90	—	—	—	—	—
	Girls	74	74	83	83	93	—	—	—	—	—
10-14	Boys	92	91	96	99	100	59	63	71	80	82
	Girls	86	90	92	94	96	55	68	67	77	82
15-19	Boys	68	77	83	89	92	27	35	35	59	57
	Girls	54	52	73	76	87	23	23	31	48	56

[a] For those aged 10-14, figures show the percentage of those in the age group and economic index category who have reached the fourth grade of primary school. For those aged 15-19, the figures indicate the percentages in each cell who have reached the third year of secondary school. Educational attainment was not examined for those in the youngest age group.

importance as an influence on attainment as opposed to enrollment, and it becomes increasingly important as children get older.

As discussed above, child fostering is common in sub-Saharan Africa, and Kinshasa is no exception in this regard. Indeed, as the biggest and most attractive "metropole" of the country, it has always been a place where rural citizens send their children to live with relatives for schooling, health care, and job opportunities. In addition, some children who experience the death of one or both parents end up living with relatives in Kinshasa. Consequently, a substantial minority of youths aged 6-19 in our data set—nearly 25 percent—were not offspring of the head of the household in which they resided. Just over a third of these youths were nephews or nieces of the household head, and almost a quarter were younger siblings.[14]

[14] Not all these individuals are fostered in to their current households. For example, some of those at the upper end of the age range being considered may be out-of-school youths who are employed in the household or who have already begun their own families but are living with their relatives in extended-family households.

Data on enrollment rates and educational attainment by age group, gender, and relationship to the head of the household (not shown here) indicate that, relative to daughters and sons of the household head, other children tend for the most part to have lower enrollment rates and educational attainment. The one notable exception to this statement is for siblings of the head vis-à-vis educational attainment: they tend to have comparable attainment to that of the head's own children, and, among 15-19-year-old males, brothers of the head actually have greater educational attainment than the head's own children.

Sibling Chain of Educational Assistance

As noted earlier, developing-country settings with strong family ties and credit constraints often are characterized by resource transfers among siblings to support the educational attainment of younger brothers and sisters. The fact that, in our data set, 10 percent of youths in Kinshasa aged 15-19 were living in their siblings' homes rather than with their parents is suggestive in this regard, as is the relatively high educational attainment of youths living in the homes of older siblings, mentioned in the preceding paragraph. Direct evidence of such resource transfers is also available from the women interviewed in our 1990 survey. They were asked about the size of their family of origin, and they were also asked who had primarily been responsible for their schooling. Nearly 80 percent of the respondents who had been to school indicated that their parents had paid for their schooling. However, as may be seen in figure 9.3, the likelihood of having had financial support from her parents declines as the respondent's birth order rises, while, correspondingly, the likelihood of obtaining such support primarily from older siblings increases.[15]

Empirical Findings: Multivariate Analyses

In this section, the educational attainment of youths aged 10-19 who were enumerated in the survey is analyzed as a function of a set of selected variables, as described in the methodology section above. Table 9.3 provides the results of weighted logistic regression analyses carried out separately for females and males aged 10-14 and 15-19.[16] These results show, with few exceptions, that,

[15] It would be most interesting to examine comparable data for males to see if there are gender differences in the sibling chain of educational assistance. Unfortunately, such data are not available.

[16] Mean values of the variables for each age group and gender are provided in appendix table 9A.1. Because our initial sample consisted of women aged 13-49, females outnumber males, especially in the 15-19 age group. This sampling-based explanation is only part of the story, however. Examination of the data shows that, in both the 10-14 and the 15-19 age groups, females are less likely than males to be children of the household head. This presumably reflects a greater propensity for females to be fostered in to households in Kinshasa, and, in the older group, it may also be a consequence of young women either working as domestics or marrying into an extended household.

Fig. 9.3 Principal source of financial support for schooling, by birth order

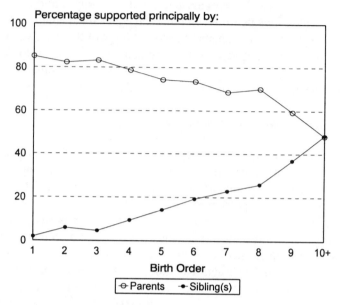

Note: Excludes women with no schooling.

among both younger (10-14) and older (15-19) females and males, age, household economic well-being, gender of the head of the household, household composition (as measured by numbers of children aged 0-5, 6-14, and 15-25 in the household), the individual's relationship to the head of the household, religion, and ethnic group are significantly related to the probability of reaching the fourth grade of primary school (ages 10-14) or the third grade of secondary school (ages 15-19). Further, pooled equations (not shown here) indicate that, all else equal, females had significantly lower educational attainment than did males. In particular, among those aged 10-14, females were roughly 20 percent less likely to attain the fourth grade of primary school than were males, while, among 15-19 year-olds, females were almost 30 percent less likely than were males to reach the third year of secondary school, all else equal.

The highly significant coefficients for the quadratic specification of age indicate that, among both female and male youths, the probability of reaching the fourth grade of primary school for those aged 10-14 increases with age, but at a decreasing rate. The same is true for the likelihood of attaining the third grade of secondary school for those aged 15-19.

The economic well-being of the household is highly significantly associated with the chances of reaching the fourth grade of primary school for the 10-14-year-olds and the third grade of high school for those aged 15-19. As may be seen in table 9.3 and in the corresponding table of marginal effects

Table 9.3 Determinants of Educational Attainment, by Age Group and Gender (coefficients from weighted logistic regressions)

Variable	Ages 10-14		Ages 15-19	
	Females	Males	Females	Males
Age				
Age	1.874**	2.108**	2.999**	3.144**
Age squared	-.044**	-.053**	-.069**	-.073**
Economic well-being				
Economic index = 0	-.651**	.027	-.044	-.140$^+$
Economic index = 1	—	—	—	—
Economic index = 2 or 3	.254**	.702**	.447**	.331**
Economic index = 4 or 5	.637**	1.526**	1.286**	1.362**
Economic index = 6+	.970**	1.470**	1.603**	1.087**
Gender of head of household				
Female	-.352*	-.227	.237$^+$	.943**
Male	—	—	—	—
Household composition				
Children aged 0-5	-.436**	.003	-.186**	-.335**
Children aged 6-14	-.186**	-.176**	-.127**	.152**
Children aged 15-25	-.035*	-.041**	-.019	-.028
Relationship to head of household				
Child	—	—	—	—
Sibling	-.299*	-.408*	-.008	.312**
Nephew/niece	-.502**	-.403**	-.164*	.098
Other	-.121	-.072	-.208**	-.566**
Religion				
Catholic	—	—	—	—
Protestant	-.064	.195**	-.486**	-.010
Kimbanguist	.486**	-.258$^+$	-.652**	-.860**
Other	-.395**	-.376**	-.530**	-.186**
None	-.210	-.466*	.737**	1.181**
Ethnic group				
Kwilu-Kwango	—	—	—	—
Bakongo North	.648**	.353**	.543**	.614**
Bakongo South	.696**	-.251**	.266**	.306**
Mongo	-.207*	-.304**	.402**	.967**
Ubangi	.377**	-.326**	.037	.185$^+$
Luba	.697**	.247**	.127$^+$	.798**
Other tribes	.285$^+$	3.120**	1.835**	-.246
Non-Congolese	1.234**	.195	.492**	.452**
Intercept	-14.883	-16.437	-31.973	-33.194
Log likelihood	-5,006.3	-4,485.5	-7,288.0	-4,639.1
Sample size	1,119	1,018	1,391	897
Mean of dependent variable	0.680	0.700	0.348	0.414

Note: For ages 10-14, the dependent variable = 1 if youth has reached the fourth grade of primary school, 0 otherwise. For ages 15-19, the dependent variable = 1 if youth has reached the third grade of secondary school, 0 otherwise.

** Significant at the .01 level, two-tailed test.
* Significant at the .05 level, two-tailed test.
$^+$ Significant at the .10 level, two-tailed test.

(appendix table 9A.2), there is for the most part a clear tendency for increases in the residential standard of living to translate into progressively higher educational attainment in all four age and gender groups. At the same time, however, the magnitudes of increments vary somewhat by age group and gender. Among the younger females, the probability of having reached the fourth grade rises consistently with household economic well-being, with an especially large increment in going from the poorest to the next-poorest group. Among the younger males, by contrast, the pattern is not quite so strong; there is no significant difference between the two poorest groups, then large increments for the next two groups, and finally a small decline for the most well-off group. Among females aged 15-19, there is no significant difference between the two poverty groups, then significantly higher educational attainment as the household standard of living increases, while among their male counterparts, there are increases across the board except in moving to the most well-off group.

The differences described above are depicted in figure 9.4, which shows (for youths aged 10-14 and 15-19, respectively) the predicted educational attainment by gender of the two poverty groups as well as the group with the highest level of economic well-being. These predicted values are derived from the equations reported in table 9.3.[17] For all groups, educational attainment increases with age. Among girls aged 10-14 (figure 9.4a), increases in economic well-being translate into increased educational attainment, and the differences by economic well-being narrow as age increases. Among boys aged 10-14 (figure 9.4b), by contrast, there is no difference in predicted educational attainment between the two poverty groups, but there is distinctly higher attainment among those from the most well-off households. For the boys, like the girls, differences in predicted educational attainment by household standard of living narrow as age increases. Among the older youths, by contrast, the differences in attainment by economic well-being tend to widen somewhat as age increases. For the females (figure 9.4c), there is essentially no difference in educational attainment between the two poverty groups, and, for the males (figure 9.4d), the corresponding difference is quite small.

A more direct perspective on gender differences by economic well-being is provided in figure 9.5, which shows (for youths aged 10-14 and 15-19, respectively) predicted educational attainment by age and gender separately for each of the two poverty groups and for the group with the highest level of well-being. In two cases (those aged 10-14 with economic index $= 1$, and those aged 15-19 with economic index $= 0$), predicted attainment is essentially the same for males and females, and, in two others (those aged 10-14 with economic index $= 6+$ and those aged 15-19 with economic index $= 1$), there are only small differences in favor of males. Only for the younger youths

---

[17] Predicted values are calculated assuming the reference characteristics: male for gender of the household head, child for relationship to household head, Catholic for religion, and Kwilu-Kwango for ethnic group. It is also assumed that there are no other youths in the household.

Fig. 9.4 Predicted educational attainment by gender, age, and economic index

a. Females, ages 10-14   b. Males, ages 10-14

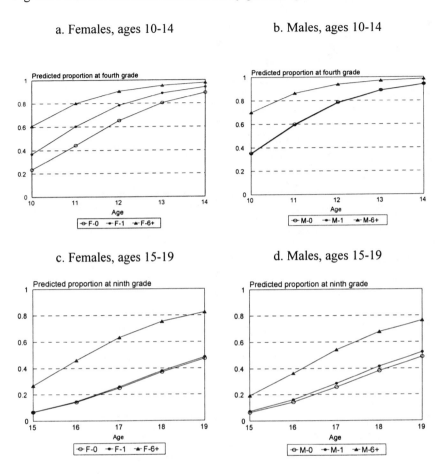

c. Females, ages 15-19   d. Males, ages 15-19

Note: Based on table 9.3, equations (1)-(4) for parts a-d, respectively.

from the lowest level of economic well-being is there a clear and consistent gender difference in favor of males. For the older youths from the highest standard-of-living group, predicted attainment for females actually exceeds that for males. This cross-sectional evidence thus strongly suggests that there is no uniform tendency for higher economic well-being to translate into reduced gender differences in educational attainment. Further, the link between these gender differences and economic well-being is also somewhat dependent on age as well: in going from the lowest to the highest level of economic well-being, there is first a narrowing and then a slight widening of gender differences among the younger youths; while, among the older youths, there is

Fig. 9.5 Predicted educational attainment by economic index, age, and gender

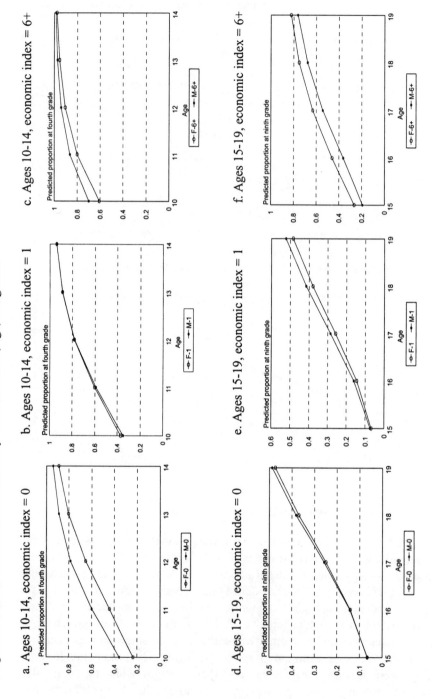

a. Ages 10-14, economic index = 0

b. Ages 10-14, economic index = 1

c. Ages 10-14, economic index = 6+

d. Ages 15-19, economic index = 0

e. Ages 15-19, economic index = 1

f. Ages 15-19, economic index = 6+

Note: Based on table 9.3, equations (1) and (2).

initially a modest widening and subsequently a reversal of gender differences.[18] The influence of gender of the household head on educational attainment varies according to the child's age and gender. Among youths aged 10-14, girls from female-headed households have significantly lower educational attainment than do those from households headed by men, while, for boys, the gender of the household head is not a significant influence on educational attainment. By contrast, among youths aged 15-19, those from female-headed households tend to have significantly higher educational attainment, especially males. These results differ somewhat from those of Lloyd and Blanc (1996), who found that educational attainment of 10-14-year-olds was generally greater for those from female-headed households and that the impact of a female head was greater for attainment of girls than for that of boys.

Household composition, as measured by the number of youths in the household aged 0-5, 6-14, and 15-25, is a statistically significant determinant of educational attainment. For the four age-gender groups analyzed, there are significant negative impacts on educational attainment of the presence of pre-school-age children in three cases. Likewise, the presence of children aged 6-14 in the household is associated with lower educational attainment in three of four cases. The former result is consistent with the findings of Lloyd and Blanc (1996) and, presumably, reflects the fact that, in Kinshasa, as elsewhere in sub-Saharan Africa, children of school age often play an important role in provision of child care to younger children in the household. The latter finding, which is consistent with a resource-dilution model, differs from the results obtained by Lloyd and Blanc (1996), who found that more children aged 6-14 was generally associated with modestly higher educational attainment. Finally, the presence of youths aged 15-25 appears to have a slight depressing effect on the educational attainment of children aged 10-14 but no impact on the educational attainment of those aged 15-19. As indicated by the table of marginal effects (table 9A.2), the magnitudes of the impacts of these household composition variables are fairly modest.[19]

Consistent with the notion that some children are fostered in primarily for child care and domestic support, we find that children living in households headed by someone other than their father or mother tend to have somewhat

[18] This reversal at the top end of the economic well-being scale among those aged 15-19 reflects the gender differences in coefficients. In going from an economic index value of 4 or 5 to one of 6 or more, there is a large jump in coefficients (and a corresponding increase in the marginal effect) for females, while there is a decline in coefficients (and a smaller marginal effect) among males. Had figure 9.5f shown predicted values for when the economic index equals 4 or 5, there would have been a distinct gender difference in favor of males, wider than that for either of the two poverty groups.

[19] We also tested for interactions between economic well-being and household composition in the light of the suggestion by Parish and Willis (1993) that household composition effects might be larger in poor households. Despite the presence of a number of statistically significant interaction coefficients, there was no support for the idea that household composition would matter more for poor households than for well-off households.

lower educational attainment than do children of the head. This is particularly the case among those aged 10-14. The notable exception to this pattern occurs among males aged 15-19, where brothers of the head of the household show significantly greater educational attainment than do the head's sons. Overall, the evidence suggests that at younger ages, child fostering frequently takes place to provide additional labor for the receiving household (Ainsworth 1992) but that, at older ages, particularly for brothers of the head of the household, it appears to contribute to enhancing opportunities for acquiring education. It should be noted, however, that, while children fostered in tend for the most part to have lower educational attainment than the children of the households where they end up, ceteris paribus, it is still possible that the fostered children are achieving higher levels of schooling than would have been the case if they had remained in their family of origin.

Religious differences in educational attainment are also evident, with some variation by both gender and age group. The one clear and consistent difference across age and gender groups is the lower educational attainment of those in the "other" religious category. There are also significant differences by ethnic group, again with variability by both age and gender. Relative to Kwilu-Kwango youths, those from the Bakongo North and Luba ethnic groups consistently have greater educational attainment.

In addition to the results reported in table 9.3 above, we have carried out some other analyses of interest. As noted earlier, education of the household head has been found to be a significant determinant of children's schooling, all else equal. While our data set does not have information on the education of the head for all households, this information is available for the subset of respondents who were either the spouse of the head or the head themselves. For the subset of children in these households, we have estimated equations similar to those in table 9.3, with level of education of the household head and the head's spouse as additional explanatory variables. The results (not shown here) indicate that, even after controlling for the household level of economic well-being and other factors, greater education of the head and the head's spouse tends to be associated with higher educational attainment for both female and male youths.

We also wanted to look at questions of sibling effects and birth order. Unfortunately, our ability to address these issues is severely compromised since we have only cross-sectional data on the composition of the household at a moment in time (i.e., we cannot identify older siblings who have already left the parental household) and the underlying behavior has a strong life cycle component to it. It is worth noting, however, that an analysis of the educational attainment of the women in the sample found that greater numbers of siblings were associated with greater educational attainment, all else equal, and that, once number of siblings was taken into account, birth order was not a significant factor (Shapiro 1999).

Conclusions and Discussion

All else equal, investments in the educational attainment of girls in Kinshasa are not as substantial as the corresponding investments in the education of boys. Despite the presence of a considerable degree of interhousehold resource transfers in support of children and their education (Shapiro et al. 1995), poverty has a substantial impact on the demand for schooling and on school enrollment and educational attainment. While increased economic well-being is associated with significantly greater educational attainment for both females and males, it is not the case that improved economic status necessarily translates into reduced gender differences in school outcomes. In particular, while gender differences in reaching the fourth grade among children aged 10-14 are greatest among the poorest households, they are smallest in this age range in the next-poorest segment of the population. By contrast, among youths aged 15-19, gender differences in reaching the ninth grade tend to emerge in moving from the poorest to the next-poorest households, and further increases in economic well-being first yield a wider difference in favor of males and then a gender difference in favor of females for those from the most well-off households.

In addition to the impact of poverty on the educational attainment of youths, it is also apparent that young children from low-income households are more likely to delay initial entry into school. Later entry, lower subsequent enrollment rates, an increased likelihood of repeating grades and eventually dropping out, and hence slower progress in reaching given educational levels all appear to be consequences of coming from poor households. Overall, then, the impact of low economic well-being on the educational attainment of women and men appears to be an important mechanism in Kinshasa contributing to the intergenerational transmission of poverty.

Our analyses have also documented statistically significant effects of household composition. There is a clear adverse impact on educational attainment associated with the presence of preschool-age children in the household. Consistent with a resource-dilution story, the educational attainment of youths is for the most part influenced negatively by the presence of other school-age youths in the household. In contrast, however, and consistent with the notion of a sibling chain of educational assistance, the schooling of older males is positively related to the presence of younger school-age children.

Finally, we have also determined that, in addition to the differences in educational attainment associated with economic well-being and household composition, youths residing in households without a parent as head of the household tend for the most part to have lower educational attainment, all else equal. Exceptions are evident in the older age group for brothers and nephews of the household head, suggestive of fostering aimed at securing better educational opportunities for these older youths. Even for other youths, however, educational attainment that is lower than that of children of the household head does not necessarily mean that child fostering for the purpose of acquiring schooling is not important; rather, it simply tells us that fostered children have enrollment rates that are lower than those of comparable children in the households where they reside. We should note that decisions regarding child fostering are likely to be endogenous with respect to decisions concerning the schooling of own children. This suggests that it would be desirable to model and analyze these decisions jointly.

As noted in chapter 1, the Congo's chronic economic crisis, going back to the mid-1970s, became acute beginning in late 1990. After several years of political and economic crisis, a civil war that began in late 1996 ended in a change of government in May 1997. Stability was brief, however; in August 1998, a new rebellion broke out. One consequence of all this turmoil is that the country's economy remains in very poor shape and has continued to deteriorate. For example, it is estimated that, in 1999, the Congolese economy shrank by 14 percent while inflation jumped to 370 percent (République Démocratique du Congo 1999).

While detailed data are not available, it appears that school enrollment rates have probably dropped somewhat (see chapter 13). Parents increasingly confront severe financial difficulties in attempting to keep their children in school. The consequences of these changes for the Congo's economic prospects in the short to medium term are grim, and their consequences for investments in children's education and for gender differences in these investments remain to be seen.

Appendix

Table 9A.1 Mean Values of the Variables in the Analyses of Educational Attainment, by Age Group and Gender

Variable	Ages 10-14		Ages 15-19	
	Females	Males	Females	Male
Age	12	11	16.9	16.9
Economic well-being				
Economic index = 0	0.268	0.27	0.262	0.262
Economic index = 1	0.154	0.155	0.147	0.165
Economic index = 2 or 3	0.245	0.247	0.255	0.205
Economic index = 4 or 5	0.175	0.169	0.174	0.183
Economic index = 6+	0.158	0.159	0.162	0.185
Gender of head of household				
Female	0.03	0.03	0.023	0.043
Male	0.97	0.97	0.977	0.957
Household composition				
Children aged 0-5	0.264	0.179	0.321	0.28
Children aged 6-14	1.64	1.7	0.353	0.331
Children aged 15-25	1.93	2.11	2.4	2.78
Relationship to head of household				
Child	0.762	0.826	0.695	0.778
Sibling	0.057	0.022	0.108	0.08
Nephew/niece	0.103	0.076	0.099	0.087
Other	0.078	0.076	0.098	0.055
Religion				
Catholic	0.55	0.573	0.57	0.562
Protestant	0.19	0.174	0.172	0.176
Kimbanguist	0.037	0.041	0.04	0.043
Other	0.2	0.2	0.199	0.204
None	0.023	0.012	0.019	0.015
Ethnic group				
Kwilu-Kwango	0.379	0.319	0.335	0.34
Bakongo North	0.082	0.076	0.076	0.092
Bakongo South	0.197	0.253	0.232	0.214
Mongo	0.067	0.093	0.081	0.084
Ubangi	0.086	0.063	0.076	0.086
Luba	0.121	0.134	0.118	0.103
Other tribes	0.02	0.02	0.02	0.023
Non-Congolese	0.048	0.042	0.062	0.058
Mean of dependent variable	0.68	0.7	0.348	0.414

Note: For ages 10-14, dependent variable = 1 if youth has reached the fourth grade of primary school, 0 otherwise. For ages 15-19, dependent variable = 1 if youth has reached the third grade of secondary school, 0 otherwise.

Table 9A.2 Marginal Effects on Educational Attainment, by Age Group and Gender

	Ages 10-14		Ages 15-19	
Variable	Females	Males	Females	Males
Age	0.129	0.107	0.168	0.183
Economic well-being				
Economic index = 0	-0.148	0.006	-0.007	-0.027
Economic index = 1	—	—	—	—
Economic index = 2 or 3	0.049	0.133	0.08	0.071
Economic index = 4 or 5	0.111	0.232	0.273	0.323
Economic index = 6+	0.153	0.227	0.352	0.256
Gender of head of household				
Female	-0.072	-0.038	0.052	0.231
Male	—	—	—	—
Household composition				
Children aged 0-5	-0.091	0	-0.038	-0.076
Children aged 6-14	-0.037	-0.029	-0.026	0.037
Children aged 15-25	-0.007	-0.007	-0.004	-0.007
Relationship to head of household				
Child	—	—	—	—
Sibling	-0.058	-0.07	-0.002	0.076
Nephew/niece	-0.103	-0.069	-0.034	0.024
Other	-0.023	-0.011	-0.043	-0.123
Religion				
Catholic	—	—	—	—
Protestant	-0.012	0.028	-0.1	-0.002
Kimbanguist	0.08	-0.043	-0.129	-0.179
Other	-0.081	-0.065	-0.108	-0.043
None	-0.041	-0.082	0.179	0.285
Ethnic group				
Kwilu-Kwango	—	—	—	—
Bakongo North	0.121	0.051	0.118	0.145
Bakongo South	0.128	-0.043	0.055	0.07
Mongo	-0.046	-0.053	0.086	0.233
Ubangi	0.075	-0.058	0.007	0.042
Luba	0.128	0.037	0.026	0.191
Other tribes	0.058	0.19	0.428	-0.051
Non-Congolese	0.162	0.028	0.118	0.111

Note: These marginal effects show the impact of each variable on the probability that a youth in the corresponding age and gender group will reach the indexed level of educational attainment (fourth grade for those aged 10-14 and ninth grade for those aged 15-19). They are calculated at the sample means of the independent variables, except that—following Liao (1994, 19)—for each grouping of dummy variables they show the difference in predicted probabilities between the realization indicated and the reference category.

Chapter 10. Extended-Family Solidarity: Interhousehold Resource Transfers in Support of Children's Schooling and Child Fostering

The analyses presented in part 2 focused on the behavior of individuals, while the preceding chapter's analysis of investments in children's education emphasized the household as a key focal point and decision-making unit. Individuals are component parts of households, and it is often useful to consider the behavior of individuals in the context of the households in which they are situated. By the same token, in sub-Saharan Africa in particular, households are part of broader social networks (typically, the clan or an extended-family subset of the clan), and what households do should be considered within the context of those broader networks.

Economic analyses of much behavior frequently focus on the household as both the unit of observation and a key decision-making unit. This approach is well adapted to industrial-country settings where nuclear households are the norm and also the locus of decision making with respect to resource allocation within the household. However, in developing countries, households are often complex, in that they may be vertically integrated and/or horizontally integrated. In addition, there are often considerable resource flows between and among households. These interhousehold resource transfers, which may involve money, labor time, and/or material goods, for the most part take place within an extended-family context. There are several different motivations for these transfers that have been cited in the literature, including but not limited to resource flows involving migrants (e.g., remittances), demand for (child) labor, and efforts to finance investments in human capital. In addition, such transfers may serve a short-run income redistribution function, and they may also have important consequences for fertility behavior.

This chapter uses data from our 1990 survey to examine interhousehold resource transfers within extended families, or what we refer to here as *solidarity* behavior. More specifically, we use the term *solidarity* to refer to resource transfers between households (in the form of money, time, and/or goods) in the absence of formal contracts. Our focus is on interhousehold resource flows that take place for the purpose of providing assistance in the schooling and fostering of children. We seek to document the prevalence and nature of such transfers and to identify and assess the factors affecting these transfers.[1]

The following section examines some pertinent literature, with emphasis on the motivations and the likely consequences of this extended-family solidarity. The data used in the chapter as well as the empirical model and hypotheses are then discussed. Empirical results are described subsequently, beginning with a descriptive overview highlighting the incidence and the sources and destinations of interhousehold resource flows. This is followed by multivariate analyses of factors influencing participation in these resource flows. The concluding section provides a brief summary, notes some limitations of our research, and attempts to assess the consequences of the Congo's economic crisis for solidarity networks.

Literature Review

As noted earlier in chapter 5, in settings where extended-family ties remain strong, many of the important activities and decisions of a household involve family members outside the immediate household. That is, household concerns and decisions often include, not just parents and their children, but also grandparents, uncles and aunts, in-laws, etc. Among the more clan-based traditional societies in sub-Saharan Africa, this type of extension embraces almost all aspects of living. In particular, children's welfare is the responsibility of the clan (Caldwell 1976).

In such societies, decisions about selling property, marrying, or sending children to school or away from home are normally cleared with clan members, who have the power to dispute any individual family decisions that may seem inappropriate. Although such decisions are increasingly becoming the responsibility of nuclear families, individual members know that the clan can be appealed to when disputes arise. Thus, the clan represents a type of system of law and order as well as a potential source of material support. While individualism is found increasingly among modern, educated, and younger families, most African families are involved in exchanges outside the nuclear household.

Several different motivations for extended-family solidarity behavior have

---

[1] The continuous flow of (illegal) immigrants from the Third World, and in particular from Africa, to industrialized countries is another very tangible manifestation of this inter- and intra-generational chain of solidarity. Using all imaginable strategies, the first family member who gets established overseas brings in the second, the second brings in the third, and so forth.

been discussed in the literature. Caldwell (1976) has argued that exchange networks are mostly motivated by economic rationality but are defined within social ends. He notes that, despite increased education and urbanization, strong ties continue between rural and urban populations, between the young and educated and older traditional family members, and generally between the rich and the poor.

Looking at remittance behavior of migrants in Botswana, Lucas and Stark (1985) argued that the concentration of transfers among family members made a strong case for altruistic motivations. At the same time, by dealing with relatives rather than strangers, participants in exchange networks within the extended family reduce transaction costs (Ainsworth 1992; Folbre 1988; Pollak 1985). In addition, when money and goods transfers are concerned, family relationships tend to be dependable because they tie individuals and families in long-term contracts. This feature is especially desirable in settings where the working of markets is uncertain (Becker 1991; Ben-Porath 1982).

When extended-family members are geographically separated, one potential benefit from exchange networks is that risk is diversified. This permits or encourages greater risk taking by any one member of the family. Thus, for example, in Botswana, Lucas and Stark (1985) found that, the greater the degree of ongoing drought in the urban families' rural area of origin, the more remittances were observed passing from the urban migrants. More generally, then, extended-family solidarity from this perspective may be seen to be motivated in part by a desire to manage risk.

Educational investments in children constitute a major component of the activities of extended families since financial markets are especially limited in their ability to provide for human capital investments. As discussed in the preceding chapter, parental investment in schooling serves to enhance the quality and earnings capacity of children, and parents typically anticipate receiving support in their old age from these same children. According to this approach, parents are concerned about their children's lifetime income. They would then give priority to actions that increase the future earnings capacities of their children, such as educating them or fostering them out to family members who might be able to offer them better opportunities. Through mutual understanding and obligation, when such children become adults with income, they often provide assistance to their parents directly, and they may also support the education of younger siblings.

The hypothesis of parental investment and subsequent repayment by children is supported by several studies of remittances in Africa. Knowles and Anker's (1981) study of income transfers in Kenya found that 34 percent of total transfers and 28 percent of total transferred income came from children to their parents. In Botswana, evidence showed that the family's own youngsters increased remittances as their level of education increased. Results from Botswana further showed that, in cases where education was provided by relatives other than own parents, children remitted more to those relatives than they did to their own parents (Lucas and Stark 1985).

The human capital investment approach suggests that much of the observed fostering of children that takes place may reflect an effort to obtain better-quality education. Alternatively, Ainsworth (1992) has proposed a child labor demand model, in which fostering occurs because of the difference between the optimal number of children needed for home production and the number of own children in the host household. She hypothesized that children are fostered to reduce the time spent in home production by working adults or by their own children whom they wish to attend school. Thus, factors that raise the net demand for child labor would lead the household to foster more children in and to send fewer out for fostering. Such factors may include higher wages for the wife (increasing the wife's opportunity cost of time in home production) or an increase in the number of own children going to school. Ainsworth tested her model using data from a 1985 survey in Côte d'Ivoire. Her findings were consistent with a child labor demand explanation and inconclusive regarding schooling investments as a motive for fostering.[2]

There are several different forms that extended-family solidarity may take. Studies in Africa and Asia have found both shared residence (vertically and/or horizontally integrated households) and interhousehold transfers of money, goods, and labor time (Butz and Stan 1982; Eloundou-Enyegue 1992; Knowles and Anker 1981). Of particular interest here are two forms of assistance: aid in support of the schooling of children and child fostering. In Africa, extended-family support plays an important role in alleviating constraints to investment in children's education. Relatives outside the household are encouraged to help with school fees and other educational expenditures. A common practice in this regard is for older children to help younger ones via establishment of a sibling chain of assistance (Simons 1994; cf. figure 9.3 above).

With regard to child fostering, Ainsworth (1992) observed in Côte d'Ivoire that approximately 20 percent of children aged 7-14 lived with families other than their own parents. Of this group, 57 percent moved from rural to urban areas, 20 percent moved from urban to rural areas, and the remaining 23 percent made either rural-rural or urban-urban moves.[3] As noted in the previous chapter, Lloyd and Blanc's (1996) analyses of Demographic and Health Surveys (DHS) data for children aged 6-14 in seven countries of sub-Saharan Africa found that, in five of the countries, 27-28 percent of the youths were not

---

[2] Ainsworth considered children aged 7-14. Hence, schooling investments would refer principally to primary schooling only, and her analyses would not identify fostering for purposes of acquiring secondary or higher schooling (likely a more common phenomenon, particularly as concerns rural-urban child fostering).

[3] Looking at income transfers more broadly, Knowles and Anker (1981) found in Kenya that both the frequency and the volume of transfers between rural and urban areas were principally from urban to rural. Evidence for Kinshasa presented below suggests that there is a net outflow of assistance from the city to rural areas.

living with a biological parent and that, in the other two countries, the percentages were 20 and 51. Mcdaniel and Zulu (1996) used DHS data from 10 sub-Saharan countries to show that child fostering is more prevalent in Southern Africa than in East or West Africa.

The immediate consequence of extended-family solidarity is to alter the income distribution. However, because over the long haul resource flows tend to move back and forth, it is important to consider net rather than gross flows. Studies in Kenya and Malaysia suggest that the effect of extended-family transfers on the general income distribution is limited (Knowles and Anker 1981; Butz and Stan 1982). However, it appears that there are notable effects in the poorest segments of the population: Knowles and Anker (1981) found that the poorest 20 percent of urban households in Kenya received almost half their total income in the form of transfers, while Butz and Stan (1982) found that among the bottom 20 percent of Malaysian households net transfers constituted 86 percent of their annual average income.

In addition to effects on income distribution, interhousehold resource transfers have also been seen as a possible influence on fertility behavior. To the extent that the responsibilities and costs of childbearing are shared within the extended family (Burch 1983), including the availability of family help for child care (Mason 1984), the costs of children are lowered to individual parents. However, efforts to identify this effect have met with mixed results. Some studies have reported a positive link between the presence of extended-family assistance and the demand for children (Burch 1983; Freedman et al. 1982), while others have found little or no association (Nag 1975; Stokes et al. 1987).

Data, Model, and Hypotheses

The data for this chapter come from a section of the survey questionnaire that focused on interhousehold resource transfers. Respondents who were married to the head of their household or who were themselves head of their household (consisting of more than 1,250 women) were asked if (since leaving their family of origin) they had ever given or received assistance from others, that assistance being focused around three distinct categories: schooling for children; lodging of children; and money to make ends meet. Those individuals who indicated either receipt or provision of such assistance were then asked with whom they had made such transfers and when they had last done so.[4] Our analyses focus on participation in the first two categories of manifestations of solidarity, overall and during the year preceding the survey.[5]

---

[4] We did not ask about the amounts of the transfers, principally because this would be a very sensitive question in Kinshasa, and also because of attendant concerns about data accuracy.

[5] For each type of transfer in which the respondent's household participated, respondents were asked in what year the most recent transfer took place. Transfers characterized in the text as occurring during the year preceding the survey were those that took place in 1990 or 1989—i.e., during the period from 0 to 18 months prior to the survey.

These two types of interhousehold resource transfers are quite different, albeit at times linked. Assistance for schooling may include relatively small-scale transfers to cover expenses for tuition, uniforms, or school supplies, for example. Also, like money to make ends meet, it tends to be provided on a sporadic basis. By contrast, assistance for lodging (i.e., child fostering) normally entails a much more significant and sustained resource transfer. As noted earlier, fostering in may take place to provide labor to the household and/or to provide children with access to educational opportunities. In any case, transfers focused around child fostering will generally be distinctly more substantial than those for children's schooling.

Giving or receiving assistance for schooling and lodging of children is expected to be closely linked to the economic well-being of individual households. Relatively well-off households are more likely to be asked to and to be able to provide support to other extended-family members and less likely to seek assistance. Presumably, differences by economic well-being should be especially important concerning assistance for child fostering. In addition to the household's economic status, its (potential) demographic composition will also influence the likelihood of participation in extended-family transfers. That is, greater numbers of children translate into a greater demand for housing services, and greater numbers of school-age children translate into greater demand for resources for schooling, all else equal.

We carry out multivariate analyses of recent (1989-1990) participation in interhousehold resource transfers. In view of the considerations outlined above, our analyses focus on the effects of different variables reflecting both the economic well-being of the household and the number, age, and sex composition of the respondent's surviving children.[6] In addition, we also control for a variety of socioeconomic characteristics of the respondent's household, such as her schooling, age, ethnic group, and religion and her husband's educational attainment, in order to test for differences in resource transfers according to these characteristics.

More specifically, four empirical models are estimated. The dependent variable in each case is a binary variable indicating whether the respondent's household had participated in a particular type of transfer (receiving assistance for schooling, receiving assistance for lodging, providing assistance for schooling, providing assistance for lodging) during the past year. The explanatory variables include a set of characteristics reflecting the level of economic well-being of the household, a set of variables reflecting the number, age, and sex composition of the respondent's surviving children, and a set of variables identifying characteristics of the respondent and her household that may influence participation in interhousehold resource transfers. The equations are estimated using weighted logistic regression.

[6] We focus on the respondent's surviving children as an ex ante "predetermined" variable vis-à-vis participation in recent manifestations of solidarity.

Our principal measure of economic well-being is the index that counts the number of functioning consumer durable goods in the household. In addition to the economic index, we include in our empirical model dummy variables identifying women who work in the labor market (employees, who for the most part work in the modern sector, and the self-employed, who are in the informal sector), with the expectation that those who regularly earn income will be more likely to give assistance and less likely to receive it, even after controlling for the measured economic well-being of the household. We also include a dummy variable in the analyses identifying female-headed households, which represented 6 percent of the total, with the expectation that these households will have less income than those headed by males, ceteris paribus (Lloyd and Blanc 1996). Consequently, such households are expected to participate more as recipients and less as donors in interhousehold resource transfers.[7]

The respondent's number of living children constitutes an initial measure of her prospective demand for resource transfers, with higher-parity women consequently expected to be more likely to receive assistance. Presumably, they would also be less likely to provide assistance. An alternate set of estimates below controls for the number of own children in different age (0, 1-5, 6-14, 15-25) and gender groups. The presence of children aged 6 and above should contribute to a greater likelihood of receiving assistance for children's schooling. Otherwise, differentiation by age and gender jointly permits one to see if there are differences across these subgroups in their impact on the solidarity behavior examined here.

The analyses include some additional variables: the respondent's and spouse's level of educational attainment, age, ethnic group, and religion. We saw in the previous chapter that parents' education was positively related to their investments in the schooling of their children. Including education here allows us to see whether those with higher levels of education are more likely to support the schooling of others—i.e., manifest a greater taste for education.

The importance attached to age in sub-Saharan Africa suggests to us that older individuals may be asked and expected to contribute to the schooling of younger members of the extended family. Consequently, we include age as a control variable. Ethnic group and religious affiliation are taken into consideration in part to allow for different group beliefs or practices to influence participation in solidarity behavior. In addition, different ethnic groups in Kinshasa vary with respect to distance to their area of origin. Consequently, there may also be variation across groups in the opportunities to participate in solidarity networks.

---

[7] Deolalikar (1993) finds differences between male- and female-headed households with regard to decision making about school enrollment of children. More generally, then, the dummy variable tests for an effect of gender of the household head on the likelihood of participation in interhousehold resource transfers.

Empirical Results

Incidence, Sources, and Destinations of Interhousehold Resource Flows

Part A of table 10.1 shows that more than one-fourth of respondents acknowledge having ever received assistance for either children's schooling or child fostering and that over two-thirds had provided such assistance. The percentages for each type of assistance individually are slightly lower, indicating that many, but not all, households active in these solidarity networks participate in transfers for both children's schooling and child fostering. The much greater incidence of assisting rather than receiving assistance presumably reflects exchanges with rural areas, in which Kinshasa is a net donor.[8] In particular, as noted in earlier chapters, the city has historically been a magnet for rural youths seeking improved educational opportunities and coming to live with extended-family members in order to take advantage of those opportunities (Capelle 1947).

As shown in part A of figure 10.1, overall nearly half the respondents indicated that their household had provided but not received assistance, while more than 20 percent had both provided and received assistance in the past. Only about one in four households had not participated in these interhousehold resource flows. The regularity and frequency with which these resource transfers take place is evidenced by the fact that 80-90 percent and more of those who had ever received or given assistance had done so during roughly the preceding year. Hence, as shown in part A of table 10.1, just over one-sixth of respondents reported having received each type of assistance in either 1989 or 1990, while half had given fostering assistance during the same period, with a slightly smaller percentage having given schooling assistance. For this recent period, nearly half the households had given but not received assistance, another 19 percent had done both, while nonparticipants in these transfers represented just over a quarter of the total number of households (figure 10.1, part B).

The high degree of participation of households in solidarity networks, both as donors and as recipients, is evident from part B of table 10.1, which gives more detailed information about multiple forms of participation. Considering each form of assistance separately, a majority of those who have been

---

[8] A couple of methodological caveats are in order here. Since questions about resource transfers were asked only of women who were either themselves head of the household or married to the household head, we have systematically excluded women (currently married or not) who live in vertically or horizontally integrated households headed by a relative. Consequently, our data likely understate receipt of assistance relative to provision. While taking this consideration into account would narrow the magnitude of the gap between giving and receiving assistance, we do not believe that it would make a particularly great difference. Further, since questions about assistance were not asked of men, we may have missed some transfer activity about which wives were not knowledgeable. This latter omission is most pertinent with respect to schooling assistance.

Table 10.1 Participation in Interhousehold Resource Transfers for Children's Schooling and Child Fostering

A. Percentages Who Received or Gave Assistance, Ever and in 1989-1990, by Type of Assistance

	Children's Schooling	Child Fostering	Schooling or Fostering
Ever received assistance for	21	21	28
Received assistance in 1989-1990 for	17	18	26
Ever gave assistance for	54	58	68
Gave assistance in 1989-1990 for	44	50	67

B. Percentages Involved in Multiple Forms of Participation, by Type of Assistance

Percentage of Those Who Ever	Received Schooling Assistance	Received Fostering Assistance	Given Schooling Assistance	Given Fostering Assistance
Received schooling assistance who also have	—	65	63	70
Received fostering assistance who also have	63	—	58	62
Gave schooling assistance who also have	24	23	—	81
Gave fostering assistance who also have	25	23	75	—

Note: Universe is women aged 15-49 who either were married with a husband who was the household head or headed their own households.

recipients of assistance have also been donors, and nearly a fourth of those who have been donors have also been recipients.[9] If the time frame under consideration were limited to 1989 and 1990, the percentages would be smaller, but not by much: they would typically be 80-90 percent of those shown in the table.

Hence, these data suggest that there is a considerable amount of transfer activity that takes place between and among households, and it is not uncommon—even when one is looking only at the recent past—to observe households that are both donors and recipients. The reciprocity of these networks is apparent: those who have received a particular form of assistance are more likely than the overall sample to have given that assistance as well, and vice versa.

The sources and recipients of assistance for schooling and fostering are shown in table 10.2. With respect to schooling, there is clear evidence of a substantial degree of transfers among siblings, with majorities of both those

[9] If the two forms of assistance are combined, three-quarters of recipient households have also been donors, while over 30 percent of donor households have been recipients.

Fig. 10.1 Distribution of households according to participation in resource transfers in support of children's schooling or child fostering

a. Ever participated

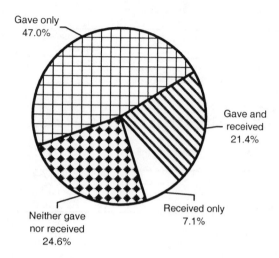

b. Participated 1989-1990

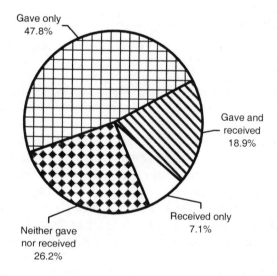

Table 10.2 Principal Sources and Recipients of Assistance for Children's Schooling and Child Fostering

Type of Assistance	Parents	Sons/ Daughters	Siblings	Nieces/ Nephews	Cousins	Aunts/ Uncles	Friends
Received schooling assistance from	23	6	50	7	4	9	6
Received fostering assistance from	37	5	33	5	2	10	3
Gave schooling assistance to	6	2	60	44	10	5	4
Gave fostering assistance to	8	2	59	44	7	3	3

Note: For each row, the universe consists of respondents reporting receipt or giving of the type of assistance indicated. Hence, e.g., of those who received schooling assistance for their children, 23 percent received such assistance from their (or their husband's) parents; of those who gave fostering assistance to other people's children, 59 percent provided such assistance to their (or their husband's) siblings. N.B: Sum of percentages in each row exceeds 100 owing to multiple donors or recipients.

receiving and those providing such assistance indicating that it was received from or given to siblings. In the former case, there is an intergenerational re-source flow, in that assistance was received from a sibling to support the schooling of one's own children. In the latter case, by contrast, the resource flow is intragenerational: 60 percent of those who indicated that they gave support for schooling indicated that it was for one or more of their siblings. The other major source of schooling assistance besides siblings is parents: nearly one-fourth of recipients benefited from support to their children from their parents. The other major destination for those who provided schooling assist-ance was nieces and nephews. This latter intergenerational transfer constitutes further evidence that siblings tend to provide assistance, not only to one an-other, but also to one another's children.

The pattern with respect to child fostering was broadly similar, in that sib-lings and parents were the main sources for those who received help and sib-lings and nieces and nephews were the main recipients of assistance.[10] Parents appear to play a more important role relative to siblings in providing fostering assistance as compared to transfers in support of children's schooling.

Multivariate Analyses of Interhousehold Resource Flows

Table 10.3 reports the coefficients from the weighted logistic regressions used to examine recent (1989-1990) provision of resources to other households. The index of economic well-being of the household is highly significantly linked to provision of both forms of assistance. Higher values of the index tend to be

---

[10] The small number of respondents who indicated that they provided fostering assistance to their parents presumably were fostering in young siblings.

Table 10.3 Analyses of Interhousehold Resource Transfers: Giving Assistance in 1989-1990

Independent Variables	Dependent Variable			
	Children's Schooling		Child Fostering	
Economic index = 0	-0.153*	-0.143*	-0.388**	-0.387**
Economic index = 1	—	—	—	—
Economic index = 2 or 3	0.294**	0.306**	0.200**	0.204**
Economic index = 4 or 5	0.732**	0.785**	0.863**	0.911**
Economic index = 6+	0.544**	0.551**	1.165**	1.197**
Not employed	—	—	—	—
Employee	0.750**	0.793**	0.504**	0.540**
Self-employed	0.289**	0.294**	0.257**	0.256**
Female head	0.241$^+$	0.187	0.636**	0.715**
No. of surviving children	-0.016	—	0.188**	—
Surviving children squared	0.0003	—	-0.023**	—
Females age 0	—	0.208**	—	0.098
Males age 0	—	-0.444**	—	-0.692**
Females age 1-5	—	0.009	—	-0.036
Males age 1-5	—	-0.046	—	0.042
Females age 6-14	—	-0.157**	—	-0.030
Males age 6-14	—	0.134**	—	0.160**
Females age 15-25	—	-0.019	—	-0.099*
Males age 15-25	—	0.141**	—	0.132**
Wife's education				
None	-0.354**	-0.307**	0.253**	0.341**
Primary	—	—	—	—
Secondary 1-2	0.582**	0.608**	0.166**	0.226**
Secondary 3-4	0.645**	0.649**	0.187**	0.240**
Secondary 5-6	0.245**	0.249**	-0.071	-0.020
University	1.005**	1.041**	-0.161	-0.138
Other	0.573**	0.476*	0.461*	0.254
Husband's education				
None	-0.960**	-0.907**	-0.121	0.019
Primary	-0.192*	-0.232**	-0.170*	-0.155*
Secondary	—	—	—	—
University	0.229**	0.210**	-0.092	-0.117$^+$
Other, don't know	-0.471**	-0.452**	-0.178**	-0.147**
Missing	-0.585**	-0.540**	-0.355**	-0.400**
Wife's age	0.116**	0.150**	0.138**	0.188**
Wife's age squared	-0.0017**	-0.0025**	-0.0020**	-0.0030**
Ethnic group:				
Bakongo North	0.159$^+$	0.225*	0.218*	0.254**
Bakongo South	-0.227**	-0.206**	-0.484**	-0.494**
Kwilu-Kwango	—	—	—	—
Mongo	-0.209*	-0.280**	0.114	0.087
Ubangi	-0.216**	-0.174*	-0.283**	-0.292**
Luba	-0.198**	-0.196**	-0.588**	-0.621**
Other tribes	-0.029	0.084	-0.183	-0.091
Non-Congolese	-0.413**	-0.322**	-0.407**	-0.316**
Religion				
Catholic	—	—	—	—
Protestant	0.080	0.115*	0.135*	0.201**
Kimbanguist	-0.042	-0.025	0.548**	0.585**
Other	0.184**	0.233**	0.231**	0.301**
None	-0.159	-0.184	-0.650**	-0.678**
Intercept	-2.573	-2.997	-2.808	-3.174
Log likelihood	-6,951.9	-6,879.4	-7,149.3	-7,083.0
Mean of dependent variable	0.434	0.434	0.490	0.490

Note: Sample size = 1,252.

** Significant at the .01 level.
* Significant at the .05 level.
$^+$ Significant at the .10 level.

associated with a substantially greater likelihood of giving assistance, especially for child fostering.[11]

Controlling for the economic index, households with women employed outside the home are also significantly more likely to provide assistance to others. Thus, the evidence is quite strong that better-off households, as well as those with working wives (especially those employed in the modern sector of the economy), are distinctly more likely to participate in resource transfers as donors. Controlling for these and other factors, female-headed households are roughly almost twice as likely to foster children in, contrary to our income-oriented hypothesis. This may reflect greater demand for labor services in the home in households headed by women.

The number of surviving children that a woman has is not linked to the propensity that her household will participate in resource transfers to other households in support of children's schooling. However, there is a curvilinear relation between women's number of surviving children and provision of assistance for child lodging: the propensity to give lodging assistance first rises as the number of surviving children increases, then diminishes after the number of children exceeds four. When one takes into account the number of surviving children in various age-gender groups that a woman has, quite a few significant coefficients are evident. Infant sons (but not daughters) are associated with a lower likelihood of providing assistance, while participation in transfers to other households is greater when a woman has sons of school age. By contrast, there is a weak and generally negative association between giving assistance and the presence of school-age daughters. This is suggestive of a gender bias in favor of males within extended families.

A woman's own educational attainment is highly significantly related to the probability that her household contributes to the schooling of children in other households. With the exception of upper-level secondary schooling, increased educational attainment of the respondent is associated with a progressively greater likelihood of providing assistance for schooling. By contrast, all else equal, women with no schooling are most likely to foster in children, while the best-educated women do not differ significantly from those with primary schooling in this regard. The findings here are consistent with our earlier notion that education likely contributes to greater tastes for schooling. This notion appears to be supported by the coefficients for husband's education. There is a clear tendency for the likelihood of provision of assistance for schooling to rise as husband's education rises, with a particularly sharp increase as one moves from husbands with no schooling to those with primary education. However, differences by husband's schooling in giving lodging assistance are small and not highly significant for the most part.

[11] For example, the estimated coefficients indicate that the odds ratios for the wealthiest households to be providing fostering assistance are almost five times greater than those of the poorest households and more than three times higher than those of the next-poorest households, all else equal.

Age is entered into the equations as a quadratic, and the significant coefficients for both terms suggest that the propensity to give assistance first rises and then falls. The magnitudes of the coefficients indicate that the increase persists only up to the early to mid-30s. Somewhat surprisingly, the turning point is not affected substantially by consideration of the age distribution of the respondent's children. In any case, these results do not support our expectation of an increasing propensity to give with age.

There are some statistically significant differences by ethnic group in participation in giving. Women from the Kwilu-Kwango area show a relatively high propensity to provide assistance for the schooling and fostering of others' children, being surpassed only by the Bakongo North women. Apart from Mongo women's comparable involvement in child fostering, all the other ethnic groups tend to be less likely to be participating in solidarity networks. Luba women in particular are significantly less likely to foster in children. Those from other countries (primarily from neighboring Angola) are relatively unlikely to provide assistance to others.

Religious differences in the provision of schooling assistance are generally modest and for the most part not statistically significant. Child fostering, however, is clearly more variable across religious groups, being relatively common among Kimbanguist women and unusual among women with no religious affiliation.

Turning now to factors associated with the receipt of assistance (table 10.4), we see that greater economic well-being tends to be associated with a lower likelihood of receiving assistance, especially for child fostering. Differences by the economic index in receipt of assistance do not appear to be as pronounced as the corresponding differences in the provision of assistance. Employment of the respondent outside the home, particularly in the modern sector, is also linked to a smaller probability of being a recipient of assistance. Contrary to our hypothesis, female-headed households do not show a markedly greater propensity to participate as recipients in solidarity networks.

The likelihood of receiving assistance tends to rise with the number of surviving children, as hypothesized. However, this increase is at a diminishing rate: beyond six children the probability of receiving support for children's schooling or fostering declines (the average number of surviving children for the women analyzed here is 3.6). Controlling for the number of surviving children by age and gender highlights some differences between assistance for schooling and for child fostering. Receipt of assistance for schooling does not appear to be strongly related to the gender of the children, although the coefficients for school-age males are a bit higher than are those for females. Women with female infants are somewhat less likely to receive such assistance, while children in all other age groups appear to contribute to a greater likelihood of receiving help with expenses for children's schooling. By contrast, all the coefficients for gender and age group in the child-fostering equation are significant, but two (for female infants and girls aged 6-14) are negative, and the

Table 10.4 Analyses of Interhousehold Resource Transfers: Receiving Assistance in 1989-1990

Independent Variables	Dependent Variable			
	Children's Schooling		Child Fostering	
Economic index = 0	-0.196*	-0.183*	0.186*	0.222**
Economic index = 1	—	—	—	—
Economic index = 2 or 3	-0.062	-0.079	-0.234**	-0.241**
Economic index = 4 or 5	-0.040	-0.062	-0.285**	-0.211*
Economic index = 6+	-0.364**	-0.374**	-0.528**	-0.550**
Not employed	—	—	—	—
Employee	-0.473**	-0.529**	-0.363*	-0.425**
Self-employed	-0.158**	-0.175**	-0.117*	-0.148*
Female head	-0.061	0.008	0.136	0.089
No. of surviving children	0.629**	—	0.540**	—
Surviving children squared	-0.048**	—	-0.042**	—
Females age 0	—	-0.226*	—	-0.454**
Males age 0	—	0.010	—	0.390**
Females age 1-5	—	0.074	—	0.151**
Males age 1-5	—	0.157**	—	0.228**
Females age 6-14	—	0.145**	—	-0.165**
Males age 6-14	—	0.173**	—	0.070*
Females age 15-25	—	0.120**	—	0.246**
Males age 15-25	—	0.228**	—	0.348**
Wife's education				
None	-0.403**	-0.411**	0.008	0.024
Primary	—	—	—	—
Secondary 1-2	-0.225**	-0.168*	0.012	0.024
Secondary 3-4	0.224**	0.260**	0.148+	0.186*
Secondary 5-6	-1.156**	-1.149**	-0.500**	-0.625**
University	0.351*	0.258	-0.326	-0.410*
Other	-2.300**	-2.409**	-0.338	-0.436
Husband's education				
None	-0.070	0.041	-1.330**	-1.418**
Primary	-0.262*	-0.264*	0.289**	0.217*
Secondary	—	—	—	—
University	0.102	0.098	0.072	0.058
Other, don't know	-0.069	-0.082	0.115	0.086
Missing	0.838**	0.724**	0.801**	0.849**
Wife's age	0.285**	0.431**	0.166**	0.463**
Wife's age squared	-0.0035**	-0.0057**	-0.0020**	-0.0066**
Ethnic group				
Bakongo North	-0.816**	-0.816**	-0.124	-0.159
Bakongo South	0.019	-0.022	0.291**	0.274**
Kwilu-Kwango	—	—	—	—
Mongo	0.611**	0.591**	1.057**	0.891**
Ubangi	0.191+	0.116	0.548**	0.506**
Luba	-0.023	-0.138	-0.050	-0.228*
Other tribes	-0.028	-0.269	0.689**	0.384*
Non-Congolese	0.698**	0.522**	-0.080	-0.307+
Religion				
Catholic	—	—	—	—
Protestant	0.097	0.104	0.439**	0.442**
Kimbanguist	0.189	0.179	-0.409*	-0.512**
Other	-0.466**	-0.447**	0.061	0.089
None	-0.080	-0.046	-0.848**	-0.835**
Intercept	-8.182	-9.398	-6.162	-9.826
Log likelihood	-4,253.3	-4,307.3	-4,543.7	-4,532.0
Mean of dependent variable	0.162	0.162	0.172	0.172

Note: Sample size = 1,252.

** Significant at the .01 level.
*   Significant at the .05 level.
+   Significant at the .10 level.

remainder are positive. Overall, then, it is apparent that having more school-age children is associated with a significantly greater likelihood of receiving assistance with respect to both children's schooling and child fostering.

There are no strong patterns of association between a woman's schooling and the likelihood of receiving assistance. Women with no schooling are relatively less likely to receive help for the schooling of their children, perhaps reflecting low enrollment rates for children of uneducated mothers. At the same time, the lowest likelihood of receiving assistance for schooling is for women with upper-level secondary education. Receipt of assistance for fostering appears to be generally low for better-educated women. With respect to husband's education, there is no pattern of differences in receipt of schooling assistance, while households in which the husband has no schooling are least likely by far to receive assistance for child fostering.

Age differences are significantly related to receipt of assistance, with the likelihood rising up to the late 30s or early 40s and then declining. Differences by ethnic group are evident with respect to receiving both types of assistance. With regard to assistance for schooling, Mongo women and those from other countries have relatively high likelihoods of being recipients, while Bakongo North women are far and away least likely to receive such assistance. Differences in receiving child-fostering assistance are also apparent, with Mongo and, to a lesser extent, Ubangi women especially likely to foster children out.

Finally, there are limited differences by religious group in receipt of schooling assistance but more substantial (and statistically significant) differerences in receiving fostering assistance. Relative to Catholics, Protestants have a high likelihood of having children fostered out, while Kimbanguists and women with no religious affiliation have distinctly lower likelihoods of receiving fostering assistance.

Conclusions and Implications

This chapter has examined resource transfers among households in Kinshasa in support of children's schooling and child fostering. Solidarity behavior is widespread, with three-quarters of all households participating as either donors of such transfers, recipients, or both. Provision of assistance is considerably more frequent than receipt, presumably reflecting the net donor position of residents of Kinshasa vis-à-vis extended-family members in rural areas. Resource flows are both intergenerational and intragenerational: parents, siblings, and nieces and nephews are the primary sources and recipients of interhousehold resource transfers.

Multivariate analyses indicate that, in general, economic well-being, the number, age, and sex of children, and other respondent characteristics such as schooling and ethnic group all influence participation in solidarity networks. At the same time, however, the influence of these different factors varies depending both on what type of assistance is being considered and on whether one is looking at receiving or giving behavior. There are several limitations of our research that should be noted. We have information on the existence of transfers but not on their magnitude. Our data may omit information concerning some transfers about which wives are not knowledgeable. We have not taken into consideration information about children of the woman's husband if they are not her children. Further, since our questions about resource transfers were asked only of respondents who were married to household heads or were themselves household heads, we have excluded consideration of young married respondents in vertically or horizontally integrated households. Consequently, we most likely understate somewhat the prevalence of receipt of assistance within Kinshasa. More fundamentally, by virtue of the fact that our data pertain to a large city, we are unable to say anything directly about resource flows to rural households. In effect, then, we must acknowledge that we have information on only a portion of the overall picture of extended-family solidarity.

Despite these limitations, the chapter's documenting of the extensiveness of solidarity networks in Kinshasa provides support for the notion that these networks serve to diffuse the costs of childbearing beyond the nuclear family. There is clearly some income redistribution taking place via these transfers since more well-off households are considerably more likely to be donors and poor households are distinctly more likely to be recipients. We also find evidence consistent with the notion that child fostering may take place to meet a household's demand for labor. At the same time, there is a long tradition in Kinshasa of rural youths coming to the city for acquisition of schooling (especially at the secondary and higher level), and the data suggest that this phenomenon was present in 1990.

The sharp economic downturn in the city's economy since the time of our survey has undoubtedly put substantial pressure on the ability of many urban households to continue to play the same role as previously in extended-family solidarity networks. Hence, we suspect that, in some cases at least, participation in these networks has diminished (Eloundou-Enyegue 1997).

Further, the high cost of education in Kinshasa appears to have increased relatively during the crisis, most likely contributing to a reduction in school enrollment rates. It may well be the case—similar to what Eloundou-Enyegue (1992) found in Cameroon—that this situation has resulted in the emergence of a flow of children from Kinshasa to rural areas, where schooling is not so expensive. In any case, the extent to which solidarity networks have been modified in the face of the economic crisis is but one of several questions that merit further research.

Chapter 11. Education and Employment in the Formal and Informal Sectors

The secular trends in both education and employment were documented in chapter 2, where we saw that the increased educational attainment of women since the 1950s has been accompanied by substantial growth in the extent of their employment outside the home. At the same time, however, the very poor overall performance of the Congolese economy since the mid-1970s means that the increased employment has been concentrated for the most part in the informal sector of the economy (as reflected in the growth in the numbers and proportions of self-employed independents; cf. table 2.5 above). Only a small minority of women working in the labor market are employed in the modern sector of the economy. In this chapter, we examine more closely the links between education and employment, with particular emphasis on the distinction between the formal and the informal sectors.

As Schultz (1993) has noted, the second half of the 20th century was characterized, not only by increasing absolute levels of education for women around the world, but also by greater schooling of women relative to that of men. Women's involvement in labor market employment has also increased over this same period. There is a substantial literature from numerous countries documenting a positive association between women's schooling and their participation in the labor market (Schultz 1993), and, as we shall see below, among women in Kinshasa there is a positive association between women's schooling and whether they are in the labor market. Further, in developing countries, women's attainment of relatively high levels of education is often a key factor facilitating access to modern-sector employment (see, e.g., Vijverberg 1993; Glick and Sahn 1997), and, in Kinshasa, women without upper-level secondary or university education have only very slim prospects for securing modern-sector employment.

As we shall see below, even relatively high levels of education do not guarantee access to modern-sector employment. Poor macroeconomic performance has effectively imposed severe constraints on the number of such jobs. One consequence of this situation is that the transition from school to work in the labor market may be lengthy, and, as a result, the likelihood of being employed will be positively related to the duration of an individual's exposure to labor market opportunities. Further, it is very possible that securing employment in the modern sector may depend as much or more on whom one knows rather than on what is known or educational credentials. In particular, family connections, contacts, and social networks to which women belong may play an important role in determining who gains access to the scarce and highly valued modern-sector jobs (see, e.g., Malhotra and DeGraff 1997, 2000).

In addition to the factors already identified as potential influences on women's labor market outcomes—educational attainment, duration since leaving school, and family connections, contacts, and social networks—household demographic composition has been shown to be linked to employment activity. In particular, a number of studies in both industrialized and developing nations have found that greater numbers of children and/or the presence of preschool-age children are associated with a lower likelihood of female involvement in the labor market (see, e.g., Shapiro and Shaw 1983; Connelly et al. 1996; Wong and Levine 1992). At the same time, some studies of urban labor markets in developing countries indicate that this prospective lower labor market participation, presumably associated with child-care responsibilities, may be offset by the presence of other individuals in the household who can assist in the provision of child care (Birdsall and Behrman 1991; Connelly et al. 1996). From a long-term perspective, a case can be made for household composition as being endogenous with respect to women's employment, as a reflection of both past fertility and perhaps also child fostering to meet household labor demand. However, we believe that it is useful to examine the associations that exist in Kinshasa between household demographic composition, on the one hand, and women's employment activity, on the other.

Ideally, our examination of education and employment would take into consideration information on wages (earnings) of workers and how these wages varied by educational attainment and by sector of employment. As noted earlier, however, we were not able to gather data on wages or earnings in our survey because of the sensitive nature of such questions in Kinshasa. Indeed, there is remarkably little evidence available, even for the modern sector of the economy, on earnings and how they are related to the educational attainment of workers. However, data from a large-scale survey of firms in the modern sector of Kinshasa's economy carried out in 1987 and analyzed by Shapiro (1992) do provide a clear indication of substantial payoffs to educational attainment for better-educated workers employed in the modern sector.

Relative to workers in occupations that typically required on the order of 4 years of secondary schooling, those in occupations requiring completion of secondary school had earnings that were roughly 35 percent higher, those in occupations where a first (3-year) university degree was required were paid more than twice as much, and those in managerial occupations requiring a 5-year university degree were paid four times as much (Shapiro 1992). While this is clearly only limited evidence for the modern sector, it does indicate the existence of quite substantial wage premiums for better-educated individuals in Kinshasa with employment in the modern sector. And, of course, it provides a basis for the observation that modern-sector employment is very highly valued, especially among individuals with high educational attainment.

The following section provides a descriptive look at education and employment in the formal and informal sectors and, in so doing, documents the predominance of better-educated women in the modern sector. We also examine the kinds of jobs in which women are engaged in Kinshasa and the links between women's employment and household economic well-being. This is followed by a section with multivariate analyses of employment status. Multinomial logit analyses are carried out to assess the roles of various factors in determining whether women are employed in the modern sector, are working in the informal sector, or are not employed or working for pay or profit outside the home. These multivariate analyses first focus on the effects of educational attainment and time since leaving school and then incorporate consideration of additional influencing factors, most notably those relating to household demographic composition and to family connections and contacts that may facilitate entry into the modern-sector labor market. The concluding section of the chapter summarizes and discusses the findings and considers the changes in women's employment that are likely to have taken place since 1990.

Education and Employment: A Descriptive Overview

Women's employment status in 1990 according to their educational attainment is shown (for women not in school) in part A of table 11.1. Overall, just under 40 percent of nonenrolled women aged 15-49 are employed, but only one out of eight women in the labor market is an employee. Nonparticipants in the labor market constitute 60 percent or slightly more of each schooling group, apart from the relatively low nonparticipation of those with university education. Hence, the data suggest that, over the range of schooling from none to upper-level secondary, there is virtually no link (or, if anything, a weak negative association) between women's education and whether they are in the labor market. We shall return to this issue below.

With respect to sector of employment, it is clear from the first part of the table that 40 percent or slightly less of each of the three lowest schooling groups are self-employed; the figure drops off, first slowly and then more rapidly, as one moves across the three highest schooling groups. Access to the modern sector (i.e., status as an employee) is effectively limited to women with at least 3 years of secondary schooling.[1] Only among women with upper-level secondary schooling or university education are more than 10 percent of the women in a given schooling group employed in the modern sector. With two-thirds of employed women working as employees, university-educated women constitute the only schooling group of which more than half of employed women are working in the modern sector.

Part B of table 11.1 shows the educational attainment of each employment status group. Relative to all nonenrolled women, those who are self-employed are slightly disproportionately more likely to be from among the three lowest schooling groups and distinctly less likely to be in either of the two highest groups. Women from the three lowest education groups are clearly underrepresented among employees: they account for 57 percent of all women not in school but only just over 10 percent of employees. At the other extreme, women in the two highest education groups, who represent 15 percent of the total of nonenrolled women, account for 57 percent of all employees.

The distribution of employment by industry and by sector (for men and women combined) in 1987 is shown in table 11.2.[2] Commerce is by far the principal industry of informal-sector workers, representing more than half the total. Agriculture, manufacturing, private services, and transport and communications are the other major industry groups represented by informal-sector workers. By contrast, employment by industry in the modern sector is somewhat more evenly distributed. Public administration accounts for almost a third of the total, manufacturing represents a fifth, and private services, transport and communications, and commerce each account for 10-13 percent of the estimated total employment in the modern sector.

Our data for 1990 demonstrate that women's employment in the informal sector in particular is much more heavily concentrated in commerce: fully 94 percent of women were engaged in commerce, principally in the sale of food products (table 11.3).[3] The remaining women in the informal sector were primarily in services, and almost three-quarters of them worked as dressmakers or seamstresses (*couturière*). As with the global data for 1987 reported in table

---

[1] As noted in chapter 2, being an employee is not equivalent to being employed in the modern sector. However, among women, virtually all independents are in the informal sector, while the vast majority of employees are found in the modern sector. Operationally, then, in this chapter we treat independents as being in the informal sector and employees as being in the modern sector.

[2] Comparison of the total data for 1987 in table 11.2 with the corresponding data from the 1984 census reveals some modest differences. These reflect assumptions made concerning industry-specific growth in employment between 1984 and 1987. The division of total employment into estimates for the informal and modern sectors was done using census data on class of worker by industry, data from other employment surveys, and assumptions about the distribution of salaried employment between the modern and the informal sectors. For further details, see Shapiro (1992).

[3] Both processed and unprocessed food are included here, and it is undoubtedly the case that a number of the women were selling unprocessed food that they had grown. Our data do not permit us to determine the size of this group of agricultural producers.

Table 11.1 Educational Attainment and Employment Status (percentage distributions)

		Educational Attainment					
			Secondary				
	None	Primary	1-2	3-4	5-6	University	Total[a]
A. Employment Status by Educational Attainment							
Not employed	60	61	61	61	63	51	61
Self-employed	40	38	37	34	23	16	35
Employee	0[b]	1	1	6	13	33	5
Total	100	100	100	100	100	100	100
B. Educational Attainment by Employment Status							
Not employed	7	29	22	26	13	3	100
Self-employed	8	32	24	26	8	1	100
Employee	1	3	7	31	34	23	100
Total	7	28	22	26	12	3	100

Note: Universe is women aged 15-49 not enrolled in school.

[a] Totals include the small number of women with "other" schooling (typically, vocational training), 50 percent of whom were self-employed and 11 percent of whom were working as employees, representing 1 and 2 percent of those employment status groups, respectively.

[b] Percentage is less than 0.5.

Table 11.2 Distribution of Employment in Kinshasa by Industry and by Sector, 1987 (percentage distributions)

	Sector		
Industry	Informal	Modern	Total
Agriculture	14.6	2.2	9.4
Mining	0.3	0.4	0.3
Manufacturing	9.8	20.0	14.1
Construction & public works	3.6	3.9	3.7
Utilities	0.2	1.4	0.7
Finance, insurance, & real estate	0.9	4.9	2.6
Transport & communications	7.6	12.3	9.5
Services—public administration	0.0	32.6	13.9
Services—private	9.8	12.7	11.1
Commerce	53.3	9.5	34.7
Total	100.0	100.0	100.0

Source: Shapiro (1992).

11.2 above, modern-sector employment of women in our survey was more varied. The majority of employees were in public and private services, but commerce, manufacturing, finance/insurance/real estate, and transportation and
communications were other industries each accounting for 8-11 percent of
women's modern-sector employment.

As may be seen in table 11.4, similar patterns are evident in our 1990 data
with respect to occupation. In the informal sector, well in excess of 90 percent
of employment is as commercial personnel, while there is substantially greater
occupational diversity in the modern sector. Women employed as administrative personnel (secretaries, accounting clerks, etc.) and as professional and
technical employees (teachers, nurses, etc.) account for more than three-
quarters of women workers in the modern sector.

Data on economic well-being and women's sector of employment are
shown in table 11.5. As in earlier analyses, economic well-being is measured
by an index that enumerates the number of working consumer durable goods
in the respondent's household. It is often argued that women's participation in
the informal sector frequently represents an effort to augment low family incomes, and the data in the table are consistent with this notion. The two poverty
groups—those from households with a value of 0 or 1 on the index—represent
half of Kinshasa's nonenrolled women of childbearing age. It is evident from
part A of the table that women in the two poverty groups are somewhat more
likely to be working in the informal sector than are other women and distinctly
less likely to be working in the modern sector. Conversely, women at the high
end of the index are disproportionately likely to be working in the modern
sector, and they are least likely (although not by a large margin) to be found in
the informal sector.[4]

Focusing on the economic well-being of the different employment status
groups (part B), it is clear that women employed in the modern sector are
substantially underrepresented in the two poverty groups and disproportionately
concentrated at the high end of the economic index. By contrast, self-employed
women are slightly overrepresented in the two poverty groups, while the economic well-being of nonemployed women is virtually identical to that for all
women. Hence, it is clear that, although women employed in the modern sector
constitute only a small proportion of all women, they are relatively affluent.

Determinants of Employment Status

The descriptive data reviewed in the preceding section provide a fairly clear
indication of the importance of acquisition of higher levels of schooling for
access to the modern sector, but no other factors influencing the likelihood of
employment in the modern sector are taken into consideration. The data
presented earlier in table 2.4 show that women's employment activity tends to

[4] Poverty status and employment status are clearly jointly related. Our purpose here is simply
to provide descriptive information on the association between the two.

Table 11.3 Distribution of Employment of Women, by Industry and by Sector, 1990 (percentage distributions)

	Sector	
Industry	Informal	Modern
Agriculture	0[a]	1
Mining	0	1
Manufacturing	0	11
Construction & public works	0	2
Utilities	0	1
Finance, insurance, & real estate	0	8
Transport & communications	0	8
Services	6	58
Commerce	94	11
Not specified	0[a]	1
Total	100	100

Source: Calculated from data.

[a] Less than 0.5 percent.

Table 11.4 Distribution of Employment of Women, by Occupation and by Sector, 1990 (percentage distributions)

	Sector	
Occupation	Informal	Modern
Professional and technical	1	32
Directors, upper-level managers	0	2
Administrative personnel	0	44
Commercial personnel	94	8
Specialized service workers	1	7
Agricultural workers	0[a]	0[a]
Nonagricultural workers	4	7
Not specified	0	1
Total	100	100

Source: Calculated from data.

[a] Less than 0.5 percent.

Table 11.5 Economic Well-Being and Employment Status (percentage distributions)

	Value on Economic Index					
	0	1	2-3	4-5	6+	Total
	A. Employment Status by Economic Well-being					
Not employed	62	57	63	62	56	61
Self-employed	37	41	33	30	30	35
Employee	2	3	5	8	14	5
Total	100	100	100	100	100	100
	B. Economic Well-being by Employment Status					
Not employed	33	17	23	18	9	100
Self-employed	34	21	21	15	9	100
Employee	11	10	21	29	29	100
Total	32	18	22	18	10	100

Note: Universe is women aged 15-49 not enrolled in school.

Fig. 11.1 Employment by age group, overall and by class of worker, 1984 and 1990

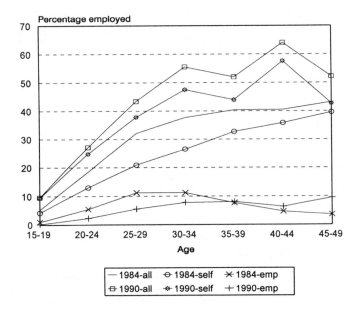

Sources: 1984: Institut National de la Statistique (1991a, tables 10, 14, pp. 68, 74); 1990: calculated from data.

be positively associated with age. This may be seen more directly in figure 11.1, which shows the percentage of women employed by age group—overall and by class of worker (self-employed and employee)—from the 1990 survey and also from the 1984 census. It is apparent from the figure that self-employment and overall employment tend to rise with age; in 1990, there is also a general increase with age in the percentage of women who are employees, but this was not the case in 1984.

At the same time, the evidence presented in table 2.1 above documents that younger cohorts of women tend to have higher levels of schooling than do their older counterparts. Conversely, women with greater educational attainment are also more likely to be relatively young and, in particular, to have limited exposure to the labor market.[5] Given their relative youthfulness and greater time in school, then, well-educated women will have a period of availa-

---

[5] Among those aged 20 and over, e.g., the median age of nonenrolled women with no schooling or primary education is 30, while, for the four groups with secondary education or higher, the corresponding medians are from 25 to 28 years. Although these absolute differences in median age are not very large, when one considers the schooling levels to which these medians correspond, it is clear that better-educated women tend to have considerably less potential (postschool) experience in the labor market, especially so for the women in the highest educational attainment groups. Indeed, among those aged 20 and over, the median number of years since leaving school exceeds 15 in the two lowest schooling groups, while in the four higher groups the median falls steadily—from 11, to 8, to 6, to 4—as educational attainment increases.

bility for employment that is comparatively brief, and this factor may offset somewhat the advantages of greater schooling in gaining access to modern-sector jobs or in becoming established in the informal sector. To put the matter a bit differently, gross differences in employment rates by educational attainment, like those shown in part A of table 11.1, may understate the net differences once age or availability for employment is taken into consideration.

In this section, then, we first examine employment status as a function, not only of educational attainment, but also of exposure to the opportunity to obtain employment (measured by the number of years since a woman left school). Weighted multinomial logit analyses are estimated to examine employment status in 1990 of women not enrolled in school, with self-employment (informal sector) and employee (modern sector) as two distinct employment outcomes contrasted against a reference group consisting of nonemployed women.[6] The coefficients reported in table 11.6 show the impact of schooling and years since leaving school[7] on the likelihood of working as an employee as compared to nonemployment and on the likelihood of being self-employed relative to non-employment, respectively. The corresponding marginal effects show the influence of schooling and exposure on the probability of being an employee and on the probability of being self-employed, respectively.[8] The discussion of these estimates will focus on the marginal effects rather than on the coefficients since they have a more straightforward interpretation.

The strong impact of educational attainment on access to the modern sector suggested by the data in table 11.1 is readily apparent here as well. The estimated effects of schooling on the likelihood of working as an employee rise steadily as educational attainment increases. The marginal effects indicate that, among the three lowest schooling groups, where modern-sector employment is negligible, there are not any significant differences; only beginning with mid-level secondary education are there statistically significant effects of schooling. Even for university-educated women, however, the estimated marginal effect of 0.12 is not particularly large, reflecting the limited access to modern-sector employment. Years since leaving school is entered as a quadratic, but only the linear term has a significant impact on the likelihood of securing work as an employee. That likelihood is quite low, however: all else equal, the estimated marginal effect of a year out of school on the probability of working as an employee is not quite 0.003.

---

[6] Multinomial logit analyses are used because there are three possible outcomes: employee; self-employed; and not employed. By restricting the analyses to women not enrolled in school, we effectively ignore the decision to remain in school vs. leaving school to seek employment or engage in household activities.

[7] For women with no schooling and those who left school prior to age 15, years since leaving school is defined as the number of years since age 15.

[8] The reported marginal effect of the kth independent variable on the probability of the jth alternative is obtained by computing estimates of the marginal effects at the means of the other variables. Greene (2000) details methods for calculating the marginal effects and associated standard errors.

Table 11.6 Multinomial Logit Analyses of the Effects of Education and Years out of School on Employment Status

Variable	Employee vs. Not Employed		Self-employed vs. Not Employed	
	Coefficient	Marginal Effect	Coefficient	Marginal Effect
Exposure				
Years out of school	0.199**	0.0027*	0.222**	0.048**
Years out squared	-0.0028	0	-0.0048	-0.0010**
Schooling level				
None	-0.332	-0.008	0.039	0.011
Primary	—	—	—	—
Secondary 1-2	1.535+	0.031	0.378*	0.072*
Secondary 3-4	3.089**	0.064*	0.445**	0.076*
Secondary 5-6	4.156**	0.090**	0.128	-0.003
University	5.564**	0.120**	0.247	0.013
Other schooling	3.821**	0.078*	0.806	0.150
Parameters				
Intercept	-6.953	-0.135	-2.395	-0.479
Log likelihood		-1,321.293		
Model chi-square		378.911**		

Note: Universe is women not enrolled in school. Sample size = 1,834.

** Significant at the .01 level, two-tailed test.
* Significant at the .05 level, two-tailed test.
+ Significant at the .10 level, two-tailed test.

The relation between schooling and self-employment, controlling for years since leaving school, is much less pronounced. There are only two statistically significant marginal effects, for women with lower- and mid-level secondary education. These women are 7-8 percentage points more likely to be self-employed as compared to those in the other schooling groups, all else equal. At the same time, years since leaving school is highly significant as a factor influencing the probability that a woman is self-employed, and, in contrast with the situation for working as an employee, there is a quite large marginal effect, initially approaching 0.05. The size and significance of this effect in conjunction with the limited variation in self-employment across educational attainment groups suggests that entry into the informal sector is fairly common for women across all schooling groups.

The implications of the equations just discussed for employment by education level, years out of school, and sector may be seen in figure 11.2. Part *a* of the figure shows the predicted probabilities of employment in the modern sector, according to the number of years since the individual has left school, for the four highest education groups, consisting of women with at least some sec-

Fig. 11.2 Predicted probabilities of employment, by education and years out of school, modern sector and informal sector

a.   Modern sector

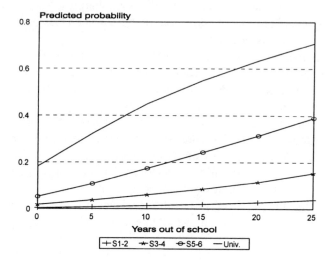

b.   Informal sector

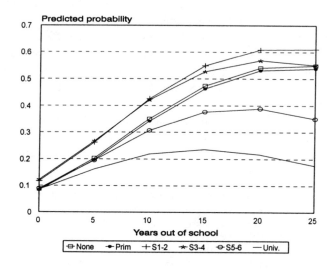

Note: Based on equations in table 11.6; only women with at least secondary education are included in panel a.

ondary schooling.[9] The limited access to the modern sector is evident: even for university-educated women, there is only about a one in three chance of being an employee 5 years after leaving school, and this rises to one in two only after more than 10 years. For women with upper-level secondary schooling, the pattern is similar, but the predicted probabilities are sharply lower, and 15 years after leaving school only about one in four of these women may be expected to be employed in the modern sector.

Part *b* of figure 11.2 shows the predicted probabilities of self-employment for each schooling group. These probabilities are greatest for the women with lower- and mid-level secondary education and lowest for the women with university and upper-level secondary schooling.[10] They generally tend to increase with years out of school, but, for the three highest educational attainment groups, there are modest declines after 15 or 20 years. Finally, it is worth noting that, with the sole exception of the university women, the predicted probabilities of employment in the informal sector are for the most part substantially higher than are those for employment in the modern sector.

Combining the predicted probabilities of modern- and informal-sector employment shows the estimated overall likelihood of being employed. As is readily apparent from figure 11.3, the probability of being employed, given the number of years since leaving school, is strongly positively related to educational attainment: university women have the highest likelihood of being employed, followed by women with upper- and mid-level secondary education, and those with primary or no schooling have the lowest levels of predicted employment. In addition, for each educational attainment group the probability rises as time since the woman left school increases. This contrasts with the data reported in table 11.1 above that suggested little relation between schooling (below the university level) and overall employment. The difference is that, here, we have taken account of the duration since leaving school, and the positive effect of this variable on the likelihood of employment in conjunction with the lower durations for better-educated women account for the pattern observed in table 11.1.

As noted at the beginning of the chapter, we have also carried out multivariate analyses controlling for other variables representing both household demographic composition and family connections and contacts that may assist

---

[9] Predicted probabilities of modern-sector employment for the two lowest schooling groups are between 0 and .01 and hence are not shown.

[10] The differences across schooling groups in predicted probabilities of self-employment, as well as those in predicted probabilities of modern-sector employment, are similar to but at the same time somewhat different from the differences in estimated marginal effects reported in table 11.6 above. That is, particularly for higher values of years out of school, the low predicted probabilities of self-employment for the two groups with the highest educational attainment would not be anticipated from looking at table 11.6. Likewise, the magnitudes of the differences in predicted probabilities of modern-sector employment are greater than those implied by the reported marginal effects. In part, this reflects the fact that the estimated marginal effects of education are calculated at the mean value of years out of school.

Fig. 11.3 Predicted probabilities of being employed, by education and years out of school

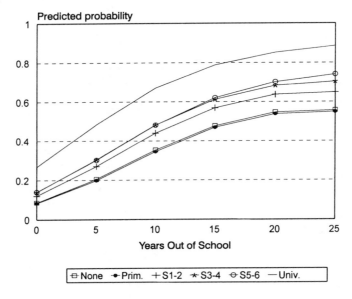

Note: Based on equations in table 11.6.

women seeking employment in the labor market. The variables for demographic composition measure the number of individuals in the household (other than the respondent) in four broad age groups: 0-5, 6-25, 26-54, and 55 and over. In addition, for the 6-25 age group, we have differentiated females and males.[11] As an indicator of family connections, there is a set of dummy variables identifying the status of the woman's husband's occupation, including one variable distinguishing those women not married.[12] The coefficients of the resulting multinomial logit equations and the corresponding marginal effects are reported in table 11.7.

Greater numbers of preschool-age children are associated with lower likelihoods of employment, as indicated by the estimated marginal effects, and this is true in both the modern and the informal sectors. While this result is

[11] Our effort to ascertain the impact of household demographic composition began with a larger set of variables counting those in more numerous age groups separately by gender. Most of the estimated coefficients and marginal effects were insignificant, and we subsequently combined age groups and genders except for the one case (ages 6-25) where there was a clear difference by gender. We have also estimated similar equations with dummy variables indicating simply whether there were people in the household in each of the groups; these estimates were similar to those shown in table 11.7 and are not reported here.

[12] We also examined ethnic and religious groups as explanatory variables linked to social networks that might assist women in gaining access to employment, but these variables were not related to employment status.

Table 11.7 Multinomial Logit Analyses of Employment Status, Controlling for Exposure, Schooling, Husband's Employment Status, and Household Demographic Composition

	Employee vs. Not Employed		Self-employed vs. Not Employed	
Variable	Coefficient	Marginal Effect	Coefficient	Marginal Effect
Exposure				
Years out of school	0.246**	0.0033*	0.238**	0.051**
Years out squared	-0.0046*	-0.0001	-0.0052**	-0.0011**
Schooling level				
None	-0.308	-0.006	-0.005	0.001
Primary	—	—	—	—
Secondary 1-2	1.429$^+$	0.026	0.362*	0.070*
Secondary 3-4	2.849**	0.054*	0.454**	0.081*
Secondary 5-6	3.908**	0.077**	0.201	0.018
University	5.172**	0.101**	0.418	0.057
Other schooling	3.818**	0.071*	0.819	0.155
Husband's employment status				
Low	—	—	—	—
Medium	0.326	0.005	0.172	0.036
High	0.837*	0.023*	-0.883**	-0.200**
Not employed	0.798	0.014	0.351$^+$	0.072$^+$
No husband	1.083**	0.022*	-0.064	-0.021
Household demographic composition				
Children 0-5	-0.283*	-0.005$^+$	-0.110*	-0.022*
Males 6-25	-0.128	-0.002	-0.054	-0.011
Females 6-25	0.185*	0.003	0.084*	0.017*
Adults 26-54	0.045	0.001	0.041	0.009
Adults 55+	0.090	0	0.256$^+$	0.056$^+$
Intercept	-7.312	-0.130	-2.469	-0.495
Parameters				
Log likelihood		-1,290.483		
Model chi-square		440.531**		

Note: Universe is women not enrolled in school. Sample size = 1,834.

** Significant at the .01 level, two-tailed test.
* Significant at the .05 level, two-tailed test.
$^+$ Significant at the .10 level, two-tailed test.

consistent with previous literature, the magnitudes of the estimated effects are small.[13] Women from households with greater numbers of females aged 6-25 are significantly more likely to be working in the informal sector, all else equal. The number of males aged 6-25 is negatively but not significantly related to the

[13] Our questionnaire asked women who had given birth within the 6 years prior to the survey to identify who principally took care of the child when they were at work. More than half the women in the modern sector relied on either a sister or a mother (including in-laws) for childcare, and another 18 percent used hired help (a maid or nanny). Among women in the informal sector identifying child-care arrangements, almost half indicated that they worked at home (selling from just outside one's residence is very common), and just over a quarter relied on either a sister or a mother. In each sector, roughly 10 percent of women had care of the youngest child performed by another of their own children.

probability that women will be employed. This suggests that there is some intrahousehold labor substitution that takes place, with school-age females (but not males) substituting for self-employed women in the performance of household chores. The presence of other adults in the household aged 55 and over appears to facilitate women's employment in the informal sector.

Family connections likely to facilitate access to modern-sector employment are presumably most pertinent vis-à-vis husband's occupational status for those women with husbands in high-status occupations (e.g., professional and upper-level managerial or administrative positions). The estimates presented in table 11.7 show that such women were significantly more likely than those whose husbands were in low-status occupations to be working in the modern sector and that, at the same time, they were significantly and substantially less likely to be self-employed. This finding suggests that high-status husbands may indeed play an important role in facilitating access to modern-sector employment for their wives. At the same time, wives of high-status husbands show a strong aversion to participation in the informal sector.

Those women whose husbands were not employed were significantly more likely than those with low-status husbands to be self-employed. These women were most likely of all the husband's occupational status groups to be self-employed, consistent with an added-worker effect whereby the wife seeks to compensate for the lack of the husband's employment income. In addition, women who were not married had a significantly greater likelihood of being employed in the modern sector.

Both household demographic composition and the variable for husband's occupational status (proxying for contacts) are significant influences on women's employment behavior in Kinshasa. Further, controlling for these variables does not, for the most part, appear to have much of an influence on the estimated effects of schooling and years out of school. More specifically, in comparing tables 11.6 and 11.7, we see that the marginal effects of schooling on the probability of working as an employee are reduced slightly when the additional variables are included and that the impact of years out of school appears to be a bit stronger. With respect to being self-employed, inclusion of the additional variables results in only very small changes in the two significant education marginal effects, along with a small increase in the effect of years out of school.

Discussion and Conclusions

In this chapter, we have examined women's employment in both the modern and the informal sectors of Kinshasa's economy, with particular emphasis on the role of women's education. It is apparent that, for the most part, high levels of education are a necessary but not a sufficient condition for gaining access to modern-sector employment. Most of this employment among women is concentrated in administrative support and professional and technical jobs.

Informal-sector employment, which overall in 1990 was seven times more common among women than was modern-sector employment, occupies roughly 35-40 percent of women in each schooling group with less than 5 years of secondary education and distinctly smaller percentages of the women with the highest levels of schooling. More than 9 in 10 women employed in the informal sector are involved in petty commerce, primarily selling food products. There is a relatively high incidence of poverty among women working in the informal sector, while those employed in the modern sector are distinctly more likely to be in households that rank highly on the scale of economic well-being.

Overall, there appears at first glance to be at most only a mild positive relation between women's education and employment: while nearly half of women with university education are employed, as compared to almost 40 percent of other women, the percentage of women at lower schooling levels who are employed ranges only from 37 to 40 and actually is inversely related to educational attainment. However, it is evident from the multivariate analyses that, once exposure to the labor market is taken into account, a much stronger positive relation between schooling and employment emerges. Further, as the number of years since leaving school increases, the likelihood that a woman will be employed, either in the modern or in the informal sector, tends generally to increase.

Our multivariate analyses of employment status also indicate that household demographic composition influences women's employment activity. Broadly speaking, greater numbers of preschool-age children appear to hinder women's participation in the labor market, while greater numbers of school-age females and older adults in the household seem to facilitate women's employment in the informal sector. Clearly, there is some intrahousehold labor substitution that takes place, and, with respect to youths of school age, this substitution is limited to females.

The family connections and contacts that women have, as proxied for by husband's occupational status, also significantly influence their employment activity. Of particular note is the fact that women whose husbands are in high-status occupations are significantly more likely to be employed in the modern sector and significantly less likely to be self-employed in the informal sector. Further, women whose husbands were not employed were more likely to be working in the informal sector.

In considering how women's employment has changed since our 1990 survey, the acute economic crisis of the first half of the decade and the continuing economic and political problems must be seen as playing a major role. With growing numbers of relatively well-educated women (reflecting the long-term trend in women's educational attainment) most likely confronting shrinking numbers of modern-sector jobs, the already difficult access to the modern sector that prevailed at the outset of the 1990s has almost certainly become even more difficult. At the same time, informal-sector activity may be presumed to have continued its long-term expansion as women seek to supplement their meager family incomes. Hence, it seems most plausible that the secular trend toward increased involvement of women in the labor market has continued. At the same time, however, the mix between modern- and informal-sector employment has undoubtedly become even further skewed in favor of the informal sector.

Chapter 12. Migration, Education, and Employment

In chapter 1, we saw that Kinshasa has historically attracted migrants from other parts of the Congo. Prior to independence, first labor recruitment of men and subsequently family reunification and also educational opportunities were important factors stimulating migration to Leopoldville (see, e.g., Lux 1962; Capelle 1947). In the first half of the 1960s migration intensified, not only because of the dismantling of colonial controls on migration, but also because the city constituted a safe haven for people fleeing from the conflicts taking place in other parts of the country (Houyoux and Kinavwuidi 1986). Subsequently, migration to Kinshasa has continued, presumably reflecting efforts by both rural residents and those from smaller urban centers to take advantage of the greater opportunities for improved well-being that the country's capital and largest city had to offer.[1]

Migration has played an important role in the city's overall growth, accounting for the bulk of that growth up through about 1970 (Houyoux and Kinavwuidi 1986, 116-118; Boute and St. Moulin 1978, 14-15).[2] The majority of the city's population consisted of migrants until 1975. Further, even as of the 1984 census, when just over 40 percent of the city's total population was made

---

[1] The poor performance of the city's economy since the mid-1970s, discussed in chapter 1 and emphasized at numerous points subsequently, might lead one to wonder why people would continue to migrate there. Part of the answer is that rural areas and the country's agricultural sector were badly neglected by the Mobutu regime (Shapiro and Tollens 1992) and, consequently, even informal-sector employment in Kinshasa frequently offered greater economic opportunity than remaining in rural agriculture (Cole and Sanders 1985). Houyoux and Kinavwuidi (1986) suggest that the flow of migrants to Kinshasa included both rural residents from neighboring provinces (Bas-Congo and Bandundu) and urban residents from more distant locations.

[2] It is net migration (inmigration minus outmigration) to the city that is relevant in considering the role of migration in contributing to the growth of the city's population. Houyoux and Kinavwuidi (1986, 116-120) provide an analysis of survey data from 1967 and 1975 indicating that outmigration from Kinshasa was negligible.

up of migrants, 65 percent of the city's adult population (aged 15 and over) were migrants (Institut National de la Statistique 1991a, table 5, p. 61).

At various points in part 2, we took migrant status into account as an explanatory variable in the analyses of fertility behavior. In brief, we saw in the appendix to chapter 4 that, in 1975, migrants (who at that time represented 74 percent of all women aged 15-49 and 87 percent of married women in that age range) had slightly higher fertility than nonmigrants. The difference in children ever born was at most 0.2, all else equal. By 1990, however, this differential was smaller (less than 0.1) and no longer statistically significant. In chapter 5, we saw evidence of differences between migrants and Kinshasa natives in the timing of key life course transitions pertinent to fertility, but it was evident that the timing of migration—most notably, whether it occurred prior to or subsequent to the onset of a woman's adolescence—was very important. Women who migrated prior to or early in adolescence but who spent most of their preadolescent years in a village or small urban center tended to initiate sexual activity, enter into a union, and begin childbearing relatively early, while women who migrated after adolescence tended to experience delayed transitions. And, in chapter 6, we found evidence of significantly lower use of modern contraception and abortion and significantly longer durations of postpartum abstinence among migrants.

In this chapter, we take a closer look at migrants as a group and examine the associations between migration, on the one hand, and education, employment activity, and economic well-being, on the other. Women migrants are often characterized as being tied movers, in the sense that their migration is frequently, not simply an individual act, but rather a move undertaken within a family context and, hence, tied to family considerations (Sandell 1977). With respect to migration to Kinshasa, this will be true, not only for adult women who moved with their husbands, but also for women who moved as young girls, migrating to the city with their entire family. At the same time, given Kinshasa's prominence as the political capital and the country's dominant place of economic activity as well as being a center for higher education, it is certainly plausible to suggest that some women may indeed move as individuals, often to take advantage of educational or job opportunities available in Kinshasa and not anywhere else in the country.[3] These considerations suggest that migrants themselves are likely to be a fairly heterogeneous group across a number of dimensions.

The following section provides an overview of several key characteristics of migrants. In particular, we examine the importance of migrants among the

---

[3] University-level education has been available elsewhere in the Congo, although much of it is oriented toward teacher training. In addition, at times in the past, university study in certain disciplines (e.g., economics, medicine, law, engineering) was either exclusively or predominantly available in Kinshasa. With respect to job opportunities, the concentration of both public and modern private-sector employment in Kinshasa makes it especially attractive to prospective migrants with high levels of education.

different age groups covered by our 1990 survey and discuss the ethnic origins of migrants in our survey. We also look at the timing of migration, in terms of both age at migration and duration since migration. This is followed by a section focused specifically on education and employment, in which the educational attainment of migrants is compared to that of nonmigrants. Employment status of migrants and nonmigrants as well as the economic well-being of the two groups are also examined. A brief concluding section summarizes and discusses the findings of the chapter.

Characteristics of Migrants

In 1990, migrants represented a little under half of women aged 15-49 in Kinshasa, down from just over 60 percent in the 1984 census. As is evident in table 12.1, and similar to what was seen in table 1.1 above for both sexes, the proportion of each age group consisting of migrants rises as age increases.[4] Hence, while only about a quarter of women aged 15-19 were migrants, the fraction rose to just over half among those aged 25-29 and to more than three-quarters among those aged 35-39. Consequently, among women aged 15-49, migrants tend on average to be a bit older than nonmigrants. Further, reflecting the longer-term trend seen in table 1.1, the percentage of migrants in each age group in 1990 is distinctly lower than the corresponding percentage in 1984.

The ethnic composition of the population of migrants may be expected to reflect the proximity to Kinshasa of the different ethnic groups, and, indeed, more than 60 percent of migrants are from the neighboring provinces of Bandundu and Bas-Congo. In addition, given that the presence in the destination of people from one's own ethnic group is likely to facilitate migration, we expect the ethnic composition of migrants to be linked to the overall ethnic composition of the city. Further, trends in this overall ethnic composition will also be relevant. Groups whose share of the city's population has been increasing may be expected to have a relatively high number of migrants compared to their overall representation in the city, while those groups with shrinking population shares can be expected to have a smaller share of migrants as compared to their share of the total population.

Fully 40 percent of the migrants as of 1990 had originated from the Kwilu-Kwango districts of Bandundu Province, making this area far and away the most important as a source of migrants to Kinshasa. In 1975, by contrast, only 28 percent of the migrant population of Kinshasa was from Kwilu-Kwango, compared to 30 percent from Bas-Congo (Houyoux and Kinavwuidi 1986, 120). Recall that, in table 1.2 above, we saw that 37 percent of women in 1990 were from the Kwilu-Kwango area and that the share of this group in

---

[4] The small decline in 1990 in the proportion of migrants in going from the 40-44 to the 45-49 age group is presumably a consequence of the relatively small sample size of the older age group in our survey.

Table 12.1 Percentage of Migrants, Women Aged 15-49, by Age Group, 1990 and 1984

Age Group	1990	1984
15-19	24	37
20-24	41	52
25-29	52	66
30-34	61	75
35-39	77	84
40-44	80	89
45-49	77	91
Total	47	61

Sources: 1990: calculated from data; 1984: Institut National de la Statistique (1991a, table 5, p. 61).

the city's population had risen substantially over the period from 1955 to 1990. Hence, the high proportion of migrants from Kwilu-Kwango in 1990 is consistent with the data presented earlier.

Indeed, there are other similarities as well between the ethnic composition of migrants and the levels and trends of representation in Kinshasa of different ethnic groups. In particular, Bakongo South women constitute the second-largest group of migrants, making up 15 percent of the migrant women of reproductive age; they are also the second-largest group overall in 1990, representing 22 percent of the total, but their share of the city's population has declined since the 1950s. Luba women represent 14 percent of the migrants, as compared to a share of 11 percent of the overall population in 1990, which in turn is a distinctly higher share than that which prevailed prior to independence. Mongo, Ubangi, and Bakongo North women represented 10, 9, and 7 percent, respectively, of the pool of migrants; in each case, the share of migrants was close to the group's overall share. The six major ethnic groups accounted for 94 percent of the total migrant population, with the remainder being equally divided between women from other tribes within the Congo and non-Congolese women.

Consider now the timing of migration in terms of the life cycle of the migrant. As may be seen in part A of table 12.2, more than 40 percent of migrants came to Kinshasa prior to reaching age 15, and the majority of these individuals arrived prior to reaching age 10. This group presumably consists primarily of women whose move took place as part of a migration by their family of origin. Thirty percent of the migrant women were aged 15-19 when they came to Kinshasa. Some of these women may have migrated to take advantage of schooling opportunities, most notably at the secondary school level, while others may have migrated as part of their family of origin, as fostered-in young women to provide labor assistance to extended-family members, or as young married women arriving with their husbands. Nearly the

Table 12.2 Age at Migration and Years since Migration, by Current Age, 1990 (percentage distributions)

Age Group	0-4	5-9	10-14	15-19	20-24	25-29	30-34	35-39	40-44	Total
	A. Age at Migration by Current Age									
15-19	19	25	30	26	—	—	—	—	—	100
20-24	9	13	17	36	25	—	—	—	—	100
25-29	6	17	14	31	23	9	—	—	—	100
30-34	10	13	18	25	18	11	6	—	—	100
35-39	4	6	18	32	25	10	4	1	—	100
40-44	4	7	12	29	23	10	8	8	0	100
45-49	5	0	5	29	16	34	6	0	4	100
All	9	14	18	30	19	7	2	1	0	100
	B. Years since Migration by Current Age									
15-19	46	22	20	11	—	—	—	—	—	100
20-24	43	2	16	15	3	—	—	—	—	100
25-29	17	28	24	12	15	3	—	—	—	100
30-34	11	14	20	22	18	10	7	—	—	100
35-39	4	4	16	34	21	14	6	1	—	100
40-44	2	9	10	11	22	33	7	7	0	100
45-49	4	0	0	21	26	28	14	1	5	100
All	22	18	18	17	13	8	3	1	0	100

Note: Universe is migrants to Kinshasa. — Not applicable.

same number (29 percent) migrated to Kinshasa at age 20 or older, with almost two-thirds of these women coming when they were aged 20-24. Migration to pursue university education is a likely motive for some of these women, but, since only a small portion of the total number of migrants have postsecondary education, it is presumably the case that the bulk of these women migrated with their husbands. Migration by women age 30 and over accounts for only 3 percent of the total.

There is some evidence in part A of the table of a relation between age group and age at migration. Women age 35 and over are distinctly less likely than younger women to have come to Kinshasa prior to age 15, while, the older a woman's current age, the greater the likelihood that she migrated after reaching age 20. There is, of course, a built-in bias toward indication of such a relation, in the sense that women in younger age groups have had little or no possibility for migrating at comparatively older ages.

Part B of table 12.2 shows the duration since migration, overall and by age group. Forty percent of all migrants had migrated within the past 10 years, another 35 percent had done so within 10-19 years, and the remaining 25 percent had migrated 20 years or more earlier. Given that migration tends to take place at relatively young ages, it is not surprising to see in the table that older migrants tend disproportionately to have migrated 20 or more years ago and that younger migrants are distinctly more likely to be relatively recent migrants.

Education, Employment, and Economic Well-Being of Migrants

We noted earlier that acquiring education may be one motive for migration. The data reported in table 12.3 suggest, at first glance, that, for many migrants, this motive is not relevant. That is, overall, migrants clearly have lower educational attainment than do Kinshasa natives. Indeed, women with either no schooling or only primary education constitute 42 percent of migrants, as compared to only 22 percent of nonmigrants.[5] Conversely, Kinshasa natives are substantially more likely than migrants to have attained either lower-level or mid-level secondary schooling. At the same time, however, the proportion of those with upper-level secondary schooling is almost identical for migrants and nonmigrants, and there is actually a higher percentage of migrants than nonmigrants with university education.[6]

These differences in educational attainment between migrants and nonmigrants are indicative of a dualistic migration stream. A relatively high proportion of migrants have little or no formal education. These women most likely include many who migrated to Kinshasa with their husbands, where the husbands were in search of better employment opportunities than those in their place of origin, and they also presumably include some women fostered in to provide labor assistance. About one in six migrants has either upper-level secondary or university education, however, and these women are most likely to have either migrated to Kinshasa while still quite young, migrated to continue their education, or migrated as individuals with relatively high educational attainment acquired elsewhere and in search of employment opportunities.

An alternate perspective on the interplay between migration and education is provided by figure 12.1, which shows the percentage of migrants who attended school after migration, in relation to their age at migration. More than 70 percent of those who migrated to Kinshasa prior to age 10 subsequently attended school, compared to 45 percent of those who migrated when aged 10-14, fewer than 20 percent of migrants at ages 15-19, and less than 10 percent of those who migrated in their early 20s. Comparison of these figures with the school enrollment data reported in chapter 2, even after allowing for the time since migration, makes it clear that, for many migrant women, having migrated put them at a disadvantage (as compared to Kinshasa natives) with respect to attending school.[7]

---

[5] The fact that migrants have less schooling than nonmigrants does not, by itself, negate the possibility of migration for the purpose of acquiring schooling. The relevant comparison in this regard is the actual education of migrants as compared to the schooling that they would have had in the absence of migration. For further discussion, see below.

[6] Calculation of educational distributions of migrants and nonmigrants limited to women who were not enrolled in school shows that only 3 percent of each group are at the university level. Hence, the higher proportion of migrants with university education shown in table 12.3 reflects migration in pursuit of higher education by women currently in school.

[7] For example, figure 2.1a above shows that, in 1975 and 1984, essentially 90 percent of all girls aged 10-14 and 60 percent or more of young women aged 15-19 were enrolled in school. These rates are substantially higher than those for migrants shown in figure 12.1.

Table 12.3 Educational Attainment of Migrants and Nonmigrants, 1990 (percentage distributions)

Migrant Status	Educational Attainment							
	None	Primary	Sec. 1-2	Sec. 3-4	Sec. 5-6	Univ.	Other	Total
Migrants	11	31	19	21	11	6	1	100
Nonmigrants	3	19	28	33	12	4	1	100

Note: Universe is women aged 15-49.

Additional evidence on migration and education is provided by a recent study looking at family influences on the educational attainment of women aged 25 and over in Kinshasa (Shapiro 1999). Controlling for parental education and survival status, cohort, and number of siblings, we found that women who spent their childhood (up to age 12) in a village ended up with about 1.5 fewer years of schooling completed as compared to those who spent their childhood in a large city (typically, Kinshasa) and that those spending their adolescence (ages 12-18) in a village had 1 year less of schooling completed, all else equal. Women whose childhood was spent in a small urban center did not have significantly lower educational attainment than those growing up in Kinshasa, but residing in a small urban center during adolescence was associated with lower educational attainment by 0.8 years.

These comparisons of the educational attainment of migrants and nonmigrants are illuminating, but it is also useful to consider the educational attainment of migrants in relation to that of women in the areas of origin. For example, data from the 1984 census show that, among women aged 10-49 elsewhere in the country besides Kinshasa, nearly half had no schooling, just over 40 percent had some primary education, and only 10 percent had gone beyond primary school (calculated from Institut National de la Statistique 1991a, table 8, pp. 31, 65). If one looks only at younger women aged 10-24, the corresponding percentages are 35, 51, and 13, respectively.

It is apparent from these figures that migrant women in Kinshasa have substantially greater educational attainment than do women in the areas of origin of these migrants.[8] While the percentage of migrants with no schooling is three to four times greater than the percentage of Kinshasa natives with no schooling (table 12.3), it is only one-third to one-fourth of the percentage of women in the rest of the country with no schooling. Likewise, while not quite 60 percent of female migrants in Kinshasa aged 15-49 have gone beyond

[8] The comparative numbers from the census are from the entire country outside Kinshasa. Alternative estimates could have been generated by weighting the populations of different provinces according to their importance in the flow of migrants (and thereby giving greater weight to Bandundu and Bas-Congo Provinces and less weight to the provinces that are more remote from Kinshasa). However, the variation in educational attainment across provinces (other than Kinshasa) is relatively modest, as evidenced in Institut National de la Statistique (1991c, table 4.1, p. 24). Hence, the alternative estimates would not be very different from the estimates reported here.

primary school, compared to nearly 80 percent of those born in the city, the figure for migrants is far above the figures of 10 percent or slightly higher for women elsewhere in the country.

Even after allowing for both schooling that takes place after migration of very young migrants and the 6-year span between the census and our survey, then, it is clear that female migrants to Kinshasa tend to be considerably better educated than women in the areas of origin. This positive selection of migrants on the basis of education is a very common finding in the literature on migration (see, e.g., Yap 1976). Further, not only are migrants self-selected on the basis of education, but they may also be selected positively in terms of their market productivity, holding education constant, as well as with respect to their motivation to control their fertility and to invest relatively heavily in the education of their children.

The employment status of migrants and nonmigrants who are not in school, overall and by educational attainment, is shown in table 12.4. Migrants are more likely to be employed than nonmigrants (43 vs. 36 percent), with the bulk of the difference reflecting employment in the informal sector. The table also provides further evidence of a dualistic migration stream and the self-selection of migrants, but this time more directly in relation to employment. Below upper-level secondary education, migrant women in each schooling group have higher employment rates than do Kinshasa natives, with the differences being considerable for women in the two lowest educational attainment groups. Just over 45 percent of migrants in these two groups are employed (virtually all self-employed), compared to nearly 28 percent of nonmigrants. Among women with university education, migrants also have a higher overall employment rate, and, while they are distinctly less likely to be self-employed, this is more than offset by a substantially greater likelihood of being employed in the modern sector.

Finally, the economic well-being of migrant and nonmigrant women is reported in table 12.5. The distributions of the two groups of women across the economic index categories are quite similar, and, indeed, to the extent that there is a difference, it is in favor of the migrants. Relative to their nonmigrant counterparts, they are slightly less likely to be in the two poverty groups at the low end of the scale and somewhat more likely to be in the two groups with the highest levels of economic well-being. These differences, especially given the educational differences between the two groups, may very well be a consequence of migrant selectivity.

Fig. 12.1 School attendance after migration, by age at migration

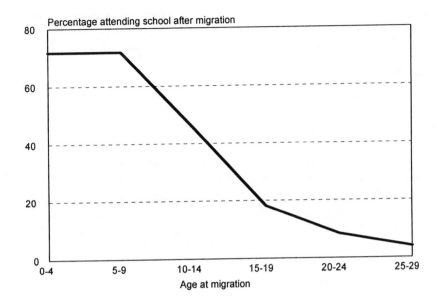

Source: Calculated from data.

Table 12.4 Employment Status by Educational Attainment, Migrants and Nonmigrants, 1990 (percentage distributions)

Migrant Status	Educational Attainment						
	None	Primary	Sec. 1-2	Sec. 3-4	Sec. 5-6	Univ.	Total
Migrant							
Not employed	54	55	58	59	68	46	57
Self-employed	45	45	40	34	16	9	37
Employee	0	0	2	7	16	45	5
Total	100	100	100	100	100	100	100
Nonmigrant							
Not employed	81	71	63	62	59	56	64
Self-employed	19	29	35	33	29	23	32
Employee	0	1	1	5	11	21	4
Total	100	100	100	100	100	100	100

Note: Universe is women aged 15-49 not enrolled in school.

Table 12.5 Economic Well-Being of Migrants and Nonmigrants, 1990 (percentage distributions)

| | Economic Index | | | | | |
Migrant Status	0	1	2-3	4-5	6+	Total
Migrant	29	16	22	19	14	100
Nonmigrant	31	18	22	17	11	100

Note: Universe is women aged 15-49.

Summary and Discussion

This chapter has provided evidence on the background characteristics of women who were migrants to Kinshasa as of 1990 and on their education, employment, and economic well-being. As in previous years, the migrant population is increasingly important in Kinshasa as one moves from younger to older individuals. Hence, among women of reproductive age, migrants are slightly older on average than are nonmigrants. For the most part, migrants came to Kinshasa when they were fairly young, but almost 30 percent of them were age 20 or older when they migrated. Almost 70 percent of the migrant women came from the neighboring provinces of Bandundu and Bas-Congo.

Migrant women are substantially more likely to have little or no schooling as compared to Kinshasa natives, and even those who migrate at fairly young ages appear to be at a disadvantage (as compared to their nonmigrant counterparts in Kinshasa) with respect to education. At the same time, the migrant population includes a slightly higher proportion of women with university education, indicative of at least some migration to take advantage of opportunities in Kinshasa for higher education or for employment requiring such education. Further, migrant women have considerably greater educational attainment than do women in the areas of orgin of the migrants, suggestive of positive self-selection of migrants.

Participation in the labor market is greater for migrants than for Kinshasa natives, and differences between the two groups are greatest at the extremes of the education distribution. Migrant women with no or only primary schooling are considerably more likely than their nonmigrant counterparts to be in the informal sector, while those with university education are essentially twice as likely to be working in the modern sector. These differences by employment status, which are likely linked to migrant selectivity, are undoubtedly a factor contributing to the slightly greater economic well-being of migrants.

We noted at the outset of the chapter that migration accounted for the major part of the city's growth up until about 1970. Since then, natural increase has been the dominant source of growth. This change in the components of growth was exacerbated in the early 1990s, when (according to foreign press reports) there was out-migration from Kinshasa in response to the onset of acute economic crisis. However, the rebellion that began in August 1998 has once again brought about a situation comparable to that prevailing in the early 1960s, in which the city is a safe haven for citizens fleeing from conflict elsewhere in the country. It seems likely, then, that there has been a resurgence of migration in recent years and in its importance in the overall growth of the city.

Part IV

Prospects for Changes in the Future

Chapter 13. Economic Crisis and Further Transitions in Education, Employment, and Fertility

We have examined changes in education, employment, and fertility in Kinshasa that took place over the bulk of the second half of the 20th century. More specifically, our data covered the period from 1955 to 1990, and we have seen that, over the course of this period, there was a remarkable transformation in the lives of women in the city. As the city has grown from a population of around 300,000 in the mid-1950s to a population at present in excess of 5 million, women have acquired schooling, become increasingly involved in the labor market, and begun to control their fertility.

These transformations are by no means unique to Kinshasa. Elsewhere in sub-Saharan Africa and in the developing world, and most notably in urban places, the second half of the 20th century witnessed dramatic increases in women's access to formal education (Colclough with Lewin 1993; Schultz 1993) and in their participation in the labor market (Schultz 1990). Fertility transition also emerged in the developing world during this period, initially in Asia and Latin America (Leete and Alam 1993; Guzmán et al. 1996). More recently, fertility transition has become increasingly evident throughout the sub-Saharan region (Tabutin 1997; Cohen 1998), most notably in urban centers and especially in capital cities (Shapiro and Tambashe 1999a; Tabutin and Schoumaker 2001). Hence, in many ways it is probably the case that what has transpired in Kinshasa is similar to changes that have taken and are taking place elsewhere in sub-Saharan Africa.

Particularly in the latter half of the span covered by the data that we have examined, these changes in Kinshasa have emerged in a context of chronic economic crisis. And, since 1990, Kinshasa and the Congo have experienced acute economic crisis in conjunction with political instability and civil war. In this brief concluding chapter, we first consider what has likely taken place with respect to women's education, employmént, and fertility over the course of the period since 1990. We then assess the near-term prospects for the economy of the Congo and its capital and the likely changes in the future in women's education, employment, and fertility within the context of an economy characterized by chronic economic crisis.

Women's Education, Employment, and Fertility in Kinshasa since 1990

As noted in chapter 1, the acute economic crisis of the early 1990s appeared to be abating somewhat by the middle of the decade (Maton and Van Bauwel 1996). Following a brief civil war and the ensuing change of government in May 1997, the new regime of Laurent Kabila showed some early signs of economic improvement, most notably with respect to inflation ("Un An après" 1998). However, the Kabila government managed to alienate Western donors and other prospective investors, and the civil war that broke out in August 1998 has proved to be exceedingly difficult to halt, despite the Lusaka peace agreement signed in August 1999. Financing the ongoing civil war has taken the major part of government resources (Bureau d'Etudes, de Recherches, et de Consulting International 2000).

Whether the accession to power of Joseph Kabila early in 2001 will change the situation remains to be seen. In any case, the country's economy is in extremely poor shape, with the agricultural, manufacturing, mining, and transportation sectors all suffering badly from the combined effects of, first, years of corruption and neglect and, more recently, protracted conflict. Further, subsequent to the outbreak of civil war in 1998, the combination of increased government expenditures to fight the war and reduced domestic production and government revenues resulted in rapidly growing deficits (Masangu 1999). As a direct consequence, inflation and monetary instability have reemerged as problems (Maton et al. 1999).

Consider now the transitions that have taken place with respect to schooling and educational attainment. We have seen evidence for the period from 1955 to 1990 of a long-term upward trend in school attendance and, ultimately, in the educational attainment of the adult population. This has been accompanied by a narrowing of the gender gap in schooling. However, the acute economic crisis of the 1990s undoubtedly reduced economic well-being for many families, effectively rendering more difficult the task of finding the resources to send children to school while at the same time raising the perceived opportunity cost of children being in school. Indeed, one report describes sending children to school as a "genuine ordeal" for parents (Bureau d'Etudes, de Recherches, et de Consulting International 2000, 3). Consequently, there is good reason to believe that the adverse economic circumstances of the 1990s most likely slowed down and perhaps even reversed the longer-term trend toward increased schooling and may also have been accompanied by a widening of the gender gap in educational attainment (Maton et al. 1999).

Evidence on these points comes from a survey of nearly 1,200 households that was carried out in Kinshasa during the middle of 1995 (Lututala et al. 1996). Data on school enrollment in 1995 by age group and gender indicate that, while there was no sign of declining enrollment among the youngest children (ages 6-9), for female and male youths in each of the 5-year age groups from age 10 to age 24 school enrollment rates were lower than for the corresponding group in 1990.[1] Among females, the declines in enrollment were modest, ranging from about 2 to 6 percentage points. Among males, by contrast, enrollment rates fell more sharply for those aged 10-19, with declines on the order of 10 percentage points (Lututala et al. 1996, table 4.7, p. 55). The fact that enrollment rates fell more for males than for females resulted in a narrowing of the gender gap in enrollment.

In view of the prevailing economic circumstances, the comparatively modest declines in school enrollment that appear to have taken place bear witness to the very strong desire that parents have to provide their children with an education. Further, this suggests that the long-term trend toward increasing educational attainment of the adult population (and especially women) has most likely continued, albeit perhaps at a slightly reduced pace.

Employment of women also increased quite substantially during the period from 1955 to 1990 and was clearly associated in part with women's increased educational attainment. This was especially the case at the top end of the educational distribution, for women with upper-level secondary or university education, who had some limited access to modern-sector employment. At the same time, however, the poor overall performance of the economy constrained the number and growth of jobs in the modern sector, and, hence, after 1975, most of the increased employment of women was to be found in the informal sector. Given the shrinkage of modern-sector employment that took place in the first part of the 1990s, in conjunction with ongoing economic adversity, it seems most plausible to surmise that the trend toward the increased employment activity of women, accompanied by a growing share of employment in the informal sector, continued during the 1990s.

A substantial study of the informal sector in Kinshasa and in the country at large (De Herdt and Marysse 1996) as well as recent research on gender relations and women's trading activities in Kinshasa (Bouchard 2000) both suggest that, during the acute economic crisis of the 1990s, the informal sector has continued to grow as part of household survival strategies in an economy in which the modern sector has undergone a "process of de-industrialization" (Sala-Diakanda 1997, 362). De Herdt and Marysse (1996, 13) estimate that, by the mid-1990s, the informal sector may have generated as much as 50 percent of urban income. In addition, some research suggests that accompanying the growth of women's economic activity has been a change in gender relations,

---

[1] Recall from chapter 2 that, owing to delayed entry, school enrollment rates have typically been higher among those aged 10-14 than among children aged 6-9.

with, perhaps, increased women's autonomy (see, e.g., Mianza 1996; Bouchard 2000). This, in turn, is likely to have implications for fertility behavior.

With respect to fertility, our earlier analyses suggest that the secular increase in schooling, and particularly the growing proportions of women with at least some secondary education, has been a very important factor contributing to the emergence of fertility decline in Kinshasa. In the 1950s, ethnic group differences in fertility were quite substantial, and women's educational attainment was so limited that it did not make sense to speak of differences in fertility by education. By 1990, however, the situation had essentially almost reversed itself—for the most part, the ethnic group differences in fertility per se had diminished considerably, and, instead, substantial fertility differences by educational attainment had emerged. Hence, to the extent that economic crisis has slowed the tendency for increased women's schooling, there would presumably be a corresponding slowdown in the pace of fertility decline. As suggested above, however, any such impact has most likely been quite modest.

In addition, there may well be more direct effects of economic crisis on fertility. For example, to the extent that adverse economic conditions result in a tendency to delay the onset of marriage, one would expect there to be a subsequent decline, not only in marriages, but also in first births (National Research Council 1993a). However, it is not clear that such an effect would persist over an extended period. At the same time, longer-term effects, such as changes in ideal or desired family size stemming from prolonged economic crisis, may also emerge. It has been suggested that economic crisis may induce or promote fertility transition (Foster 1993; Lesthaeghe 1993; Palloni et al. 1993), and Eloundou-Enyegue et al. (2000) have provided considerable evience of such a crisis-induced fertility decline in Cameroon, especially in urban areas (see also Eloundou-Enyegue 1997).

In a recent effort to assess the national level of fertility in the Congo at present, we considered potential influences on fertility, including factors such as women's schooling, economic crisis, civil war, socioeconomic development (or, more accurately, the lack thereof), and urbanization (Shapiro and Tambashe 2001a). Overall, we concluded that, despite the absence of the sort of socioeconomic development that has historically been broadly associated with fertility transition, factors such as economic crisis, increased women's educational attainment, and urbanization had probably contributed to a decline in fertility, and we speculated that the total fertility rate might have fallen from just above 6 to a level of 5.5. Correspondingly, we believe that the decline in fertility in Kinshasa between 1975 and 1990 that we have documented earlier in this book has continued since 1990.

By how much fertility may have fallen remains to be seen. As suggested above, the educational attainment of adult women has presumably continued to increase, and growth in women's labor market activity and perhaps autonomy may also have contributed to further declines in fertility. Between 1975 and 1990, the total fertility rate in Kinshasa fell by at least 1.5.[2] If the pace of decline (0.1 per year) had continued through the 1990s, then as of 2000 Kinshasa would have had a total fertility rate of approximately 4.7. By way of comparison, we note that, for the 15 countries of sub-Saharan Africa that have had at least one Demographic and Health Survey (DHS) and reported fertility for the capital city or region, the (unweighted) average total fertility rate (TFR) for the capital in the most recent survey is 4.02. If one excludes those countries for which the national TFR is below 5.5, eight countries remain, and the average TFR in the capital for those countries is 4.75 (Shapiro and Tambashe 1999a). Hence, our "continued linear decline" hypothesis leads us to an estimate of the TFR in Kinshasa as of 2000 (4.7) that seems quite consistent with data from the Demographic and Health Surveys.

Whether the decline in fertility maintained its pace, slowed somewhat, or accelerated in the face of acute economic crisis is not known. However, it is worth noting that Ngondo (1996, table 3, p. 427) provides evidence indicating that trends toward increasing age at marriage and higher proportions never married, which had begun in the mid-1970s, continued through the mid-1990s. These are trends that one would expect to be associated with ongoing fertility decline.

Further, we saw evidence in chapter 7 of growth over time in contraceptive prevalence and in the efficacy of contraception throughout much of sub-Saharan Africa, indicative of growing demand for fertility control. This has occurred in numerous countries, with quite different economic circumstances and prospects. We believe that the same phenomena most likely characterize Kinshasa, thereby facilitating continued fertility decline, as may be seen elsewhere in large African cities (Shapiro and Tambashe 1999a; Tabutin and Schoumaker 2001). Indeed, all things considered, it is possible that the fertility decline in Kinshasa may even have accelerated somewhat. However, we must acknowledge that this is primarily speculation on our part, and how far fertility has fallen is, at this point, something that we just do not know.

Future Prospects

The Congo's economy can be expected to continue in a state of crisis at least until the civil war has ended. And, once that happens, prospects for real economic improvement will still remain only on the distant horizon: private investors and donors will need to be convinced that there is a government seeking to promote real and widespread development, and the task of rehabilitation of the economy will be enormous and time-consuming. In brief, then, ongoing crisis will likely characterize the economy for a good number of years to come.

[2] As noted in chapter 3 (table 3.2), our best estimates of the total fertility rate (TFR) in Kinshasa are 7.5 for 1975 and 5.67 for 1990. However, those estimates are based on different methodologies. Using the same methodology (see n. 7, chapter 3) yields estimates of the TFR of 7.2 and 5.67 for 1975 and 1990, respectively, implying a decline of 1.53 over a period of 15 years.

Another factor relevant here in considering future prospects is mortality. One very plausible likely outcome of continuing economic crisis is increased mortality (Barrère et al. 1999). Indeed, increased mortality was reported nationally for the 1995 survey conducted in the Congo (Enquête Nationale sur la Situation des Enfants et des Femmes au Zaïre), and attributed to the "deterioration in the overall socioeconomic situation of the country" (République du Zaïre 1996, 59). From the perspective of the Easterlin framework for fertility analysis, rising mortality would be expected ultimately to have a pronatalist effect since it would reduce the supply of children and, hence, reduce motivation to control fertility. Over the long haul, then, increased mortality might tend to have an impact of slowing the fertility decline.

In considering mortality, it is desirable as well to assess the situation with respect to HIV/AIDS. Mortality from HIV/AIDS is another element in consideration of Kinshasa's demographic future. In 1990, the American director of Projet SIDA, a joint U.S.-Congolese AIDS project affiliated with the Centers for Disease Control, reported in a public presentation that HIV prevalence in the adult population of Kinshasa was estimated at 7 percent and appeared to have been steady over the preceding 3 years. A study of HIV prevalence in Kinshasa that was published in 1994 found the incidence of HIV among women of reproductive age to be on the order of 6-7 percent and stable over a 3-year period in the late 1980s (Batter et al. 1994). A subsequent study carried out in 1997 that collected data on HIV prevalence (primarily in Kinshasa but also elsewhere in the country) and compared it to estimates going back to the late 1980s concluded that, "despite the social disruption, the rapid decline in health-care provision, and the decrease in funding in health education programmes, our results show that the HIV seroprevalence rates remain relatively low and stable in DRC" (Mulanga-Kabeya et al. 1998, 908). While it is certain that AIDS has increased mortality in Kinshasa from what it otherwise would have been, the impact is probably considerably lower than that in urban centers in East and Southern Africa, where HIV prevalence is distinctly higher.

Consider, then, the likely future prospects for women's education, employment, and fertility in Kinshasa. The adverse economic circumstances likely to prevail in Kinshasa's future suggest that parents seeking to send their children to school will continue to face a genuine ordeal in their efforts to realize that objective. Whether this will lead to further declines in school enrollment rates, greater than the modest declines that have already been observed, and to an end to the trend toward increased educational attainment among adults remains to be seen. At best, however, it seems likely that the continuing adverse economy will ultimately slow the trend toward a better-educated population, and hence on this count the trend toward lower fertility is likely to slow as well. Whether the crisis will ultimately lead some parents to revise their desired numbers of children (Eloundou-Enyegue 1997) and thereby contribute to lower fertility remains to be seen.

Women's employment seems destined to remain high for a long time to come. Our analyses in chapter 4 did not find evidence that, all else equal, employment in the informal sector was associated with lower fertility. On this count, then, the increased involvement of women in the informal sector since 1990 might be expected not to have much of an impact on fertility. Again, however, there are other possible effects, including the greater women's autonomy alluded to by some observers as part of the process of women's increasing involvement in securing economic support for the household. If greater women's autonomy translates also to stronger desires by women to limit their own fertility, this increased involvement in the labor market in the context of ongoing economic crisis might contribute to continuing fertility decline.

All things considered, then, we believe that fertility in Kinshasa is likely to continue to decline in the coming years. At the same time, under the circumstances prevailing there, we believe that it is likely that the pace of the decline will slow somewhat. What we have seen in Kinshasa parallels the fertility transition that is presently unfolding in urban places throughout much of the continent. In fact, our expectations for Kinshasa are similar to what we expect for much of sub-Saharan Africa: fertility transition will continue, but it may be somewhat unsteady, and the big question—how far will the transition proceed? —remains an open one.

Appendix: Major Ethnic Groups in Kinshasa

We have elsewhere described Kinshasa as "an ethnic mosaic" (Shapiro and Tambashe 1997a), and this appendix provides some documentation to this effect. The 1975 survey of the city, which covered 10 percent of Kinshasa's households and more than 163,000 persons, identified individuals from well over 300 distinct tribes. Our own 1990 survey of women aged 13-49, with a total sample size of only 2,450, identified women from over 200 different tribes. In some cases, these tribes are part of well-defined broad ethnic groups, such as the Bakongo or the Mongo. However, in many other cases, there is considerable heterogeneity across tribes.

In order to provide quantitative analyses by ethnic group, we needed to aggregate the large number of small groups into a reasonable number of categories. To this end, we relied largely on the work of Jan Vansina (1966).[1] Figure A.1 shows the 15 "cultural regions" of the Congo proposed by Vansina.

There are relatively few individuals in Kinshasa from the easternmost part of the country. Conversely, since the Bakongo are well represented in Kinshasa and can be readily distinguished according to whether they are from north or south of the Congo River,[2] we have subdivided Vansina's region 8 (Kongo), corresponding to Bas-Congo Province, into two.

Our classification scheme, then, resulted in six broad major ethnic groups. In addition to the two Bakongo subgroups that correspond to Vansina's region 8, we have a large group that comprises Vansina's regions 9 (Bas Kasai) and 10 (Entre Kwango-Kasai). Because the principal tribes in this heterogeneous group are from the Kwilu and Kwango Districts of Bandundu Province, we refer to this group as the Kwilu-Kwango group. Note, then, that this designation is in fact a geographic one and not an ethnic category. These first three groups

[1] Vansina's work was the basis for the coding scheme for tribes that was used in the 1975 survey and in our 1990 survey.
[2] Those from south of the river are for the most part originally from closer to Kinshasa, while those from north of the river (including individuals from Bas-Fleuve District of Bas-Congo Province) typically originated farther from the city.

Fig. A.1 Cultural regions of the Congo

Source: Jan Vansina (1966).

Note: One of Vansina's 15 groups, pigmy hunters, is not shown on the map because of its geographic dispersion.

2   Région de l'Ubangi
3   Région de l'Uele
4   Région de l'Itimbiri-Ngiri
5   Région de la Cuvette Centrale
6   Région Balese-Komo
7   Région du Maniema
8   Région Kongo
9   Région de Bas Kasai
10   Région de l'Entre Kwango-Kasai
11   Région du Kasai-Katanga
12   Région Lunda
13   Région Tanganyika-Haut Katanga
14   Région du Kivu
15   Région du Nord-est

accounted for 46 percent of the city's population of reproductive-age women in 1955, more than 60 percent in 1975, and almost 70 percent in 1990.

The remaining three groups represented a little under a fifth of the population of reproductive-age women in 1955 and about a quarter in both 1975 and 1990. The fourth group is the Mongo ethnic group, corresponding to Vansina's very large region 5 (Cuvette Centrale). Most of the Mongo in Kinshasa are from the southern part of Equateur Province, with some also from northern Kasai Oriental Province (the Tetela) and from northern Bandundu Province.

Our fifth group comprises Vansina's regions 2 (Ubangi) and 4 (Itimbiri-Ngiri). The principal tribes in this group are primarily from the northern part of Equateur Province, but just over a fifth of the group comes from Orientale Province. We call this group the Ubangi group.

The final group is the Luba and related category. Codes for this group correspond to Vansina's regions 11 (Kasai-Katanga) and 13 (Tanganyika-Haut Katanga). However, the principal tribes from this group in Kinshasa are largely from region 11, originating in the provinces of Kasai Oriental and Kasai Occidental.

Table A.1 shows the principal tribes for each of these six broad ethnic groups in 1975 and 1990 (principal tribes are defined operationally as those with at least 10 percent of the population of the broad group in at least one of the two years). This criterion yields 20 tribes, which, combined, represented approximately 63 percent of the city's population of reproductive-age women in 1975 and more than 70 percent of the estimated corresponding population in 1990.

For the most part, there is a fair degree of stability in the composition of each of the broad groups between the two years, with the notable exception of the huge increase in the proportion of the Luba and related group identifying themselves as Luba. We believe that that increase reflects a greater tendency as of 1990 for individuals in Kinshasa to identify with the broader group rather than with a small component tribe.

Table A.2 shows the composition of the city's population of reproductive-age women, according to these broad ethnic groups, for 1955, 1975, and 1990. Clearly, their relative share of the population has increased over time (largely at the expense of non-Congolese Africans, most notably Angolans). Further, the share of the Kwilu-Kwango group has increased sharply over time, while the relative size of the Bakongo South group has diminished somewhat.

Table A.1 Principal Tribes of the Major Ethnic Groups in Kinshasa, 1975 and 1990 (percentages indicate tribe's share of broader group)

Ethnic Group	1975	1990
Bakongo North (north of the Congo River)		
Manyanga	57.1	56.8
Yombe	35.2	37.0
Bakongo South (south of the Congo River)		
BesiNgombe	14.3	13.2
Mbata	10.7	8.2
Ndibu	20.5	24.2
Ntandu	37.6	38.4
Kwilu-Kwango (Bas Kasai, Entre Kwango-Kasai)		
Mbala	17.6	12.2
Suku	11.1	16.0
Yaka	20.7	34.5
Yansi	16.2	12.7
Mongo (Cuvette Centrale)		
Mongo	52.9	50.5
Tetela	18.2	23.2
Ubangi (Ubangi, Itimbiri-Ngiri)		
Lokele	6.4	12.3
Mbuja	26.2	30.4
Ngbandi	10.5	12.0
Ngombe	21.1	16.2
Luba and related (Kasai-Katanga, Tanganyika-Haut Katanga)		
Bakwa Kalondji	11.4	3.3
Lulua	14.9	4.0
Luba	15.5	68.2
Songye	11.0	3.4

Sources: Calculated from survey data.

Table A.2 Composition of the Female Population of Reproductive Age, by Ethnic Group, Kinshasa, 1955, 1975, and 1990 (percentage distributions)

Ethnic Group	1955	1975	1990
Bakongo North	7.1	10.0	7.6
Bakongo South	30.5	25.9	22.1
Kwilu-Kwango	8.4	25.9	37.0
Mongo	5.6	7.5	7.3
Ubangi	7.2	7.7	7.8
Luba and related	5.1	9.3	11.1
Subtotal	63.9	86.3	92.9
Other groups	36.1	13.7	7.1
Grand total	100.0	100.0	100.0

Sources: 1955: calculated from Congo Belge (1957a, table 18); 1975 and 1990: calculated from survey data.

Note: Data on women of reproductive age in 1955 by ethnic group were limited to 25 principal tribes in the city. Hence, the data slightly understate the share of each of the six groups in the city's population because minor tribes in each group are not included in the figures for the group (and are included instead in the "other groups" category). Fully 25 percent of the city's total population of women of reproductive age were from either Angola or French Equatorial Africa (mostly Angola).

References

African Population Policy Research Center. 1998. *Fertility Decline in Kenya: Levels, Trends, and Differentials*. Nairobi, Kenya: African Population Policy Research Center, Population Council.

Agyei, William K. A., and John B. Ssekamatte-Ssebuliba. 2000. "Social Disruption as a Factor Influencing Infant and Child Survival in Uganda." *Genus* 61, nos. 1-2: 221-244.

Ainsworth, Martha. 1992. "Economic Aspects of Child Fostering in Côte d'Ivoire." Living Standards Measurement Study, Working Paper no. 92. Washington, DC: World Bank.

Ainsworth, Martha, Kathleen Beegle, and Andrew Nyamete. 1996. "The Impact of Women's Schooling on Fertility and Contraceptive Use: A Study of Fourteen Sub-Saharan African Countries." *World Bank Economic Review* 10, no. 1 (January): 85-122.

Allison, Paul D. 1984. *Event History Analysis: Regression for Longitudinal Event Data*. Beverly Hills, CA: Sage Publications.

Anderson, K. H. and M. A. Hill. 1983. "Marriage and Labor Market Discrimination in Japan." *Southern Economic Journal* 49: 941-953.

Bachrach, C. A. and M. C. Horne. 1987. *Married and Unmarried Couples, United States, 1982*. Vital and Health Statistics, ser. 23, no. 15. Washington, DC: U.S. Government Printing Office.

Baeck, L. 1956. "Léopoldville, phénomène urbain africain." *Zaïre* X, no. 6 (June): 613-636.

Bakutuvwidi, Makani, Lewu Niwembo Kinavwidi, and Jane T. Bertrand. 1991. *Fécondité et planification familiale—Kinshasa, 1988*. Kinshasa, Zaire: Département de Santé Publique (PSND); New Orleans: Tulane University School of Public Health and Tropical Medicine.

Bakutuvwidi, Makani, Niwembo Kinavwidi, and Ann Way. 1985. *Planification familiale, fécondité, et santé familiale au Zaïre, 1982-1984*. Kinshasa, Zaire: Institut National de la Statistique.

Barrère, Bernard, Goram Mboup, and Mohammed Ayad. 1999. *Enquêtes démographiques et de santé en Afrique de l'Ouest: Résultats des enquêtes démographiques et de santé réalisées au Burkina Faso (1998-99), au Cameroun (1998), en Côte d'Ivoire (1998-99), et au Togo (1998)*. Calverton, MD: Macro International Inc.

Barreto, Thália, Oona M. R. Campbell, J. Lynne Davies, Vincent Fauveau, Véronique G. A. Filippi, Wendy J. Graham, Masuma Mamdani, Cleone I. F. Rooney, and Nahid F. Toubia. 1992. "Investigating Induced Abortion in Developing Countries: Methods and Problems." *Studies in Family Planning* 23: 159-170.

Batter, V., B. Matela, M. Nsuami, T. Manzila, M. Kamenga, F. Behets, R.W. Ryder, W. L. Heyward, J. M. Karon, and M. E. St. Louis. 1994. "High HIV-1 Incidence in Young Women Masked by Stable Overall Seroprevalence among Childbearing Women in Kinshasa, Zaire: Estimating Incidence from Serial Seroprevalence Data." *AIDS* 8, no. 6 (June): 811-817.

Becker, Gary S. 1991. *A Treatise on the Family*. Enlarged ed. Cambridge, MA: Harvard University Press.

Becker, Gary S., and H. Gregg Lewis. 1973. "On the Interaction between the Quantity and Quality of Children." *Journal of Political Economy* 81, no. 2, pt. 2: S279-S288.

Becker, Stan. 1999. "Measuring Unmet Need: Wives, Husbands, or Couples?" *International Family Planning Perspectives* 25, no. 4: 172-180.

Behrman, Jere R., Robert A. Pollak, and Paul Taubman. 1986. "Do Parents Favor Boys?" *International Economic Review* 27, no. 1: 33-54.

Ben-Porath, Yoram. 1982. "Economics and the Family—Match or Mismatch? A Review of Becker's *A Treatise on the Family.*" *Journal of Economic Literature* 20, no. 1 (March): 52-64.

Bicego, George T., and J. Ties Boerma. 1993. "Maternal Education and Child Survival: A Comparative Study of Survey Data from 17 Countries." *Social Science and Medicine* 36, no. 9: 1207-1227.

Birdsall, Nancy, and Jere R. Behrman. 1991. "Why Do Males Earn More Than Females in Urban Brazil: Earnings Discrimination or Job Discrimination?" In *Unfair Advantage: Labor Market Discrimination in Developing Countries*, ed. Nancy Birdsall and Richard Sabot, 147-170. Washington, DC: World Bank.

Blanc, Ann K., and Naomi Rutenberg. 1990. "Assessment of the Quality of Data on Age at First Sexual Intercourse, Age at Marriage, and Age at First Birth in the Demographic and Health Surveys." In *An Assessment of DHS-I Data Quality* (DHS Methodological Reports, no. 1), ed. A. K. Blanc and N. Rutenberg. Columbia, MD: Institute for Resource Development.

Blanc, Ann K., and Naomi Rutenberg. 1991. "Coitus and Contraception: The Utility of Data on Sexual Intercourse for Family Planning Programs." *Studies in Family Planning* 22: 162-176.

Blanc, Ann K., and Shea O. Rutstein. 1994. "The Demographic Transition in Southern Africa: Yet Another Look at the Evidence from Botswana and Zimbabwe." *Demography* 31, no. 2 (May): 209-215.

Bolamba, Antoine-Roger. 1949. *Les Problèmes de l'évolution de la femme noire.* Elisabethville: Editions de l'Essor du Congo.

Bongaarts, John. 1978. "A Framework for Analyzing the Proximate Determinants of Fertility." *Population and Development Review* 4: 105-132.

Bongaarts, John. 1991. "The KAP-Gap and the Unmet Need for Contraception." Working Paper no. 23. New York: Population Council.

Bongaarts, John, and Judith Bruce. 1995. "The Causes of Unmet Need for Contraception and the Social Content of Services." *Studies in Family Planning* 26, no. 2: 57-75.

Bongaarts, John, Odile Frank, and Ron Lesthaeghe. 1984. "The Proximate Determinants of Fertility in Sub-Saharan Africa." *Population and Development Review* 10, no. 3 (September): 511-537.

Bongaarts, John, and Robert G. Potter. 1983. *Fertility, Biology, and Behavior: An Analysis of the Proximate Determinants.* New York: Academic Press.

Bongwele, Onanga, Douglas Nichols, Miatudila Malonga, Anne Whatley, Nadine Burton, and Barbara Janowitz. 1986. *Determinants and Consequences of Pregnancy Wastage in Zaire: A Study of Patients with Complications Requiring Hospital Treatment in Kinshasa, Matadi, and Bukavu.* Research Triangle Park, NC: Family Health International.

Bouchard, Hélène. 2000. "Rapports de genre, stratégies des femmes dans l'exercice du micro-commerce à Kinshasa (République Démocratique du Congo)." Ph.D. diss., Department of Sociology, Université de Québec à Montréal.

Boult, B. E., and P. W. Cunningham. 1991. "Black Teenage Pregnancy: An African Perspective." *Early Child Development and Care* 74: 103-107.

Boute, Joseph, and Léon de Saint Moulin. 1978. *Perspectives démographiques régionales, 1975-1985.* Kinshasa: Département du Plan, République du Zaïre.

Bozon, M. 1993. "L'Entrée dans la sexualité adulte: Le Premier Rapport et ses suites." *Population* 48, no. 5: 1317-1352.

Bruaux, P., J. Cerf, and A. Lebrun. 1957. "La Lutte contre les affections vénériennes à Léopoldville." *Annales de la Société Belge de Médecine Tropicale* 37, no. 6 (December): 801-813.

Bukasa, Albert Gislain. 1951. "De l'éducation de la femme noire." *La Voix du Congolais* 7, no. 61 (April): 172-177.

Bulatao, Rodolfo A., and Ronald D. Lee, with Paula E. Hollerbach and John Bongaarts, eds. 1983. *Determinants of Fertility in Developing Countries.* Washington, DC: National Academy Press.

Burch, Thomas K. 1983. "The Impact of Forms of Families and Sexual Unions and Dissolution of Unions on Fertility." In *Determinants of Fertility in Developing Countries*, ed. Rodolfo A. Bulatao and Ronald D. Lee, with Paula E. Hollerbach and John Bongaarts, 532-561. Washington, DC: National Academy Press.

Bureau d'Etudes, de Recherches, et de Consulting International (BERCI). 2000. *Une Pauvreté insupportable.* Kinshasa, BERCI.

Butz, William P., and Peter J. E. Stan. 1982. "Interhousehold Transfers and Household Structure in Malaysia." *Population and Development Review* 8, suppl.: 92-115.

Caldwell, John C. 1976. "Toward a Restatement of Demographic Transition Theory." *Population and Development Review* 2, nos. 3-4 (September/December): 321-366.

Caldwell, John C., I. O. Orubuloye, and Pat Caldwell. 1992. "Fertility Decline in Africa: A New Type of Transition?" *Population and Development Review* 18: 211-242.

Capelle, Emmanuel. 1947. *La Cité indigène de Léopoldville*. Elisabethville, Belgian Congo: Centre d'Etude des Problèmes Sociaux Indigènes.

Carolina Population Center. 1984. "Pubertal and Social Factors of Adolescent Sexuality and Hormone Supplement." Report to the National Institute of Child Health and Human Development. Chapel Hill: University of North Carolina.

Charles, V. 1948. "Le 'Mal démographique' de Léopoldville." *Zaïre* 2, no. 8 (October): 897-901.

Chernichovsky, Dov. 1985. "Socioeconomic and Demographic Aspects of School Enrollment and Attendance in Rural Botswana." *Economic Development and Cultural Change* 34, no. 2: 319-332.

Cleland, John G., and Jerome K. van Ginneken. 1988. "Maternal Education and Child Survival in Developing Countries: The Search for Pathways of Influence." *Social Science and Medicine* 27, no. 12: 1357-1368.

Cochrane, Susan H. 1979. *Fertility and Education: What Do We Really Know?* Baltimore: Johns Hopkins University Press.

Coeytaux, Francine M. 1988. "Induced Abortion in Sub-Saharan Africa: What We Do and Do Not Know." *Studies in Family Planning* 19: 186-190.

Cohen, Barney. 1993. "Fertility Levels, Differentials, and Trends." In *Demographic Change in Sub-Saharan Africa*, ed. Karen A. Foote, Kenneth H. Hill, and Linda G. Martin, 8-67. Washington, DC: National Academy Press.

Cohen, Barney. 1998. "The Emerging Fertility Transition in Sub-Saharan Africa." *World Development* 26, no. 8: 1431-1461.

Colclough, Christopher, with Keith Lewin. 1993. *Educating All the Children: Strategies for Primary Schooling in the South*. Oxford: Oxford University Press.

Cole, William E., and Richard D. Sanders. 1985. "Internal Migration and Urbanization in the Third World." *American Economic Review* 75, no. 3 (June): 481-494.

Comhaire-Sylvain, Suzanne. 1968. *Femmes de Kinshasa: Hier et aujourd'hui*. Paris: Mouton & Co.

Congo Belge. Service des Affaires Indigènes et de la Main-d'Oeuvre (AIMO). 1957a. *Enquêtes démographiques: Cité Léopoldville*. Fascicule no. 1. Léopoldville, Congo: AIMO.

Congo Belge. Service des Affaires Indigènes et de la Main-d'Oeuvre (AIMO). 1957b. *Enquêtes démographiques: Territoire suburbain de Léopoldville*. Fascicule no. 2. Léopoldville, Congo: AIMO.

Connelly, Rachel, Deborah DeGraff, and Deborah Levison. 1996. "Women's Employment and Child Care in Brazil." *Economic Development and Cultural Change* 44, no. 3: 619-656.

Dackam, N. R. 1990. *L'Education de la mère et la mortalité des enfants en Afrique*. Les Cahiers de l'IFORD (Yaoundé, Cameroon), no. 2.

Davis, Kingsley, and Judith Blake. 1956. "Social Structure and Fertility: An Analytic Framework." *Economic Development and Cultural Change* 4: 211-235.

DeGraff, Deborah S., Richard E. Bilsborrow, and Alejandro N. Herrin. 1996. "Children's Education in the Philippines: Does High Fertility Matter?" *Population Research and Policy Review* 15, no. 3: 219-247.

DeGraff, Deborah S., and Victor de Silva. 1996. "A New Perspective on the Definition and Measurement of Unmet Need for Contraception." *International Family Planning Perspectives* 22, no. 4: 140-147.

De Herdt, Tom, and Stefaan Marysse. 1996. *L'Économie informelle au Zaïre: (Sur)vie et pauvreté dans la période de transition*. Cahiers Africains nos. 21-22. Paris: Editions L'Harmattan.

Demographic and Health Surveys. Various country reports. Columbia, MD: Institute for Resource Development/Macro Systems, Inc.; Calverton, MD: Macro International, Inc.

Denis, J. 1956. "Léopoldville: Etude de géographie urbaine et sociale." *Zaïre* 10, no. 6 (June): 563-611.

Deolalikar, Anil B. 1993. "Gender Differences in the Returns to Schooling and in School Enrollment Rates in Indonesia." *Journal of Human Resources* 28, no. 4: 899-932.

Dhanis, E. 1953. "Recrutements de main d'oeuvre chez les Bayaka." *Zaïre* 7, no. 5 (May): 489-496.

Dixon-Mueller, Ruth B., and A. Germain. 1992. "Stalking the Elusive 'Unmet Need' for Family Planning." *Studies in Family Planning* 23, no. 5: 330-335.

Easterlin, Richard A. 1973. "Relative Economic Status and the American Fertility Swing." In *Family Economic Behavior: Problems and Prospects,* ed. E. B. Sheldon. Philadelphia: J. B. Lippincott Co.

Easterlin, Richard A. 1975. "An Economic Framework for Fertility Analysis." *Studies in Family Planning* 6: 54-63.

Easterlin, Richard A. 1996. *Growth Triumphant: The 21st Century in Historical Perspective.* Ann Arbor: University of Michigan Press.

Easterlin, Richard A., and Eileen M. Crimmins. 1985. *The Fertility Revolution: A Supply-Demand Analysis.* Chicago: University of Chicago Press.

El Deeb, B., and John B. Casterline. 1988. "Determinants of Contraceptive Use." In *Egypt: Demographic Responses to Modernization,* ed. A. M. Hallouda et al., 527-573. Cairo: Central Agency for Public Mobilisation and Statistics.

Eloundou-Enyegue, Parfait Martial. 1992. *Solidarité dans la crise ou crise des solidarités familiales au Cameroun? Evolutions récentes des échanges entre villes et campagnes.* Les Dossiers du CEPED, no. 22. Paris: Centre Français sur la Population et le Développement, December.

Eloundou-Enyegue, Parfait M. 1997. "Demographic Responses to Economic Crisis in Cameroon: Fertility, Child Schooling, and the Quantity/Quality Tradeoff." Ph.D. diss., Department of Rural Sociology, Pennsylvania State University.

Eloundou-Enyegue, Parfait M., C. Shannon Stokes, and Gretchen T. Cornwell. 2000. "Are There Crisis-Led Fertility Declines? Evidence from Central Cameroon." *Population Research and Policy Review* 19, no. 1: 47-72.

Ferry, Benoît, and David P. Smith. 1983. "Breastfeeding Differentials." *WFS Comparative Studies,* no. 23. Voorburg, Netherlands: International Statistical Institute.

Fisher, Andrew A., Mbadu Muanda, Barbara Mensch, and Robert Miller. 1991. "A Situation Analysis of the Family Planning Program of Zaire: A Comparison of Three Service Delivery Systems." Kinshasa, Zaire: Projet des Services des Naissances Désirables and Population Council.

Folbre, Nancy. 1988. "The Black Four of Hearts: Toward a New Paradigm of Household Economics." In *A Home Divided: Women and Income in the Third World,* ed. Daisy Dwyer and Judith Bruce, 248-262. Stanford, CA: Stanford University Press.

Foster, Andrew. 1993. "The Effects of Economic Fluctuations on Marriage and Fertility in Sub-Saharan Africa." Paper presented at the annual meeting of the Population Association of America, Cincinnati, OH, 1 April.

Frank, Odile. 1983. "Infertility in Sub-Saharan Africa: Estimates and Implications." *Population and Development Review* 9, no. 1: 137-144.

Freedman, Ronald, Ming-Cheng Chang, and Te-Hsiung Sun. 1982. "Household Composition, Extended Kinship, and Reproduction in Taiwan, 1973-1980." *Population Studies* 36, no. 3 (November): 395-411.

Gage-Brandon, Anastasia J., and Dominique Meekers. 1993. "Sex, Contraception, and Childbearing before Marriage in Sub-Saharan Africa." *International Family Planning Perspectives* 19, no. 1: 14-18.

Gage, Anastasia J., and Dominique Meekers. 1994. "Sexual Activity before Marriage in Sub-Saharan Africa." *Social Biology* 41: 44-60.

Glick, Peter, and David Sahn. 1997. "Gender and Education Impacts on Employment and Earnings in West Africa: Evidence from Guinea." *Economic Development and Cultural Change* 45, no. 4 (July): 793-823.

Glick, Peter, and David Sahn. 2000. "Schooling of Girls and Boys in a West African Country: The Effects of Parental Education, Income, and Household Structure." *Economics of Education Review* 19: 63-87.

Goldman, Noreen, Ann Pebley, and G. Lord. 1984. "Calculation of Life Tables from Survey Data: A Technical Note." *Demography* 21, no. 4: 647-653.

Gouvernement Central de la République du Congo. Ministère du Plan et de la Coordination Economique. 1961. *Tableau général de la démographie congolaise: Enquête démographique par sondage, 1955-1957: Analyse générale des résultats statistiques.* Léopoldville, Congo: Ministère du Plan et de la Coordination Economique.

Greene, William H. 2000. *Econometric Analysis,* 4th Edition. Upper Saddle River, NJ: Prentice-Hall.

Grummer-Strawn, Laurence, and James Trussell. 1990. "Computing the Mean Duration of Breastfeeding from Current-Status Data." Office of Population Research, Princeton University (October). Paper presented at the annual meeting of the Population Association of America, March 1991, Washington, DC.

Guzmán, José Miguel, Susheela Singh, Germán Rodríguez, and Edith A. Pantelides, eds., 1996. *The Fertility Transition in Latin America.* Oxford: Clarendon Press.

Hagenaars, Aldi, and Klaas de Vos. 1988. "The Definition and Measurement of Poverty." *Journal of Human Resources* 23, no. 2: 211-221.

Harrison, K. A. 1985. "Childbearing, Health, and Social Priorities: A Survey of 22,774 Consecutive Births in Northern Nigeria." *British Journal of Obstetrics and Gynaecology* 92, suppl. no. 5: 1-120.

Hogan, Dennis P. 1986. "Maternal Influences on Adolescent Family Formation." In *Family Relations in Life Course Perspective*, ed. I. Kertzer and Z. S. Blau, 147-165. Greenwich, CT: JAI Press.

Houyoux, Joseph, and Kinavwuidi Niwembo. 1986. *Kinshasa, 1975.* Kinshasa, Zaire: Bureau d'Etudes, d'Aménagement et d'Urbanisme; Brussels: ICHEC. Originally published as *Etude démographique de Kinshasa* (Kinshasa: Bureau d'Etudes, d'Aménagement et d'Urbanisme, 1977).

Hulstaert, G. 1951. "L'Instruction des filles." *Aequatoria* 14, no. 4: 129-130.

Institut National de la Statistique, avec la Coopération de l'Assistance Technique Française. 1969. *Etude socio-démographique de Kinshasa, 1967—Rapport général.* Kinshasa: Office National de la Recherche et du Développement, République Démocratique du Congo.

Institut National de la Statistique. 1991a. *Zaïre/Kinshasa. Recensement scientifique de la population–Juillet 1984—Caractéristiques démographiques.* Vol. 1. Kinshasa: Institut National de la Statistique, Ministère du Plan et Aménagement du Territoire, République du Zaïre.

Institut National de la Statistique. 1991b. *Zaïre: Recensement scientifique de la population–Juillet 1984–totaux définitifs.* Kinshasa: Institut National de la Statistique, Ministère du Plan et Aménagement du Territoire, République du Zaïre.

Institut National de la Statistique. 1991c. *Zaïre: Un aperçu démographique: Recensement scientifique de la population, 1984.* Kinshasa: Institut National de la Statistique, Ministère du Plan et Aménagement du Territoire, République du Zaïre.

Institut National de la Statistique. 1993. *Projections démographiques: Zaïre et régions, 1984-2000: Recensement scientifique de la population–1984.* Kinshasa: Institut National de la Statistique, Ministère du Plan et Aménagement du Territoire, République du Zaïre.

Janowitz, Barbara, and J. Smith. 1984. "Pregnancy Intervals, Breastfeeding, and Contraception." In *Reproductive Health in Africa: Issues and Options,* ed. B. Janowitz, J. Lewis, N. Burton, and P. Lamptey, 40-47. Research Triangle Park, NC: Family Health International.

Jolly, Carole L., and James N. Gribble. 1993. "The Proximate Determinants of Fertility." In *Demographic Change in Sub-Saharan Africa*, ed. Karen A. Foote, Kenneth H. Hill, and Linda G. Martin, 68-116. Washington, DC: National Academy Press.

Kahn, Joan R., and K. Anderson. 1991. "Intergenerational Patterns of Teenage Fertility." Paper presented at the annual meeting of the Population Association of America, Washington, DC, 21-23 March.

Kiernan, K. E., and I. Diamond. 1983. "The Age at Which Childbearing Starts: A Longitudinal Study." *Population Studies* 37: 363-380.

Kikassa, Mwanalessa. 1979. "La Population scolaire zaïroise, 1960-75." *Zaïre-Afrique*, no. 134 (April): 209-220.

Knodel, John, and Gavin W. Jones. 1996. "Post-Cairo Population Policy: Does Promoting Girls' Schooling Miss the Mark?" *Population and Development Review* 22, no. 4 (December): 683-702.

Knowles, James C., and Richard Anker. 1981. "An Analysis of Income Transfers in a Developing Country: The Case of Kenya." *Journal of Development Economics* 8, no. 2 (April): 205-229.

Kobiane, Jean-François. 1998. "Les Déterminants de la demande scolaire au Burkina Faso: Approche sous l'angle des stratégies familiales." Louvain-la-Neuve, Belgium: Université Catholique de Louvain. Typescript.

Kritz, Mary M., Douglas T. Gurak, and Bolaji Fapohunda. 1992. "Sociocultural and Economic Determinants of Women's Status and Fertility among the Yoruba." Paper presented at the annual meeting of the Population Association of America, Denver, CO, 2 May.

Lamal, F. 1954. "L'Exode massif des hommes adultes vers Léopoldville: Les Basuku du Territoire de Feshi, District du Kwango." *Zaïre* 8, no. 4 (April): 365-377.

Larsen, Ulla. 1989. "A Comparative Study of the Levels and the Differentials of Sterility in Cameroon, Kenya, and Sudan." In *Reproduction and Social Organization in Sub-Saharan Africa*, ed. R. J. Lesthaeghe, 167-211. Berkeley and Los Angeles: University of California Press.

Leete, Richard, and Iqbal Alam, eds. 1993. *The Revolution in Asian Fertility: Dimensions, Causes, and Implications*. Oxford: Clarendon Press.

Lehrer, Evelyn. 1985. "Log-Linear Probability Models: An Application to the Analysis of Timing of First Birth." *Applied Economics* 17: 477-489.

Lesthaeghe, Ron J. 1989a. Introduction to *Reproduction and Social Organization in Sub-Saharan Africa*, 1-12. Berkeley and Los Angeles: University of California Press.

Lesthaeghe, Ron J. 1989b. "Production and Reproduction in Sub-Saharan Africa: An Overview of Organizing Principles." In *Reproduction and Social Organization in Sub-Saharan Africa*, ed. R. J. Lesthaeghe, 13-59. Berkeley and Los Angeles: University of California Press.

Lesthaeghe, Ron J. 1993. "Are There Crisis-Led Fertility Transitions?" Paper presented at the 1993 annual meeting of the Population Association of America, Cincinnati, OH, 1 April.

Liao, Tim Futing. 1994. *Interpreting Probability Models: Logit, Probit, and Other Generalized Linear Models*. Sage University Paper Series on Quantitative Applications in the Social Sciences, 07-101. Thousand Oaks, CA: Sage.

Lloyd, Cynthia B. 1991. "The Contribution of the World Fertility Surveys to an Understanding of the Relationship between Women's Work and Fertility." *Studies in Family Planning* 22, no. 3: 144-161.

Lloyd, Cynthia B. 1994. "Investing in the Next Generation: The Implications of High Fertility at the Level of the Family." In *Population and Development: Old Debates and New Conclusions*, ed. R. Cassen, 181-202. Washington, DC: Overseas Development Council.

Lloyd, Cynthia B., and Ann K. Blanc. 1996. "Children's Schooling in sub-Saharan Africa: The Role of Fathers, Mothers, and Others." *Population and Development Review* 22, no. 2 (June): 265-298.

Lokota, E. P. 1992. "L'Economie informelle à Kinshasa: Fait nouveau ou permanent?" *Les Cahiers du CEDAF* 3-4: 161-178.

Lucas, Robert E. B., and Oded Stark. 1985. "Motivations to Remit: Evidence from Botswana." *Journal of Political Economy* 93, no. 5 (October): 901-918.

Lututala, M., a Pitshandenge Ngondo, and Beya Mukeni. 1996. *Dynamique des structures familiales et accès des femmes à l'éducation au Zaïre: Cas de la ville de Kinshasa*. Kinshasa, Zaire: Department of Demography, University of Kinshasa.

Lux, André. 1962. *Le Marché du travail en Afrique noire*. Léopoldville, Congo: Institut de Recherches Economiques et Sociales, Université Lovanium de Léopoldville.

Maggwa, A. B. N. and E. N. Ngugi. 1992. "Reproductive Tract Infection in Kenya: Insights for Action from Research." In *Reproductive Tract Infections: Global Impact and Priorities for Women's Reproductive Health*, ed. Germain et al. New York: Plenum Press.

Malhotra, A., and D. S. DeGraff. 1997. "Entry versus Success in the Labor Force: Young Women's Employment in Sri Lanka." *World Development* 25, no. 3: 379-394.

Malhotra, A., and D. S. DeGraff. 2000. "Poverty, Marital Status and Young Women's Employment in Sri Lanka." In *Women, Poverty and Demographic Change*, ed. B. Garciá. Oxford: Oxford University Press.

Mankiw, N. Gregory, David Romer, and David N. Weil. 1992. "A Contribution to the Empirics of Economic Growth." *Quarterly Journal of Economics* 107: 407-421.

Masangu, Jean-Claude. 1999. "Nouvelles Dispositions de change en République Démocratique du Congo: Adresse du gouverneur de la Banque Centrale." *Congo-Afrique*, no. 339 (November): 517-524.

Mason, Karen O. 1984. *The Status of Women: A Review of Its Relationships to Fertility and Mortality*. Ann Arbor: Population Studies Center, University of Michigan.

Maton, Jef, Koen Schoors, and Annelies Van Bauwel. 1999. "Congo 1965-1997." Ghent, Belgium: Gent University, November.

Maton, Jef, and Annelies Van Bauwel. 1996. "Zaïre, 1996: Analyse des chiffres mensuels et trimestriels: La Politique macro-économique au premier semestre, 1996." Ghent, Belgium: Gent University, October.

Maxwell, Nan L. 1987. "Influences on the Timing of First Childbearing." *Contemporary Policy Issues* 5: 113-122.

Mbumba, Ngimbi. 1982. *Kinshasa, 1881-1981: 100 Ans après Stanley, problèmes et avenir d'une ville*. Kinshasa, Zaire: Centre de Recherches Pédagogiques.

McDaniel, Antonio, and Eliya Zulu. 1996. "Mothers, Fathers, and Children: Regional Patterns in Child-Parent Residence in Sub-Saharan Africa." *African Population Studies*, no. 11 (October): 1-28.

Meekers, Dominique. 1994. "Sexual Initiation and Premarital Childbearing in Sub-Saharan Africa." *Population Studies* 48, no. 1: 47-64.

Meekers, Dominique, Anastasia J. Gage, and Li Zhan. 1995. "Preparing Adolescents for Adulthood: Family Life Education and Pregnancy-Related School Expulsion in Kenya." *Population Research and Policy Review* 14, no. 1: 91-110.

Meheus, André. 1994. "Women's Health: Importance of Reproductive Tract Infections, Pelvic Inflammatory Disease, and Cervical Cancer." In *Family Planning Targets in Relation to Fertility Reduction and Reproductive Health Care in ECA Member States, 61-91*. Addis Abeba: United Nations, Economic Commission for Africa.

Mianza, Gertrude. 1996. *Femmes africaines et pouvoir: Les Maraicheres de Kinshasa*. Paris: L'Harmattan.

Michael, Robert T. 1973. "Education in Nonmarket Production." *Journal of Political Economy* 81, no. 2, pt. 1: 306-327.

Michael, Robert T., and Nancy Tuma. 1985. "Entry into Marriage and Parenthood by Young Men and Women: The Influence of Family Background." *Demography* 22, no. 4: 515-544.

Mincer, Jacob. 1974. *Schooling, Experience, and Earnings*. New York: Columbia University Press, for the National Bureau of Economic Research.

Moore, Kristin A., and Sandra L. Hofferth. 1980. "Factors Affecting Family Formation: A Path Model." *Population and Environment* 3: 73-98.

Mortara, G. 1949. "Fertility and Reproduction Rates." In *Methods of Using Census Statistics for the Calculation of Life Tables and Other Demographic Measures*, 40-60. New York: United Nations.

Muhuri, P. K., A. K. Blanc, and S. O. Rutstein. 1994. *Socioeconomic Differentials in Fertility*. Demographic and Health Surveys Comparative Studies, no. 13. Calverton, MD: Macro International Inc.

Mukadi, Luaba Nkamba. 1979. "Aperçu historique de l'enseignement au Zaïre (1880-1960)." *Zaïre-Afrique*, no. 134 (April): 199-208.

Mulanga-Kabeya, C., N. Nzilambi, B. Edidi, M. Minlangu, T. Tshimpaka, L. Kambembo, L. Atibu, N. Mama, W. Ilunga, H. Sema, K. Tshimanga, B. Bongo, M. Peeters, and E. Delaporte. 1998. "Evidence of Stable HIV Seroprevalences in Selected Populations in the Democratic Republic of the Congo." *AIDS* 12, no. 8 (August): 905-910.

Nag, Moni. 1975. "Marriage and Kinship in Relation to Human Fertility." In *Population and Social Organization*, ed. Moni Nag, 11-54. The Hague: Mouton.

National Research Council. Working Group on Demographic Effects of Economic and Social Reversals. 1993a. *Demographic Effects of Economic Reversals in Sub-Saharan Africa*. Washington, DC: National Academy Press.

National Research Council. Working Group on Factors Affecting Contraceptive Use. 1993b. *Factors Affecting Contraceptive Use in Sub-Saharan Africa*. Washington, DC: National Academy Press.

National Research Council. Working Group on Adolescent Fertility. 1993c. *Social Dynamics of Adolescent Fertility in Sub-Saharan Africa*. Washington, DC: National Academy Press.

Newcomer, S., and J. Richard Udry. 1987. "Parental Marital Status Effects on Adolescent Sexual Behavior." *Journal of Marriage and the Family* 49: pp. 235-240.

Ngom, Pierre, Godwin Apaliya, Nathan K. Mensah, Alex Nazzar, and Fred N. Binka. 1999. "Gender Differentials in Educational Attainment among the Kasese-Nankana of Northern Ghana." In *Third African Population Conference: The African Population in the 21st Century*, 3: 523-535. Dakar, Senegal: Union for African Population Studies.

Ngondo, a Pitshandenge Iman. 1980. *De la nuptialité et de la fécondité des polygames: Le Cas des Yaka de Popokabaka*. Tervuren, Belgium: Musée Royal d'Afrique Centrale.

Ngondo, a Pitshandenge. 1996. "Nucléarisation du ménage biologique et renforcement du ménage social à Kinshasa." *Zaïre-Afrique*, no. 308 (October): 419-444.

Nzita Kikhela, D. 1989. *Techniques for Collection and Analysis of Data on Perinatal Mortality in Kinshasa, Zaire*. Ottawa, ON: International Development Research Centre.

Oni, G. A. 1985. *The Effects of Women's Education on Postpartum Non-susceptible Period in Ilarin, an Urban Community in Nigeria.* Ann Arbor: Mich.: University Microfilms International.

Page, Hilary J. 1989. "Childrearing versus Childbearing: Coresidence of Mother and Child in Sub-Saharan Africa." In *Reproduction and Social Organization in Sub-Saharan Africa,* ed. Ron J. Lesthaeghe, 401-441. Berkeley and Los Angeles: University of California Press.

Palloni, Alberto, Kenneth Hill, and G. P. Aguirre. 1993. "Economic Swings and Demographic Changes in the History of Latin America." Paper presented at the annual meeting of the Population Association of America, Cincinnati, OH, 1 April.

Panzarine, S., and J. Santelli. 1987. "Risk Factors for Early Sexual Activity and Early Unplanned Pregnancy." *Maryland Medical Journal* 36: 927-931.

Parish, William L., and Robert J. Willis. 1993. "Daughters, Education, and Family Budgets: Taiwan Experiences." *Journal of Human Resources* 28, no. 4: 863-898.

Patel, M. A., et al. 1988. "Family Planning Accessibility as a Determinant of Contraceptive Use and Birth Rate: The Case of Nigeria." Chicago: Rush University, Center for Health Management Studies.

Pebley, Anne R., and Wariara Mbugua. 1989. "Polygyny and Fertility in Sub-Saharan Africa." In *Reproduction and Social Organization in Sub-Saharan Africa,* ed. Ron J. Lesthaeghe, 338-364. Berkeley and Los Angeles: University of California Press.

Piripiri, L., et al. 1989. *Pratiques sexuelles et perception du risque d'attraper le SIDA chez les adolescents scolarisés de la ville de Kinshasa.* Kinshasa, Zaire: Ecole de Santé Publique, Université de Kinshasa.

Pitt, Mark M., Mark R. Rosenzweig, and Md. Nazmul Hassan. 1990. "Productivity, Health, and Inequality in the Intrahousehold Distribution of Food in Low-Income Countries." *American Economic Review* 80, no. 5: 1139-1156.

Poirier, Jean, Victor Piché, and Ghyslaine Neill. 1989. "Travail des femmes et fécondité dans les pays en développement: Que nous a appris l'enquête mondiale de la fécondité?" *Cahiers Québécois de Démographie* 18, no. 1: 159-183.

Pollak, Robert A. 1985. "A Transaction Cost Approach to Families and Households." *Journal of Economic Literature* 23, no. 2 (June): 581-608.

République Démocratique du Congo. 1999. *Reconstruire l'etat et l'économie du Congo après la guerre: Stratégies de sortie de crise.* Kinshasa: République Démocratique du Congo.

République du Zaïre. Ministère du Plan et Reconstruction National. 1996. *Enquête nationale sur la situation des enfants et des femmes au Zaïre en 1995.* Kinshasa: République du Zaïre, Ministère du Plan et Reconstruction National.

République du Zaïre, Societa d'Ingegneria e Consulenza Attivita Industriali, and Département de Démographie/Université Catholique de Louvain. 1977. *Etude démographique de l'Ouest du Zaïre.* Vol. 1, *Méthodologie.* Louvain-la-Neuve, Belgium: Université Catholique de Louvain.

République du Zaïre, Societa d'Ingegneria e Consulenza Attivita Industriali, and Département de Démographie/Université Catholique de Louvain. 1978a. *Etude démographique de l'Ouest du Zaïre.* Vol. 3, *Mouvement de la population: Nuptialité, fécondité, mortalité, migrations.* Louvain-la-Neuve, Belgium: Université Catholique de Louvain.

République du Zaïre, Societa d'Ingegneria e Consulenza Attivita Industriali, Département de Démographie/Université Catholique de Louvain, and Centre de Recherches Sociologiques/Université Catholique de Louvain. 1978b. *Synthèse des études démographiques de l'Ouest du Zaïre, 1974-1977.* Louvain-la-Neuve, Belgium: Université Catholique de Louvain.

Retel-Laurentin, Anne. 1974. *Infécondité en Afrique noire: Maladies et conséquences sociales.* Paris: Masson & Co.

Rockefeller Foundation. 1992. *Population Sciences Division Strategy: Mobilizing Resources to Satisfy Unmet Demand for Contraception and Complete the Demographic Transition.* New York: Population Sciences Division.

Romaniuk, Anatole. 1961. *L'Aspect démographique de la stérilité des femmes congolaises.* Léopoldville: Studia Universitatis "Lovanium," Institut de Recherches Economiques et Sociales, Editions de l'Université.

Romaniuk, Anatole. 1967. *La Fécondité des populations congolaises.* Paris: Mouton.

Romaniuk, Anatole. 1968. "The Demography of the Democratic Republic of the Congo." In *The Demography of Tropical Africa,* by William Brass et al., 241-341. Princeton, N.J.: Princeton University Press.

Romaniuk, Anatole. 1980. "Increase in Natural Fertility during the Early Stages of Modernization: Evidence from an African Case Study, Zaire." *Population Studies* 34, no. 2: 295-310.

Rosenzweig, Mark R., and T. Paul Schultz. 1982. "Market Opportunities, Genetic Endowments, and Intrafamily Resource Distribution: Child Survival in Rural India." *American Economic Review* 72, no. 4: 803-815.

Sala-Diakanda, Daniel. 1997. "Zaïre: Une Evolution démographique inquiétante, liée à la désintégration du tissu socio-économique." In *La Population du monde: Enjeux et problèmes* (Cahier no. 139), ed. Jean-Claude Chasteland and Jean-Claude Chesnais, 359-383. Paris: Presses Universitaires de France/Institut National d'Etudes Demographiques.

Sala-Diakanda, Mpembele. 1980. *Approche ethnique des phénomènes démographiques: Le Cas du Zaïre*. Louvain-la-Neuve, Belgium: Cabay Libraire-Editeur S.A., for Département de Démographie, Université Catholique de Louvain.

Sandell, Steven H. 1977. "Women and the Economics of Family Migration." *Review of Economics and Statistics* 59: 406-414.

Sathar, Zeba A., and V. C. Chidambaram. 1984. *Differentials in Contraceptive Use*. WFS Comparative Studies, no. 36. Voorburg, Netherlands: International Statistical Institute.

Sathar, Zeba A., and Cynthia B. Lloyd. 1994. "Who Gets Primary Schooling in Pakistan? Inequalities among and within Families." *Pakistan Development Review* 33, no. 2: 103-134.

Schultz, T. Paul. 1987. "School Expenditures and Enrollments, 1960-1980: The Effects of Income, Prices, and Population Growth." In *Population Growth and Economic Development: Issues and Evidence*, ed. D. Gale Johnson and Ronald D. Lee, 413-476. Madison: University of Wisconsin Press.

Schultz, T. Paul. 1989. "Accounting for Public Expenditures on Education." Paper presented at a conference on human capital and economic growth, Buffalo, N.Y.

Schultz, T. Paul. 1990. "Women's Changing Participation in the Labor Force: A World Perspective." *Economic Development and Cultural Change* 38, no. 3: 457-488.

Schultz, T. Paul. 1993. "Investments in the Schooling and Health of Women and Men: Quantities and Returns." *Journal of Human Resources* 28, no. 4: 694-734.

Sethuraman, S. U. 1981. *The Urban Informal Sector in Developing Countries*. Geneva, Switzerland: International Labor Organization.

Shapiro, David. 1992. "Labor Markets in Kinshasa and Bandundu." Report prepared for Cornell University Food and Nutrition Policy Program. Pennsylvania State University, Department of Economics.

Shapiro, David. 1996. "Fertility Decline in Kinshasa." *Population Studies* 50, no. 1 (March): 89-103.

Shapiro, David. 1999. "Family Influences on Women's Educational Attainment in Kinshasa." Working paper. Pennsylvania State University, Department of Economics. Originally prepared for the CICRED Seminar on Educational Strategies, Families, and Population Dynamics, Ouagadougou, Burkina Faso, November 1999.

Shapiro, David, and Lois B. Shaw. 1983. "Growth in the Labor Force Attachment of Married Women: Accounting for Changes in the 1970s." *Southern Economic Journal* 50, no. 2 (October): 461-473.

Shapiro, David, Gacheke Simons, and B. Oleko Tambashe. 1995. "Extended-Family Solidarity: Interhousehold Resource Transfers for Children's Schooling and Child Fostering in Kinshasa." Working paper. Pennsylvania State University, Department of Economics. Originally presented at the annual meeting of the Population Association of America, San Francisco, April 1995.

Shapiro, David, and B. Oleko Tambashe. 1994a. "The Impact of Women's Employment and Education on Contraceptive Use and Abortion in Kinshasa, Zaire." *Studies in Family Planning* 25, no. 2: 96-110.

Shapiro, David, and B. Oleko Tambashe. 1994b. "Poverty, Women's Schooling, and Economic Activity in Kinshasa." Working paper. Pennsylvania State University, Department of Economics.

Shapiro, David, and B. Oleko Tambashe. 1997a. "Education, Employment, and Fertility in Kinshasa and Prospects for Changes in Reproductive Behavior." *Population Research and Policy Review* 16, no. 3 (June): 259-287.

Shapiro, David, and B. Oleko Tambashe. 1997b. "Ethnicity, Education, and Fertility in Kinshasa, Congo." Working paper. Pennsylvania State University, Department of Economics. Originally presented at the annual meeting of the Population Association of America, Washington, DC, March 1997.

Shapiro, David, and B. Oleko Tambashe. 1998. "Ethnicity, Education, and Fertility Transition in Kinshasa, Congo." Working paper. Pennsylvania State University, Department of Economics. Originally presented at the International Union for the Scientific Study of Population Seminar on Reproductive Change in Sub-Saharan Africa, Nairobi, Kenya, November 1998.

Shapiro, David, and B. Oleko Tambashe. 1999a. "Fertility Transition in Urban and Rural Areas of Sub-Saharan Africa." Working paper. Pennsylvania State University, Department of Economics. Originally presented at the Chaire Quetelet Symposium in Demography, Catholic University of Louvain, Louvain-la-Neuve, Belgium, October 1999.

Shapiro, David, and B. Oleko Tambashe. 1999b. "Gender, Poverty, and School Enrollment in Kinshasa, Congo." In *Third African Population Conference: The African Population in the 21st Century,*3: 587-615. Dakar, Senegal: Union for African Population Studies.

Shapiro, David, and B. Oleko Tambashe. 2001a. "Fertility in the Democratic Republic of the Congo." Working paper. Pennsylvania State University, Department of Economics. Originally presented at the UN workshop "Prospects for Fertility Decline in High-Fertility Countries," July 2001.

Shapiro, David, and B. Oleko Tambashe. 2001b. "Gender, Poverty, Family Structure, and Investments in Children's Education in Kinshasa, Congo." *Economics of Education Review* 20, no. 4 (August): 359-375.

Shapiro, David and Eric Tollens. 1992. *The Agricultural Development of Zaire.* Aldershot, U.K.: Avebury/Ashgate Publishing Ltd.

Simons, Gacheke. 1994. "Extended Family Structure and Interhousehold Resource Transfers for Child Rearing." Master's thesis, Department of Economics, Pennsylvania State University.

Skoufias, Emmanuel. 1994. "Market Wages, Family Composition, and the Time Allocation of Children in Agricultural Households." *Journal of Development Studies* 30, no. 2: 335-360.

Standing, G. 1983. "Women's Work Activity and Fertility." In *Determinants of Fertility in Developing Countries: A Summary of Knowledge,* ed. R. A. Bulatao et al., 416-438. Washington, DC: National Academy Press.

Stokes, C. Shannon, Felicia B. LeClere, and Yeu-Sheng Hsieh. 1987. "Household Extension and Reproductive Behaviour in Taiwan." *Journal of Biosocial Science* 19, no. 3 (July): 273-282.

Studer, M., and Arland Thornton. 1987. "Adolescent Religiosity and Contraceptive Usage." *Journal of Marriage and the Family* 49: 117-128.

Tabutin, D. 1982. "Evolution régionale de la fécondité dans l'ouest du Zaïre," *Population* 37, no. 1: 29-50.

Tabutin, Dominique. 1997. "Les Transitions démographiques en Afrique Sub-Saharienne: Spécificités, changements ... et incertitudes." In *International Population Conference, Beijing 1997,* 1: 219-247. Liège, Belgium: International Union for the Scientific Study of Population.

Tabutin, Dominique, and Bruno Schoumaker. 2001. "Une Analyse régionale des transitions de fécondité en Afrique Sub-Saharienne." Institut de Démographie, Université Catholique de Louvain. Typescript. Orginally presented at the general congress of the International Union for the Scientific Study of Population, Salvador, Brazil.

Tambashe, B. Oleko. 1984. *Niveau et corrélats de la fécondité des mariages à Kinshasa: Examen par les variables intermédiaires.* Louvain-la-Neuve, Belgium: Cabay Libraire-Editeur.

Tambashe, B. Oleko, and David Shapiro. 1991. "Employment, Education, and Fertility Behavior: Evidence from Kinshasa." Final report to the Rockefeller Foundation. Kinshasa, Zaire: Département de Démographie, Université de Kinshasa.

Tambashe, B. Oleko, and David Shapiro. 1996. "Family Background and Early Life Course Transitions in Kinshasa." *Journal of Marriage and the Family* 58, no. 4 (November): 1029-1037.

Thomas, Duncan. 1990. "Intra-Household Resource Allocation: An Inferential Approach." *Journal of Human Resources* 25, no. 4: 635-664.

Thomas, Duncan, and Ityai Muvandi. 1994a. "The Demographic Transition in Southern Africa: Another Look at the Evidence from Botswana and Zimbabwe." *Demography* 31, no. 2 (May): 185-207.

Thomas, Duncan, and Ityai Muvandi. 1994b. "The Demographic Transition in Southern Africa: Reviewing the Evidence from Botswana and Zimbabwe." *Demography* 31, no. 2 (May): 217-227.

"Un An après, le Congo de Kabila." *Jeune Afrique* (Paris), no. 1948 (12-18 May 1998): 85-224.

UNICEF. 1993. *The Progress of Nations.* New York: UNICEF.

United Nations. 1967. *Manual IV: Methods of Estimating Basic Demographic Measures from Incomplete Data.* Population Studies, no. 42. New York: Department of Economic and Social Affairs, United Nations.

United Nations. 1986. *Education and Fertility: Selected Findings from the World Fertility Survey Data*. New York: Population Division, United Nations.

United Nations. 1987. *Fertility Behavior in the Context of Development: Evidence from the World Fertility Survey*. New York: Population Division, United Nations.

United Nations. 1988. *Mortpak-Lite: The United Nations Software Package for Mortality Measurement*. Population Studies, no. 104. New York: Department of International Economic and Social Affairs.

United Nations. 1990. *Patterns of First Marriage: Timing and Prevalence*. New York: Population Division, United Nations.

United Nations. 1991. *World Population Prospects, 1990*. New York: Population Division, United Nations.

United Nations. 1994. *Family Planning Targets in Relation to Fertility Reduction and Reproductive Health Care in ECA Member States*. Addis Ababa, Ethiopia: Economic Commission for Africa.

United Nations. 1995a. *Abortion Policies: A Global Review*. Vol. 3, *Oman to Zimbabwe*. New York: Population Division, United Nations.

United Nations. 1995b. *World Population Prospects: The 1994 Revision*. New York: Population Division, United Nations.

United Nations. 1996. *Urban Agglomerations, 1996*. New York: Population Division, United Nations.

United Nations. 1998. *World Population Prospects: The 1996 Revision*. New York: Population Division, United Nations.

United Nations Population Fund (UNFPA). 1989. *State of the World Population*. New York: United Nations.

Van Bulck, G. 1956. "La Promotion de la femme au Congo Belge et au Ruanda-Urundi: A propos de la XIIe Session du Congrès Colonial National (23-24 Novembre 1956)." *Zaïre* 10, no. 10 (December): 1067-1074.

van de Walle, Etienne. 1993. "Recent Trends in Marriage Ages." In *Demographic Change in Sub-Saharan Africa*, ed. Karen A. Foote, Kenneth H. Hill, and Linda G. Martin, 117-152. Washington, DC: National Academy Press.

van de Walle, Etienne, and Andrew D. Foster. 1990. *Fertility Decline in Africa: Assessment and Prospects*. World Bank Technical Paper no. 125. Washington, DC: World Bank.

Vansina, Jan. 1966. *Introduction a l'ethnographie du Congo*. Kinshasa: Editions Universitaires du Congo.

Vijverberg, Wim. P. M. 1993. "Educational Investments and Returns for Women and Men in Côte d'Ivoire." *Journal of Human Resources* 28, no. 4: 933-974.

Waka, Philomene Nankara. 1998. "Feminisation de la pauvreté au Congo-Kinshasa." *Revue de Droit Africain*, no. 5 (January): 18-28.

Wassa, Ferdinand. 1951. "Education de la femme noire." *La Voix du Congolais* 7, no. 59 (February): 81-82.

Westoff, Charles F. 1992. *Age at Marriage, Age at First Birth, and Fertility in Africa*. World Bank Technical Paper no. 169. Washington, DC: World Bank.

Westoff, Charles F., and Akin Bankole. 1995. *Unmet Need: 1990-94*. Demographic and Health Surveys Comparative Studies, no. 16. Calverton, MD: Macro International.

Westoff, Charles F., and Luis H. Ochoa. 1991. *Unmet Need and the Demand for Family Planning*. Demographic and Health Surveys Comparative Studies, no. 5. Columbia, MD: Institute for Resource Development.

Whyms. 1956. *Léopoldville, 1881-1956*. Brussels: Office de Publicité, S.A.

Wong, Rebeca, and Ruth Levine. 1992. "The Effect of Household Structure on Women's Economic Activity and Fertility: Evidence from Recent Mothers in Mexico." *Economic Development and Cultural Change* 41, no. 1: 89-102.

Yap, Lorene. 1976. "Internal Migration and Economic Development in Brazil." *Quarterly Journal of Economics* 90, no. 1: 119-137.

Zulu, Eliya. 1998. "Levels and Trends of Proximate Determinants of Fertility in Kenya." In *Background Papers on the Analysis of Secondary Data in Four Kenya National Demographic and Health Surveys, 1977-1993*. Nairobi, Kenya: African Population Policy Research Center, Population Council.

Index